VIRGINIA WATER

NEIGHBOUR TO
WINDSOR GREAT PARK

A View in Windsor Great Park, 1780s, Benjamin West—A squatter returns to his family from wood gathering; in the distance a hunt is in full cry with Windsor Castle in the background.

VIRGINIA WATER

NEIGHBOUR TO WINDSOR GREAT PARK

DOROTHY DAVIS

Phillimore

2009

Published by
PHILLIMORE & CO. LTD
Chichester, West Sussex, England
www.phillimore.co.uk

ISBN 978-1-86077-490-4

Printed and bound in Great Britain

For Ron

Contents

List of Illustrations

Acknowledgements

I am grateful to Her Majesty The Queen for her gracious permission to reproduce pictures from the Royal Collection and a photograph from the Royal Photograph Collection and for the privilege of viewing prints and consulting documents in the Royal Library at Windsor Castle. I am especially indebted to the Hon. Lady Roberts, Librarian of the Royal Library, for her generous help and encouragement over many years, and to Bridget Wright of the Royal Library for her scholarly guidance.

It was Raymond South's reference to 'a bundle of yellowed documents' in the Public Record Office that led me to explore the wealth of information to be found in the Crown Estates Papers (CRES) in the National Archives at Kew. I am indebted to him, the staff at the National Archives and also the staff at the London Metropolitan Archives.

My many visits to Surrey History Centre were a delight and I am grateful to all the staff there, especially Julian Pooley, for sharing their expertise. In fact, everywhere I sought help and information it was generously given. I am glad to acknowledge the help of Caroline Benson of The Museum of English Rural Life, Sarah Skinner, Keeper of Fine Art at the Castle Museum, Nottingham and Brendan Carr of Reading Museum and for permission to reproduce pictures from their collections.

I am also grateful to P.B. Everett, Deputy Ranger of Windsor Great Park, and Mark Flanagan, Keeper of the Gardens, for supplying information and granting permission to reproduce a photograph. Molly Bootes and her colleagues at Runnymede Borough Council also kindly answered numerous questions.

I am much indebted to Graham Dennis and John End for allowing me to use items from their collections and for sharing their enthusiasm for their localities. Mary Dunk, great granddaughter of Percy Willmer Pocock, formerly of Beeches, Egham Hill, kindly allowed me access to the Pocock family archive; Audrey and Donald Walker shared information on the Cheesman genealogy and Anne Long provided a transcript of her father's Second World War diaries.

My researches began long ago when I first became a volunteer at the Egham Museum and discovered it was a mine of information. I am grateful to the members of Egham-by-Runnymede Historical Society, who have collected, transcribed and indexed so many resources over the years, and to the Egham Museum Trust for allowing access to the collection and generously granting permission to reproduce some of its pictures and photographs.

Closely associated with both Egham and Chertsey Museums and with Royal Holloway, University of London, is the Sidney A. Oliver Charitable Settlement. Its Trustees have also been generous in making their archives available. The late John Hardaker, during his period as Trustee, was particularly supportive of my work.

I am grateful to Alan Bostock, who so often came to my rescue with his camera, and to the many local people who shared their memories with me. I am particularly indebted to Jill Hyams for help, especially with research into First World War newspaper archives, and to Jill Williams and Chris Rowley for constructive comments on the original manuscript. Vivien Bairstow, Jeanne Faucherre, Diana Fear, Pamela Maryfield, Margaret and Peter White, Joy Whitfield and Richard Williams supplied information and references.

Lastly my greatest debt is to my late husband, Ron, my fellow researcher and my most helpful and supportive critic.

Dorothy Davis, 2008

Illustration acknowledgements

The illustrations are reproduced by kind permission of the following, to whom any application for use should be made: The Royal Collection © 2007 Her Majesty Queen Elizabeth II: Frontispiece (RCIN 406917), 3, (RL 14616), 7 (RCIN 711290), 11 (RL 14331), 14 (RL 14318), 17 (RL 14647), 18 (RL 14642), 25 (RL 17866), 44 (RL 14618), 74 (Royal Photographic Collection), 77 (RCIN 402584), 91 (RL 20816), 106 (Crown Estate Commissioners); The Egham Museum Trust: 1 (B646), 4 (PR101), 6 (PR115), 13 (PR8), 20 (PR263), 23 (PR117), 24 (PR15), 30 (PR193), 31 (PR176), 34 (PR275), 42 (PR165), 46 (PR188), 47 (PR151), 48 (PR150), 49 (PR174), 54 (PR306), 56 (PR197), 60 (PR189), 87 (EMT P1054), 99 (EMT P471), 103 (P2020), 109 (P4324); John Hardaker Collection: 8; The National Archives: 9 (PRO MR1/279), 36 (PRO CRES 2/58), 45 (PRO CRES 2/58), 93 (PRO CRES 35/2824); The Castle Museum, Nottingham: 22 (NCM 1945-142); The Reading Museum Service © Reading Borough Council: 28 (REDMG 1931.250.1), all rights reserved; John End Collection: 27, 35, 75, 79, 80, 82, 84, 92, 94 , 98, 100-1; Surrey History Service: 37 (SHC QS 2/6 1790 p. 27/2), 69, *Pictorial Times*, Vol. II, 1843, p.17 (SHC PX/56/73), 95 (SHC 7502/ES/17B p.10); The Museum of English Rural Life, The University of Reading: 40 (35/6740), 41 (5/733); Wentworth Auction Rooms Catalogue: 81; Graham Dennis Collection: 19, 33, 53, 64, 65, 76, 83, 97, 102; Mavis Collier ©1985: 73 (EMT PR129); Jill Williams Collection: 90; Pocock Family Archive (Mary Dunk Collection): 96; Crown Estates Office: 106. The following figures incorporate information from more then one source: 10 (PRO MPE1/565, MR1/687 & SHC QS 2/6 1790), 21 (PRO MR1/280 & MPE1/1493), 29 (PRO MPE1/565 & 1493), 38 (PRO MPE1/1493 & 565, MR1/687 & SHC QS 2/6 1790). Other figures can be found in the following publications: 12 (John Norden's Plan in William Menzies's *The History of Windsor Great Park & Windsor Forest*), 26 (facing p.324 in Hughes's *A History of Windsor Forest*), 63 (facing p.360 in *The Memoirs of George IV* by Robert Huish, 1831), 51 and 67 (Frontispiece and facing p.85, respectively. in *A Descriptive and Historical Account of Egham and the Environs*, printed by C.C. Wetton, *c.*1840, EMT B5), 57 (Sothebys, London, Roberts, 1997, p.462). Figure 68 is based on The Plan of the Parish of Egham, May & Collins, 1856. Figures 16, 55, 70, 86, 89, 104 and 107 are from private collections.

Introduction

Virginia Water, described in the *Shell Guide* of 1977 as 'the lushest residential suburb in the country', is 21 miles from London on the main road to the south-west of England, the present A30. It is three miles from Egham and five from Windsor. The present village shares its name with the lake at the southern end of Windsor Great Park, created by William Augustus, Duke of Cumberland, after the Battle of Culloden in 1746. Indeed the history of the park, the road on its south-eastern boundary and the settlements in its vicinity are intricately bound up together.

The area was part of Windsor Forest and so subject to the idiosyncrasies of forest law. The poor, sandy, acidic soil meant that the land was of little agricultural value and it provided the greater part of the common land of the manor: it was the poorest part of the parish of Egham. Daniel Defoe in the 1720s compared the area to the 'Arabia Deserta'.

The term Virginia first appears in a map and documentation in the mid-17th century, while 18th-century maps show a hamlet of the name at the point where the stream, commonly called the Virginia Stream or Virginia Water, flowed out of Windsor Great Park and crossed the main road to the south-west. When William, Duke of Cumberland, became Ranger of the Park in 1746 and landscaped the southern end of the park, he had no need to search for a name for his newly created lake, as there was one ready at hand—Virginia Water. In the later enlargement of the lake the hamlets of Virginia and nearby Egham Wick, together with at least 230 acres of surrounding land, were absorbed into the park. More land was taken into the park in the 19th century but by then new communities had emerged at Virginia Water and at Egham Wick.

There have been many extensive and scholarly histories of Windsor Great Park written in the last 150 years. Of particular significance is Jane Roberts's *Royal Landscape: The Gardens and Parks of Windsor*, a detailed historical and topographical study that is an inspiration and an essential point of reference

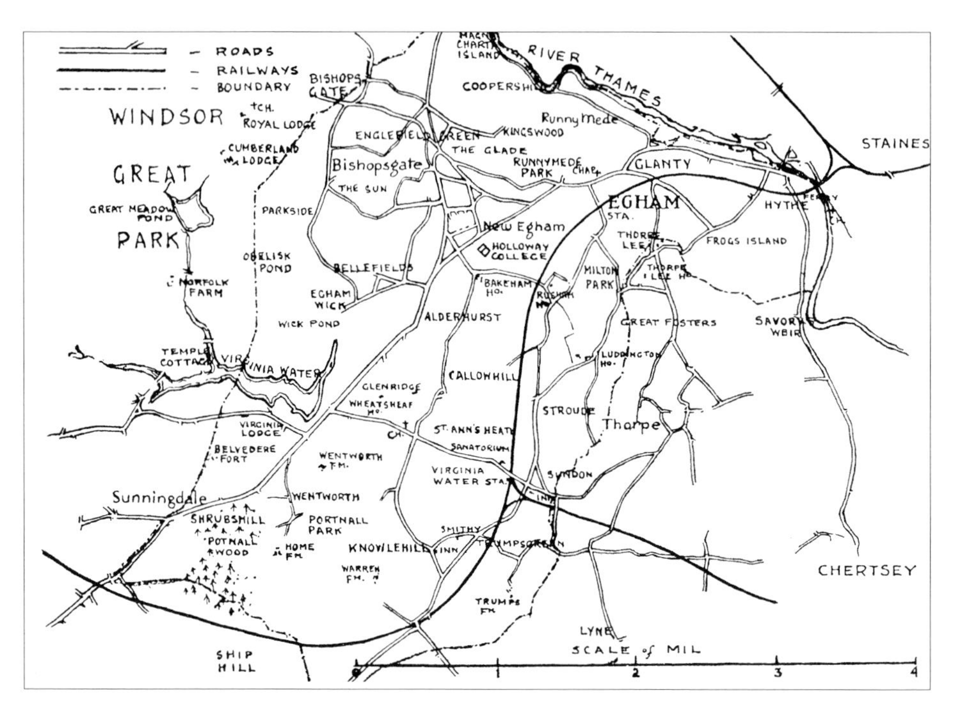

1 *Map of the district, 1928.*

for other writers. The present work looks at the development of the park from outside the pales, and to tell the story I have used, whenever possible, the words of the people involved: letters and reports from the men working in the park, quotations in vestry claims, diaries, recollections and local newspapers.

I have tried to show how the local inhabitants were affected by royal decrees, how they lost land or found work because of the proximity of a great royal estate and how royal influence infiltrated even into the vestry meetings of Egham parish and affected particularly the lives of the poor. It is the story of royal officials and rebels, house owners and tenants, road builders and highwaymen. It ventures into the park legally with gardeners, labourers and gamekeepers and illegally with poachers and scavengers. It notes the changes at Virginia Water from protected royal domain to popular pleasure park.

This is, however, only a small part of Virginia Water's rich historical tapestry: several estates and the five hamlets that make up the unusual conglomeration that is the modern village retained their independent histories.

Dorothy Davis, 2008

Chapter One

From Forest and Waste to Hamlets and a Turnpike Road: the 12th to mid-18th Centuries

The early history of Virginia Water is difficult to unravel, as the area was only a small part of several larger units. Bronze Age and Roman ditches have been found at St Ann's Heath[1] and the Roman road from *Londinium* to *Calleva Atrebatum*, modern Silchester, traversed it.[2] This road is clearly shown as the 'Devil's Highway' on Ordnance Survey maps of Berkshire, near the Surrey border to the north of the road to the south-west, the present A30. It is known that the Romans crossed the River Thames at *Pontes*, modern Staines, and that finds have been made in the Bakeham area. Between Sunningdale and Staines, however, the route can only be conjectured. The area immediately south and east of the present lake has been much disturbed over the centuries, having been in turn heathland, hamlet and royal park, while the old roads to the south-west and to Windsor crossed it. A survey of 1982 found embankments and ditches within the present bounds of Windsor Great Park in the woods at Fort Belvedere and also to the east of the lake at Virginia Water.[3]

Two significant Anglo-Saxon place names in the area are associated with the road to the south-west. 'Herepaethford' (Harpesford), meaning 'ford on the main road', pinpoints the location to the meeting place of the river and the road, while, a mile to the south-west, 'Shrubbeshedde' (Shrubs Hill) was said in a medieval version of Chertsey Abbey's foundation charter to be 'by the way that goeth to Winchestre'.[4] The river itself, known in medieval times as the 'Redewynde' and later as the Red(e)bourne or Bourne, flowed under the main road, passing Trotsworth and Thorpe on its way to the Thames at Chertsey.[5]

In Anglo-Saxon times the area now known as Virginia Water was part of the vill of Egham. With the neighbouring settlements of Thorpe, Chertsey and Chobham it was held by the Chertsey Abbey of St Peter, founded in 666 by Frithuwold, sub-regulus of Surrey. The abbot remained the overlord of these lands through the Norman Conquest and into the medieval period.

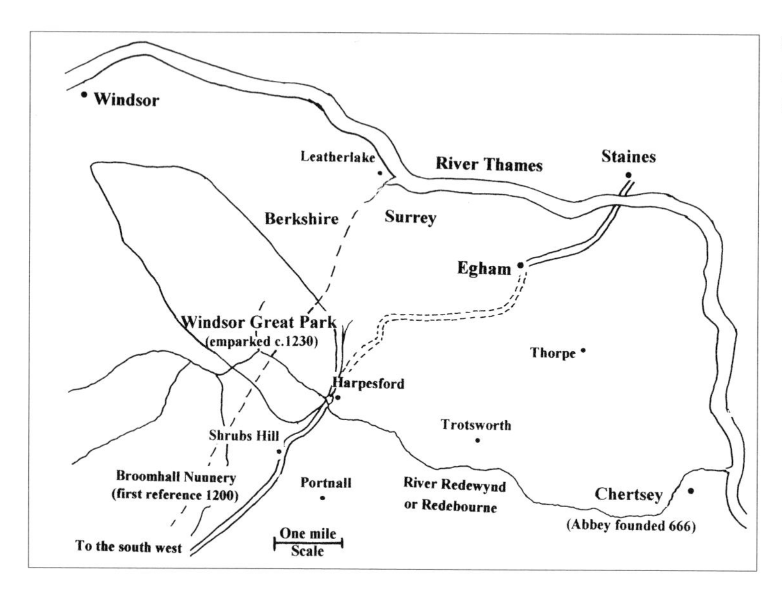

2 *Diagram of Egham and environs in the 13th century.*

Through his officials he leased out properties to tenants, collected rents and administered points of law and rights of inheritance in his courts.

The area to the south of the main road, as far west as Broomhall, was part of the manor and parish of Egham but was sparsely populated. There were only two medieval settlements in the vicinity, Portnall and Trotsworth; most of the land was the common heath or wasteland of the parish. Although poor by agricultural standards, the common was valuable in its own right for its provision of extra pasturage for cattle and above all as a source of fuel. Commoners could collect fallen wood, cut turf and, in the areas nearer the river, dig for peat. Each customary tenant was entitled to take up four cartloads of turves for his winter use; in return he had to give the abbot one cartload.[6]

By ordinary manorial custom the holders of existing settlements were not discouraged from encroaching on heath land. Small pieces of waste were valuable to free and copyhold tenants as rough grazing and sometimes for the cropping of trees and underwood.[7] Chertsey Abbey authorised such encroachments. In 1304 such a piece of land was granted to Henry Mylton but with the abbey reserving the right to the crop of alder growing there. During the short reign of Richard III (1483-5) a moor of alderwood and underwood as well as some heath land were granted to John Mersh, along with a considerable acreage of established enclosures in the Stroude/ Bakeham area.[8] Tenants could also extend their landholdings by clearing and enclosing nearby pieces of common, which increased the value of their estates.

This practice was not, however, encouraged by royal officials, for these lands and the neighbouring waste were also claimed as part of Windsor Forest. The fact that Egham's common land was in the forest inhibited the taking-in and improvement of heath land, which was happening in other parts of the county.[9] While encouraging good husbandry on his estates the abbot could find himself in direct conflict with the will of the monarch, whose chief interest in the land was its potential for hunting.

Much of north-west Surrey and east Berkshire was ideal hunting country, being close to the royal estate at Windsor and having an abundance of open, scrubby land interspersed with patches of woodland. In such an environment the king could enjoy good sport and an exciting chase while the deer had secure places to rest and browse between hunts.

A forest was not by definition a dense wood, but a mixed habitat over which the monarch had sole right of hunting and whose inhabitants were subject to forest law. This law sought to protect both the creatures of the chase and the herbage, shrubs and trees that provided their food and shelter. In the forest the deer reigned supreme; the needs of the husbandman, together with his fields and settlements, were subservient to the requirements of the game. No commoner might kill a deer even if it was laying waste to his crops. Men from the local community were elected as verderers to settle disputes concerning 'vert and venison'.[10] The forester, trying to enforce forest law on the ground, often met with antagonism. In 1270 Richard Bataylle, forester of Bagshot, complained that the men of Egham and Thorpe hindered him in carrying out his office.[11]

3 *View in Windsor Forest, 1796, Paul Sandby—A forest was a mixed habitat where agriculture and rural industries co-existed with the requirements of the hunt.*

In the reign of Henry II (1154-89) the Knights of Surrey were aggrieved when the king claimed their county as part of Windsor Forest. They fought an extensive campaign with the Crown to have Surrey disafforested. It was Henry's son, Richard I, who finally agreed that only that part of the county north of Guildford Downs and west of the river Wey should remain forest. This area became known as the Bailiwick of Surrey as it was outside the jurisdiction of the county sheriff but subject to its own forest bailiff. The parishes of Chertsey and Egham were supposed to be excluded.[12]

The Great Charter, agreed by King John and the barons in 1215, included several clauses relating to forests. The most important was the promise to disafforest those territories only made forest in the reign of his father, Henry II. John also agreed to abolish all evil customs connected with forests and foresters.[13] He died only a year later and it was left to his successor, Henry III, when he came of age, to grant a new forest charter with only a small piece of Surrey remaining in the forest. The boundaries were named as 'Bromhull' (Broomhall), 'Sorbes-hull' (Shrubs Hill), Harpesford and 'Loderslake' (Leatherlake) on the Thames, all near the border of Surrey with Berkshire. The abbot agreed to the new charter on condition that his tenants were exempt from the authority of the king's officials.[14]

During the 12th century, part of the forest south of Windsor Castle was emparked; that is, a pale or fence was built to make a secure enclosure for the deer, with a park keeper appointed to see to their welfare. During the 1240s Henry III built a moated manor house on the river that later became known as Virginia Water. The enclosure by then extended five miles south from the castle into Surrey towards the main road to the south-west. This became Windsor Great Park.[15]

Attempts were made by the Crown in the reigns of Edward I and Edward II to reclaim Surrey as part of the ancient forest. On the succession of the young Edward III in 1327, representatives of the county seized their opportunity and demanded a new assessment of the forest boundaries. Officials on both sides made a perambulation of the disputed area and it was agreed that no part of Surrey was in the forest. The boundary line was much as it had been in the reign of Henry III. That part of the county north of Guildford Downs and west of the river Wey—the old Bailiwick of Surrey—remained a purlieu of the forest, a tract of land on the borders of a forest once regarded as part of it, and so still subject to certain restrictions. The king retained some hunting rights there and owned the deer that strayed into it, a ranger being appointed to round up any straggling animals.[16]

One group of inhabitants were treated with tolerance when they encroached on forest land. They were the 'nuns of the forest', whose priory of St Margaret had been established at Broomhall on the Surrey and Berkshire borders by 1158. The nunnery had been endowed with some land in both counties and allowed by successive Plantagenet monarchs to add to it by clearing and even enclosing forestland. The lifting of some of the constraints of forest law was the nuns' reward for their harsh environment so long as they always remembered the cardinal rule that the deer must be allowed to come and go freely.[17]

The nuns and their servants not only laboured in an unfriendly landscape but were the only providers of dole along a lonely stretch of the road to the south-west. It has been suggested that the gateway of their priory, facing onto the main road, became a refuge or 'hutch' from which bread could be distributed to poor travellers.[18] Among the Surrey lands granted to the priory were several pieces in the Virginia Water area, including land at Harpesford, where the river running out of the park crossed the main road, and a woodland called Knowle Grove, about a mile and a half to the south-east.[19]

The superiors of the Abbey of Chertsey lived in a different style from their poor sisters at Broomhall. The abbot, as landlord of much of north-west Surrey, retained hunting rights on his own manors. He was allowed to keep dogs and to hunt foxes, hares and wild cats in the forest and elsewhere.[20] Certain tenants on the manors of Egham and Thorpe had a right to graze animals in the park in the summer. In return for this privilege they had to send 20 cartloads of hay to Windsor Castle each year for feeding the deer.[21]

The combination of open heathland and woodland, as well as the sparse habitation of the forest, created certain dangers. When in 1235 the king's justices travelled to the Hundred of Godley court, where the affairs of Egham, Chertsey and Chobham were administered, they confirmed that a man known as Reynold, found dead on Egham heath, had been murdered by persons unknown. Evidence of his 'Englishry' was presented to the court and thus the hundred was saved from penalties that would have ensued had the victim been of Norman blood.[22] The implementation of justice was not easy. In 1325 the abbot appealed to the king to appoint an extra coroner to the Chertsey court as men were dying in gaol before appeals could be heard. If, on the other hand, the abbot attempted to send prisoners from Chertsey to the king's gaol at Guildford for appeal, his men were ambushed on the way and the accused freed by their friends. On this occasion the abbot's request was speedily granted.[23]

It is possible that by this time the road from Harpesford to Windsor that ran along the eastern boundary of Windsor Great Park was in use. By the beginning of the 14th century, less than a mile along this track, the names of the moors are given for the first time in the Chertsey Cartularies as Suthbroke (Southbrook) and Wykbroke. There was also a land-holding family called atte Wyke, which suggests that there may have been a 'wic' or farmstead in the area that later became Wick Farm and hamlet.[24]

The fact that deer were enclosed in Windsor Great Park attracted poachers, especially local men who knew the terrain better than park officials. For most of the monastic period the de Trotsworth family held the sub-manor of that name, which is part of modern Virginia Water. In June 1329 John de Trotsworth and Robert, son of Richard de Trotsworth, were accused with others of having 'broke[n] the king's park at Wyndesore, county Berks., hunted, carried away deer and assaulted Thomas le Parker, the king's servant'. Some months later they were pardoned and bound over to be of good behaviour but further investigations were set afoot to find the people responsible for the illegal hunting and assault.[25]

The main road to the west also attracted crime. In 1381 at Parkhurne (Parkcorner) at the southern end of Windsor Great Park, a red horse, three gowns and two pairs of hose, valued at 30s., were stolen from Richard de Yerdesley. A Staines man, John Bradfield, was accused of the theft but later pardoned.[26]

There was a mill at Harpesford in the 13th century, owned from about 1274 by Chertsey Abbey. In 1314, however, Edward II sent his keeper of the park to the abbot, requesting him to allow the king to have the mill. Edward wished his chaplains in the park to have use of the mill, presumably for profit. The abbot, who 'dared not gainsay the king', agreed, but nothing was put in writing.[27] The abbot obviously felt the injustice of the king's actions in taking over the mill, for almost immediately after the dethronement of Edward II the abbot petitioned his successor, the 15-year-old Edward III, for the restoration of his property. The new king, or rather his regency council, seemed only too anxious to undo the actions of Edward II and ordered the matter to be investigated before a jury and in the presence of the keeper of the mill, who would 'show the king's right'. By the second month of Edward III's reign (March 1327) judgement had already been reached. The jury accepted the abbot's story; it must have helped his case that the keeper of the mill failed to attend the hearing. The property that had been worth 13s. 4d. in 1316 had increased in value to 20s. by 1327.[28]

Arguments also occurred between king and abbot over the maintenance of the bridge over the stream at Harpesford. When the ford became a bridge is not known. In 1473 it was described as being a common wooden bridge, 24ft long and 8ft wide and, moreover, to be broken and in disrepair. Such a state of affairs was causing grave harm to the king's people and their right of carriage. The Crown declared that it was customary for the abbot to mend the bridge, but the abbot demurred. Eventually, in 1475 an inquiry was held; the jury found that the abbot was not responsible—after all, the bridge was on the king's highway to Winchester.[29] This road played an important role in Egham's development: the town's oldest inn, the *Catherine Wheel*, owned by Chertsey Abbey, was in existence as early as 1507, when Richard Adamson was granted the lease.[30]

At the beginning of the 16th century Jane Rawlyngs, the last prioresses of Broomhall nunnery, became increasingly rash in granting long leases to unscrupulous tenants. William atte Wyke was able to renew his lease of Knowle Grove for 55 years at a rental of 40s., while Roberd Gunner of Egham was allowed to lease 'one parcelle of lande with a water lying in

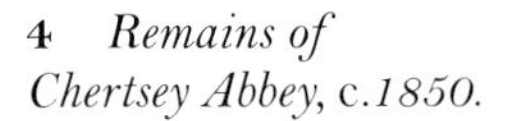

4 *Remains of Chertsey Abbey*, c.*1850*.

Eweshote called harpers fforde', along with several other pieces of land in Egham, for an absurdly long term of 200 years. Some of these Egham lands remained in private hands when the nunnery was suppressed in 1521 and its remaining assets, including one piece of land at Harpesford, put into the tenure of St John's College, Cambridge. The woodland at Knowle Grove, however, caught the eye of Henry VIII because of its hunting potential and he paid the college 1s. for each of its 44 acres.[31]

The delicate power game between the Abbot of Chertsey and the monarch ceased when Chertsey Abbey itself was dissolved in 1537. The monarch became lord of the manor of Egham as well as remaining lord of the forest. The question of whether or not north-west Surrey was part of Windsor Forest remained a point of contention between king and commoner. Forest charters had mostly excluded it, but its past history as part of the forest and its natural landscape told against it.

Some local men also acquired land at dissolution. John Worsopp held land to the south-east of the park pales 'in a place called the Weeke', which he passed on to his son, Edward, a London merchant. By 1564 the estate consisted of some 20 acres of arable and pasture land as well as a stretch of woodland and tenements when Edward sold it to William Russell, a keeper in Windsor Great Park, for £60.[32]

Smaller properties neighbouring the farm were carved out of the heathland at Wick. One such smallholding consisted of a tenement, barn, orchard and garden by the little stream on the west of the Windsor road, as well as three acres of land to the east of the road. In 1598 it was in the possession of the Gallises, a yeoman family that came to Egham from Dartford.[33]

For the yeomen and labourers who lived in the disputed areas of the forest the precise boundary was an academic consideration. Whatever the charters decreed, they were in an unenviable situation; a hunt in full cry would not

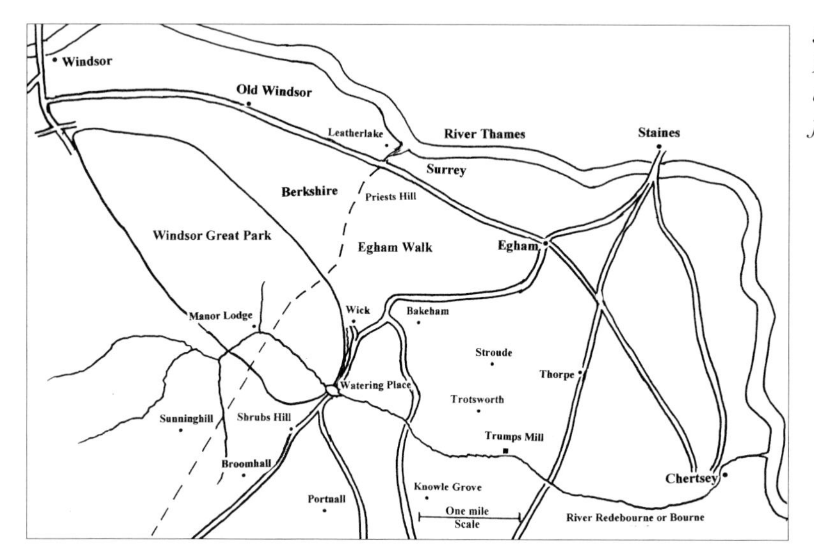

5 *Diagram of Egham and environs as a purlieu of the forest.*

halt at a line on a map. The commons and wasteland of the manor of Egham as well as Knowle Grove and the small enclosures of cultivated land between would still be hunted over.

Growing commercial prosperity in Tudor England demanded better links between London and such centres of trade as Southampton, Salisbury and Exeter. As trade increased, the main road to the south-west and the towns on it became more important and in 1555 each parish was made responsible for the upkeep of that section of the highway that ran through it.

During the reign of Elizabeth I some of the heathland seems to have been used for the pasturing of sheep. In the summer of 1569 two Egham women, Bridget, wife of John Appletree, and Agnes, wife of John Aire, were accused of 'breaking and entering a common at Egham' on six separate occasions and stealing sheep from Robert Skete, Christopher Pinkneys and Robert Bateman. Both women were spinsters by trade and perhaps were in the habit of visiting the common to collect discarded wool. The evidence that made them chargeable to such a serious crime must have been of doubtful quality for they both received a royal pardon in March 1571.[34]

Towards the end of the 16th century local yeomen were legally acquiring pieces of Egham's wasteland, not only for clearance but also for the use or marketing of the valuable deposits of peat to be found there. One hundred acres, known variously as the Peat Pitts, the Bog or the *King's Head* Waste from its long association with the landlords of the Egham inn of that name, were sited along the north bank of the River Redbourne and east of the main road. Another valuable piece, also in freehold ownership, lay south of the river and was commonly known as Child's Waste. Only the owner or his tenant had the right to remove turf or peat from these pieces of land but commoners could graze cattle there. The land was not enclosed but the boundaries were well known.[35]

Forest law still did its best to deter encroachment and defaulters were brought before the Swainmote court. In 1579 John Cowper, a major lessee of the manor of Egham, was accused of building cottages on forest land. He claimed that he had permission for encroachments for three of his sub-tenants, 'all of which do no hurt to the forest'. Forest officials had sometimes to accept that encroachment was unavoidable: his plea was accepted and his tenants allowed to remain.[36]

Other infringements against forest law also came under the jurisdiction of the Swainmote. Young wood had to be protected from deer browsing it too early and at the same court Richard Kellifet of Rusham in Egham and John Osborne of Cowarth in Berkshire were summoned for allowing this. Another offender was Henry Lane of Portnall, himself a sub-forester. He was presented at the Swainmote for taking several cartloads of wood from Priest's Hill on the borders of Egham and Old Windsor. On another occasion, he found a deer carcass with a fractured foot and distributed the meat to the poor.[37]

When James I succeeded to the English throne in 1603 he needed to make himself familiar with his new domain and, as a keen huntsman, get to know his forests. John Norden was commissioned to make a map of Windsor Forest that he completed for the king in 1607. The map clearly shows Surrey within the bounds of the forest but the text states that all that land east of the Berkshire county boundary was in the Surrey Bailiwick. James was wise enough to avoid confrontation on forest matters.

By the beginning of the 17th century, land within comparatively easy reach of London was attracting the capital's investors. One such was Francis Anthony, a Doctor of Physic, who had acquired the farmhouse and the small estate at Wick.[38] For his investment he received a quarterly rent of £7 10s. from his gentleman tenant, George Mortimer.[39] In 1621 Dr Anthony put the estate, which by then he claimed to be much more than a mere farm, referring to it as 'my Manor of Wicke', on the market. He sold it for £255 and the conveyance of the house in which he lived in St Bartholomews, London. The new purchasers were also speculators and three years later Wick Farm (and reputed manor) was sold on again for £400, a vastly increased price compared with that of 1564.[40] In the intervening years, however, the acreage had grown. Wick Farm adjoined common land both to the north and the south, so there were plenty of opportunities for the tenant farmer, in agreement with the owner, to assart scrubland, clear it and fertilise it until it was indistinguishable from the old enclosures.

For the less fortunate in society the problem of poverty, which had increased in Elizabeth's reign, continued. Merchants, justices on circuit, royal messengers and officials of state were welcome on the roads and in the towns, as they had money to spend. Less welcome were the beggars and vagrants and those being moved from parish to parish in accordance

6 *Egham East Entrance, the road to the south-west with the King's Head on the left .*

with the Poor Law Acts of 1597 and 1601. As each parish was responsible for its own paupers, it had no alternative but to ruthlessly exclude anyone who had no right of settlement. Many of these unfortunates, being hounded from one parish to another, never reached their intended destination but died miserably on the road, as recorded in the parish registers. In 1612 Alice Sanders, a beggar woman, 'posted from place to place' and belonging to the parish of St Edmunds in Salisbury, was buried in Egham churchyard. Another woman, Elizabeth Greatwood, also died on the road, while being returned, tithing by tithing, to Hilmarton in Wiltshire in 1620.

Even pauper burials were quite costly to the parish and every effort was made to move vagrants on as speedily as possible. They might be given 6d. or even three times that amount to get out of the parish. Women could bargain for more, especially if they were accompanied by children or were pregnant. A baby born by chance on a parish road might later claim settlement there. In July 1604 Dorcas Farington unexpectedly gained an Egham birthright. She was the daughter of Thomas, a yeoman from Berkshire, whose wife, Elizabeth, 'suddenly fell in travail of birth upon the way in her journey'. The offspring of other less respectable travellers might merely be recorded by their Christian name with no incriminating surname or parental details to cause the overseers problems in the future.

There was fear of strangers because they might bring disease to a community. In 1606 Mary, the daughter of John Jocky, a Scot, died of the plague while passing through Egham. Less than a year later Mary Palmer, a way-going woman, died of the plague and was buried where she was found dead. An increased number of pauper funerals and possible settlements, the need to pay off a few vagrants and even an increased risk of catching the plague were acceptable risks if a town could also grow rich from passing traffic.

Charles I, more reckless than his father, sought to reclaim all of Surrey for the forest and, to the dismay of the poor labourer, the deer proliferated. Matters became so bad by 1636 that everyone holding land in the common fields of Egham had to pay 12d. annually for every acre sown with winter corn to provide wages for honest men to watch the fields and 'preserve them from the spoil of deer'. As late as 1662 four men were still employed in this task.[41]

In 1640 the Long Parliament took the matter in hand and appointed a commission to enquire once more into Windsor Forest's bounds.[42] Two Egham men, Richard Mountain and William Kirkham, were named as jurymen. Feeling in Egham was, however, running high; many were unwilling to await the outcome of judicial processes. On 31 August 80 to 100 people gathered in broad daylight with the intention of killing the king's deer. In September even more men entered woods and attacked the deer. John Green and William Purse of Egham even threatened the keepers.[43] Green and Purse, together with Robert Mills and Daniel Coggs, were accused of killing deer and committing riots in Egham Walk. Their defence was that their actions had not taken place in the forest. They were arrested by a Parliamentary messenger but such was the sense of outrage aroused that he was attacked and his prisoners released.[44] Henry, Earl of Holland, Chief Justice in Eyre of the Forests, south of Trent, as well as steward of the manor of Egham, ordered the locks on the gates of Windsor Great Park to be changed: there were too many keys and unauthorised people continued to take in cattle and horses for pasturage.[45]

The commission reported in 1642 that no part of Surrey was in the forest except the park at Guildford. This was followed by a somewhat petty retaliation against the people of Egham by the Earl of Holland, who seemed obsessed with domestic animals within the pales. He stopped all agistment—the right to browse cattle in the park in summer. This aroused more substantial opposition: 17 Egham gentlemen and yeomen signed and presented a most strongly worded petition to the earl asking for this ancient right to be restored.[46] Two of the signatories were the jurymen, Mountain and Kirkham. Several others identifying themselves with the protest farmed in the vicinity: Daniel Wickes or Atwick of Bakeham and Thomas Rolfe of Stroude. William Gibson and John Slarke at Englefield Green were also close neighbours of the park. Equality was in the air and they claimed to have respect for the king's rights as for their own. The threat of violence was also there: 'the rude multitude have threatened to pull down the pales of the park and lay it all to common'. There was obviously long-term resentment not only of the constraints imposed upon them by forest law, but also of the very existence of the Great Park. The petitioners had informed his lordship in their first sentence that 'a great part of the park has been taken out of the commons belonging to the parish'.[47]

The inhabitants of Berkshire sent a similar petition but by then the king and his servants had greater concerns than the insolent demands of a few forest yeomen. By October that year Charles I was engaged in battle with his Parliament at Edge Hill; the English Civil War had begun. That same month Colonel Venn took Windsor Castle for Parliament and with it the neighbouring areas.

Many of Egham's inhabitants, with their recent history of rebellion in the forest, would have welcomed the Parliamentary presence, and this must have been known to Royalist intelligence. In an attempt to regain Windsor for the king in November 1642, his nephew, Prince Rupert, set up camp for a few days in Egham. During his stay his men lived off the local farmers and innkeepers in the manner of invading armies. Egham's vicar, William Reyner, seems to have been especially targeted for his puritan beliefs, for his books were looted as well as his household possessions and farm crops.[48]

The new master of Wick Farm, John Fabian, like many other local men, also suffered losses in the Royalists' brief but disruptive incursion. Prince Rupert, however, failed to reclaim Windsor, and the surrounding area remained firmly in the hands of Parliament. Fabian continued to support the Parliamentary cause, serving as one of the Inquisitors of the Parish of Egham.[49]

The Parliamentary army in control of Surrey, however, was hardly less ruthless in exploiting the countryside than the Royalists had been. Fabian was owed £60 for the continual quartering of soldiers at his house, 'being 2 myle from the town' and for the pigs they had consumed. On another occasion he claimed £30 10s. for lost sheep, corn and other goods.[50]

Unlike many previous owners of the reputed manor of Wick, Fabian was a local man, formerly of Thorpe. He lived on the estate and it is tempting to speculate that it was he who built, or rebuilt, the farmhouse in the style shown on later plans to provide himself with a residence in keeping with the dignity of a gentleman. The house was assessed under the Hearth Tax of 1669-70 as having seven hearths.

In 1654, only a year before his death, John Fabian, in agreement with his son, also John, sold the manor for £800. A survey conducted the following year found the estate to consist of 110 acres. It had increased massively in size and value since William Russell had bought its 27 acres in 1564 for £60. The Fabians had done well from their purchase of 1624. In the Deed of Feoffment the Fabians appointed as lawful attorney 'our wellbeloved friend, Daniel Wicks'.[51] He was their neighbour, holding the Bakeham lands to the east of the main road, and had been one of the signatories protesting against the loss of manorial rights in a petition to Charles I. At the same time as they relinquished possession of the manor, the Fabians acquired for their own use a comparatively modest property nearby, consisting of dwelling house with barns, orchard, garden and three little plots of land, totalling three-and-a-half acres.[52]

Like other royal lands, Windsor Great Park was sequestrated by Parliament during the Commonwealth and divided into small estates that eventually came into the hands of Parliamentary officers. Deer were no longer a priority. Much of the land at the southern end the park, like the land outside its pales, was of little value in agricultural terms. A map made at the restoration of the monarchy shows fields to the north and north-east of Shrubs Hill with such names as 'Old Warren', 'Conny Warren', 'Conny Land' and 'Bromly's Warren'.[53] Rabbit farming was one form of husbandry in which a light sandy soil could provide its owner with a livelihood.

By the mid-17th century a small assart had been made on wasteland outside the park pales on its south-eastern boundary: the house built on it was given the name of 'Virginia'. The building is shown as a drawing on the Official Survey of the Great Park made in 1662 for Charles II on his restoration to the throne.[54] By this time some gentry families had interests in the New World colony of Virginia.[55] Perhaps the owner of the plot had such a connection and, being enthusiastic for the puritan cause like many of his Egham neighbours, named his house accordingly.

After the restoration of Charles II, Windsor Great Park was returned to the Crown and to its previous function as a deer park. The inhabitants of Egham were wary. In 1664 they once more presented a petition, reminding the king that Surrey was not in the forest and highlighting the problems of a man trying to eke out a living under forest constraint:

> The poor dayly labourer that hath only a cottage and sowing a bushel of corne after he hath been at hard labour all day, must watch that small quantity of corne all night, or els the deere will devour that as well as all his garden fruits and soe speedily come to the parish to be maintained.[56]

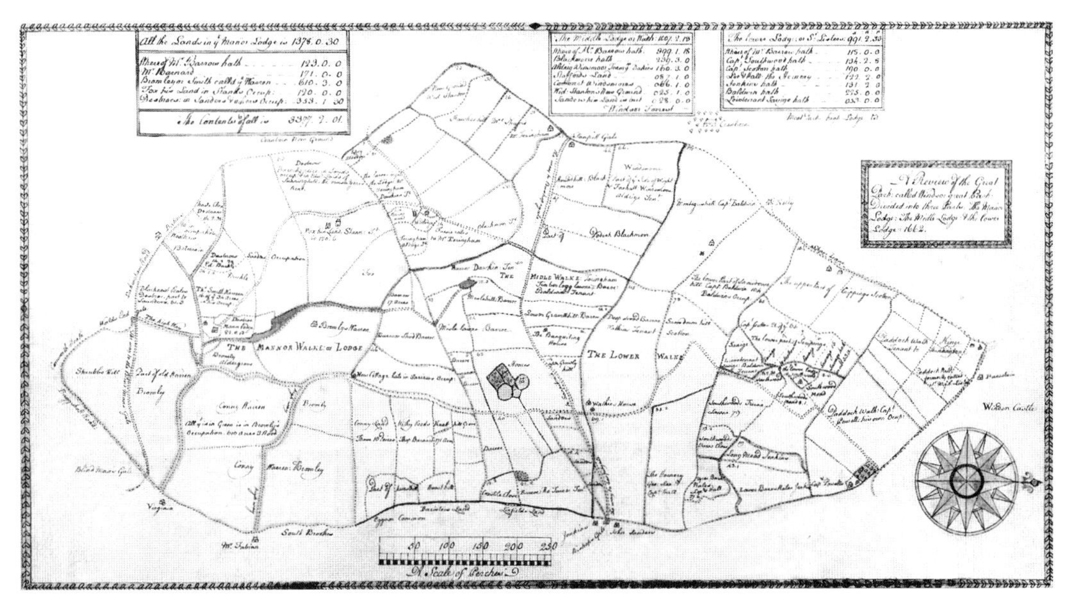

7 *A Review of the Great Park called Windsor Great Park, 1662.*

The petition further pointed out that the gamekeepers were not the good honest yeomen of old, but poor, needy fellows who lived by extortion or killing deer themselves. One under-keeper, John Saunders, was described as a poor man, living in Red Deer or Egham Walk in 1653.[57]

Rebellious commoners claimed to be unable to distinguish the waste of the manor of Egham from Windsor Great Park. The southern part of the park was, indeed, more hunting country than parkland and, as such, and being some distance from Windsor, it doubtless came last in priority for repair to its palings and rides. The land on both sides of the park pales was scrubby, boggy and prone to flooding, with another stream flowing in from the hamlet of Wick forming a watering place by the road.

The main road to the west and the stream that flowed out of the park were the dominating features of the area at the southern end of the royal estate. In monastic times this area was known as Harpesford, a name particularly associated with the mill and the bridge there. At some time, as yet unknown, the mill ceased working: it does not appear on Norden's map of Windsor Forest made in 1607, while Trumps Mill, further downstream, does (see Figure 5.)

Variations of the place-name 'Harpesford' continued to appear in legal documents to identify a one-acre close at Parkcorner in the parish of Egham. The Egham burial registers recorded a tragic accident there in December 1664. An old man, accompanied by two children, was travelling from the west. The water was running very high when they reached the bridge at Parkcorner, where the main road crossed the river. The boy, aged only 11 or 12, turned back to help his sister across, fell into the water and was drowned.

Harpesford was copyhold of the manor of Broomhall and was owned in medieval times by the nunnery of Broomhall and later by St John's College, Cambridge. The records of their Courts Baron show that the land was held by John Sanders, alias Goodwin, and his descendants from 1666 to 1785. The family was well known in Egham in the late 16th and early 17th centuries, but this particular branch seems to have migrated to London where they were engaged in coach-making and associated trades (Appendix II).

Gradually the name Harpesford fell into disuse. A cluster of dwellings grew on either side of the main road where the stream from Windsor Great Park emerged. The name Virginia, from the house built there, began to appear more often in documents and on maps as an identifiable hamlet.

The first reference to Virginia is found in the Egham parish registers and coincidentally concerns a John Saunders, almost certainly the poor park keeper previously mentioned. When a nurse child of his wife died and was buried in Egham in 1656, the parish clerk was conscientious enough to add that the family was 'of Vergeny'. He did not need to do this—Virginia was part of the parish of Egham. In September 1668, when the wife of 'Goodman Sanders' was buried, the helpful note 'of Virginie' was again added.

There was also a Backar family at Virginia in the 1670s. William Backar would seem to have been a man of some substance, he and his wife being given the courtesy titles of Mr and Mrs in the registers. Their daughter, Dorothy, was baptised in May 1677, the ceremony taking place 'at the house, the child being very ill'. Four months later she died. The Burgis or Burgees family lived at Virginia House, just off the main road, Mr Randall Burgees being buried from there in August 1690.

As more travellers used the roads a series of strip maps were produced, based on a survey carried out by John Ogilby between 1671 and 1675. The section between Egham and Bagshot included a place name that appears on no other maps, that of 'New England', where the hamlet of Virginia should have been. The name has a logical, if somewhat distant connection, with the new colonies. In 1614 Captain John Smith, in carrying out mapping operations in North America, renamed the northern part of Virginia as New England. One wonders if the mapmaker, Ogilby, or his informants jokingly thought that the hamlet of Virginia in Surrey had been similarly renamed. Alternatively it is possible that Virginia seemed to coachmen and travellers alike such an isolated and desolate spot on the road that it might just as well have been in a distant colony. In Charles Bridgeman's Plan of Windsor Forest, surveyed in about 1720, the hamlet is clearly named as Virginia.

Resentment over interference from forest officers continued on the edge of Windsor Great Park, breaking out in 1679 in dangerous riots. Several 'idle and ill-disposed persons' from Egham were accused of being in the possession of guns, prongs, bills, clubs and staves, with the intent to kill deer. Certain local magistrates tried to arrest the six or seven ringleaders

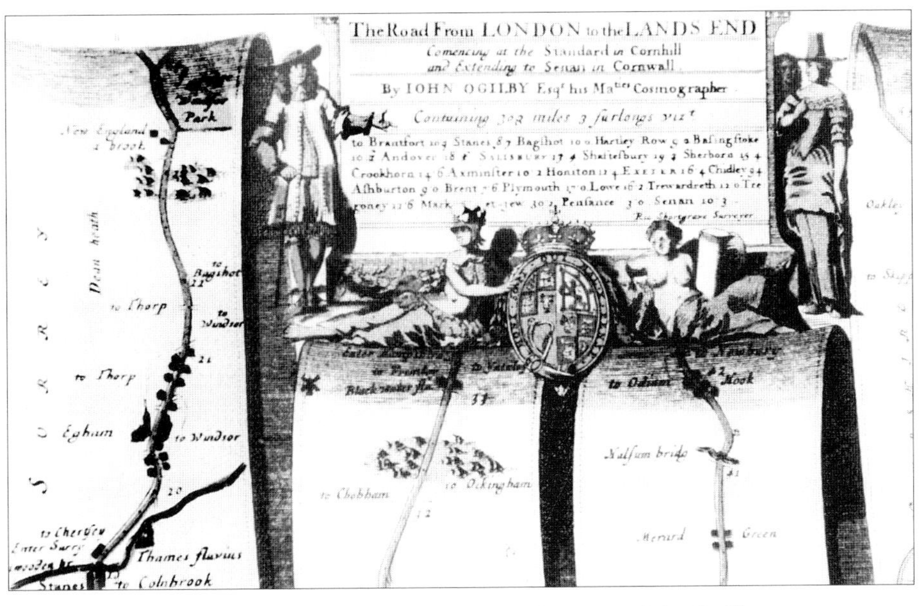

8 *Road to London from Land's End, 1671-5, John Ogilby.*

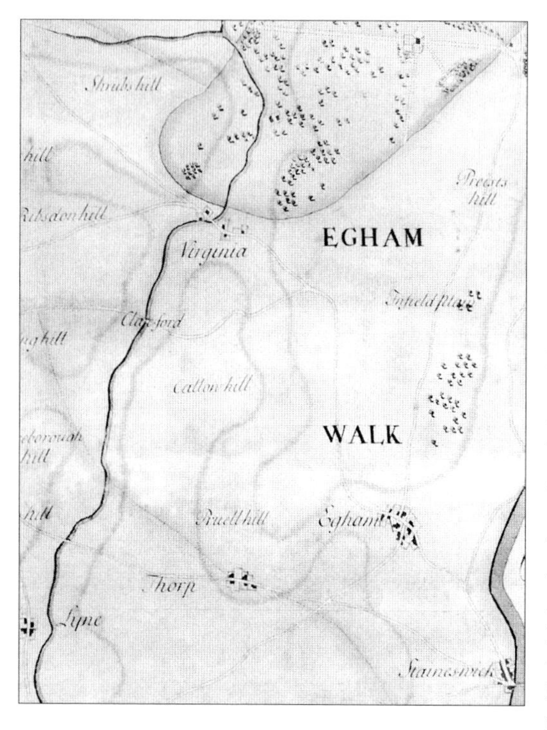

9 *Detail from The Plan of Windsor Forest, c.1720, Charles Bridgeman.*

but were opposed by about forty other inhabitants, who behaved very tumultuously. They chanted their unanimity with the accused ('They would all alike one and all!') and refused to surrender their guns. The High Sheriff of Surrey was ordered to bring William Mathews and Henry Rolfe, the two leaders of the riot, to the Privy Council to answer the charges.[58]

Two prisoners were indeed taken by royal messengers, but were rescued by Daniel Atwick, described in the Privy Council report as a gentleman. He was the descendant of tanners and farmers of Bakeham, a respected local man whose father had been one of the signatories to the petition reminding Charles I that Surrey was outside the forest. The sheriff was ordered to bring Atwick to London and to do all he could to suppress the riots and bring the ringleaders to justice 'so as others may be deterred from the like practices'.[59] The establishment, however, found little co-operation among the gentry of Egham. They protected their own and warded off the power of forest and government officials alike. Atwick seems to have remained at liberty.

By this time the hamlet of Wick, two miles from Egham, was bigger than Virginia, being named as a village in some deeds. Its centre was at a point where two streams met, one flowing in from the north and the other from a spring in Bakeham fields to the north-east. The farm or manor house stood on the banks of the stream as did meadowland and some other small properties. A deed of 1681 provides an exact description of its location: the land 'abuts upon Windsor Park pales on the west, the great Road to Bagshott on the east, Dean Common on the south, Wick Heath on the north'. By this time, however, the value of Wick Farm's land had decreased dramatically. This may have been the result of deflation or because the land was neglected by absentee landlords and unsupervised tenants. In 1681 the estate was once more in the hands of City of London merchants who sold the property to Thomas Denton, steward of the manor of Egham, for only £500.[60]

The cottages 'in a certain village called the Wick in Egham' continued to change hands. John Fabian, the younger, had no children and so, in accordance with his will, proved in 1685, his property passed to his wife,

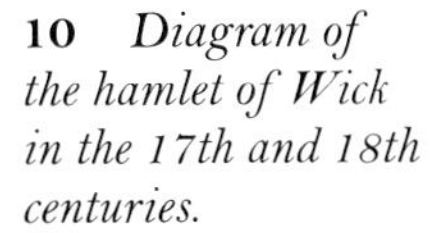

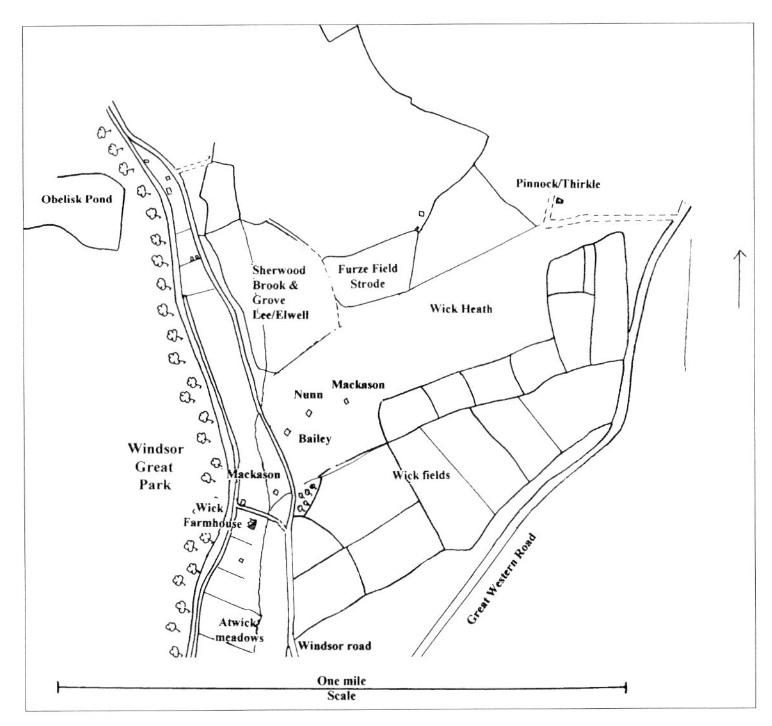

10 *Diagram of the hamlet of Wick in the 17th and 18th centuries.*

Ann, and then to his brother-in-law, Arnold Mills, who in 1697 sold it on. Four years after her husband's death Ann seems to have remarried, Egham's parish register recording the wedding of an Ann Feaben to John Hanks in 1689. Hanks was a carpenter who, in December that same year, was granted a lease of a cottage, barn and a rood of land at Wick.[61]

Henry Strode, the future founder of one of Egham's major charities, recorded in his diary in April 1700 that Hanks was working with the bricklayers and the labourers on Strode's new house at the Wick. Strode believed in sourcing his building materials locally whenever possible and sent his employees to Virginia for gravel: 'Our folks fetched a load of gravel from Virginia house and after carried dung.'[62]

In 1708 Marmaduke Bramley sold the tenement, garden and orchard at Wick that had once belonged to the Gallis family for £30. The three acres on the opposite side of the Windsor road were not included. The new owner of the property was William Ventum, a corn chandler of Egham.[63] The cottage only remained in his family for a short while, however, for his son, also William, sold it to Andrew Mackason in 1716. Mackason was in the process of turning the profits from his successful butcher's shop in Egham Street into property.[64]

In August 1728 Mackason acquired more land at Wick, a tenement, orchard, garden and yards as well as two-and-a-half acres of land from John Hanks.[65] If this was the same property that the Hanks family had held in 1697, it must have been much enlarged over 30 years by encroachment on the neighbouring heath. Ventum and Hanks continued to be remembered in field names long after they had left the area: even as late as 1790 some pasture at Wick, owned by Mackason, was still called Hankses while a piece of copyhold land at Wick was still known as Ventum's Field in 1782.[66]

Soon after the accession of the first Hanoverian monarch, George I, the conflict between king and commoner on the definition and law of the forest intensified. The Steward of the Forest Court of Windsor attempted to regain the supremacy of the rights of the king and his deer even in the 'purlieus' or fringes of the forest. As a result, in 1720, groups of men, often disguised, armed and with their faces blackened, roamed Windsor Forest, killed deer and assaulted forest officers. They became known as the 'Blacks'.[67] The government was fearful that Jacobite rebels might sow seeds of sedition in any such disaffected groups, and so their suppression was ordered.

The forest officer charged with driving the 'Blacks' out of Windsor Forest was Baptist Nunn. He had been born into royal service, being the son of Robert Nunn, who served Baptist May, Ranger of Windsor Great Park for Charles II.[68] Baptist Nunn was baptised in Sunningdale parish church in 1681 and clearly named after his father's patron. He did well in the family tradition and was eventually appointed chief gamekeeper for all the area within three miles of the castle and was also responsible for Cranbourne, Old Windsor and Egham Walks. In addition he served as Deputy Steward of the Swainmote court. Included in his powers were the rights to issue licences for hunting game other than deer and for the cutting of turf and timber.[69]

From Baptist's will, proved in 1742, it would appear that he had no family of his own, though he remained close to his brothers and sisters. The tradition of royal service continued into the next generation with Baptist's nephew, Robert, occupying the lodge at Sandpit Gate as Gentleman Deputy Surveyor of His Majesty's Woods.[70] Baptist was free from close domestic ties to police his territory ruthlessly between the spring of 1722 and the summer of 1723. He was constantly on the move, interviewing witnesses, paying spies and reporting to his masters in London. Not surprisingly, both he and his property were subject to attack. He reported in August 1722: 'Fresh Ravages nightly committed and fresh threatenings from all parts, deer killed everywhere in daytime and keepers insulted.' He travelled with guards and keepers and was even allocated a detachment of soldiers to support him in the forest.[71] It was his task to implement The Black Act (9 George I cap.22). It became law in June 1723 and made punishable by death or transportation many of the deeds that the inhabitants of Egham had committed in the past: the killing or wounding of the king's deer, the forceful rescue of someone lawfully in custody and inciting others to join in such activities.

Most of the incidents occurred in Berkshire but Virginia Water and Englefield Green did not escape Nunn's perambulations. In May 1722 he stayed at Bishopsgate with two prisoners, some guards and keepers and on another occasion at Virginia Water. In April 1723 he was again at Virginia

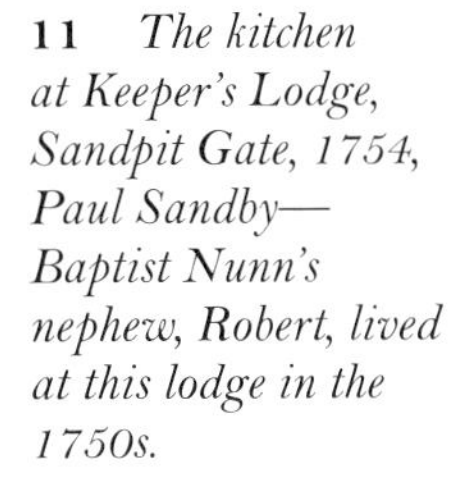

11 *The kitchen at Keeper's Lodge, Sandpit Gate, 1754, Paul Sandby—Baptist Nunn's nephew, Robert, lived at this lodge in the 1750s.*

Water but found the person he was to meet there, presumably an informer, gone. The London newspapers reported that numerous arrests were made in May 1723 throughout the forest area, including Egham and Virginia Water.[72] No great seditious plot was uncovered. In the immediate aftermath four men were executed for murder at Reading and four eventually transported from Reading gaol to Maryland; others were fined or imprisoned.[73]

By the summer of 1724 Windsor Forest was once more safe enough for George I to enjoy the chase there.[74] Daniel Defoe, touring the country that summer, also found the area agreeable, with the forest 'open for riding, hunting and taking the air for any gentlemen that please'.[75]

Baptist Nunn went from strength to strength in establishment terms. He was well rewarded for his work in apprehending the 'Blacks'. He was given more honours, becoming Porter of the Outward Gate and Janitor of Windsor Castle in 1723 and under-keeper at Linchford Walk in 1726. By 1734 he had become a keeper, a position of higher social status.[76] In 1730 he bought for £95 a cottage and half an acre of land that had been held of the manor of Egham since 1695 by his father, Robert Nunn, then described as a gentleman and living at Old Windsor. By the time of his death Baptist had property at Warfield, Winkfield, Virginia Water and Egham Wick as well as a considerable sum of money amassed through his several salaries and his dealings with government and forest departments. He left his nieces and nephews well provided for.[77]

By the beginning of the 18th century, road traffic had greatly increased. It was no longer reasonable to expect parishes to maintain national thoroughfares to newly required higher standards. In an Act of Parliament of 1718 for the improvement of roads on the south side of London it was stated that they were almost impassable during the winter.[78] By 1727 it was clear that 'part of the great Road leading to several trading Towns in the west of this Kingdom ... is become very ruinous and bad'. An Act of Parliament of 1728 (1 George II cap.6) enabled the setting up of a turnpike trust to improve the Great Western Road between the powder mills on Hounslow Heath in the county of Middlesex and the Basingstone near Bagshot in Surrey. It would be known as the Bedfont & Bagshot Turnpike Trust. More than two hundred trustees were listed in the Act and were empowered to build turnpikes and tollhouses and to appoint surveyors and toll collectors. The aim was simple: to keep the road in good repair by raising tolls on the traffic passing through. The heaviest vehicles, coaches or wagons drawn by five or six horses, those likely to do most damage to the road surface, would pay the most (9d.), while a single unladen horse or ass would be charged only 1d.[79]

All the parishes along the road were represented among the two hundred trustees. The representatives from Egham were its vicar, Thomas Beighton; landowners Adrian Moore and Richard Wyatt, senior, Sir Edmund Elwell from Englefield Green and the Bartholomews from Rusham. The presence of Baptist Nunn, guardian of the park and forest, described as a gentleman, ensured that the Crown was kept informed of whatever happened on the road that bordered Windsor Great Park. To promote efficiency only five trustees needed to be present for decisions to be made.[80]

The first meeting of the trustees was held on 1 May 1728 at the *Red Lion*, Bagshot, with several members of the Egham gentry and yeomanry present. They clearly wanted to ensure that the instruction in the act was carried out: that the western part of the road, 'being the most ruinous', was to be the first repaired. Adrian Moore, head lessee of the manor of Egham, advanced £1,000, with the proposed tolls as his security, so that work could begin.[81] Egham yeoman Henry Brumbridge was appointed surveyor. As well as having overall responsibility for the progress of the work, he controlled one work team. Local farmers were asked to supply further teams, no more than 10 on any one day, which worked from between six and seven in the morning to between two and three in the afternoon: 'Those that come first to go of first.' This would enable the workers to attend to urgent tasks about the farms in the remaining hours of daylight. Working alongside the teams were labourers, each group organised by a foreman. They were expected to work a 12-hour day and were not allowed to have a dinner break until the teams stopped work.[82] Such employment was a welcome additional source of income for local men, usually dependent on the vagaries of the rural economy.

Trustees' meetings were held frequently that summer, usually at the *Red Lion* in Egham and occasionally at the *Angel* in Staines. Work began on cutting back the trees on Egham Hill and improving ditching. Landowners were instructed to keep their hedges trimmed and their ditches scoured so as not to cause any kind of nuisance on the road. Gravel in large quantities was essential to improve the surface of the road and fortunately was locally available in plenty.[83] No reference has been found to 'New England' in the Bedfont & Bagshot Turnpike minutes; indeed, its use as a substitute for Virginia appears only in road directives.

The establishment of the turnpike roads had encouraged the building of more inns in the towns on its route. On its outskirts there was also a need for more humble accommodation for carters, wagoners and packhorse riders. The *Pack Horse* on Egham Hill, the *Red Lion* at Shrubs Hill and the *Broomhall Hutt*, thought by some to be the successor of the nuns' refuge on the main road, met this need. An inn called the *Wheatsheaf* was established in Baptist Nunn's old house at Virginia by an enterprising man called John Atkins.[84]

By the mid-18th century the name Virginy, Virginia or Virginia Water was in common use for the hamlet and the gate into the park as well as the house, while the river was called Virginy Brooke or Virginia Water.[85] The hamlet might well have developed as a village on the main road but in its proximity to the pales of a great royal estate lay the seeds of its demise.

The hamlet of Wick was a compact and recognisable community in the 18th century, less than a mile from Virginia, with a farm, several smaller properties, common land and a stream. It was agriculturally viable with meadow, pasture, arable land and woodland and supported about fourteen families. To the west of Wick stream was meadow and pasture ground, most of it belonging to Wick Farm but some five acres were owned by the Atwick family. Ownership of this land included the right to graze all cattle on Wick Heath and also to cut turf there.[86]

The heath was a valuable asset to any rural community, not least because it provided, often to the annoyance of the steward of the manor, the means of acquiring land. Some time in the 18th century, to the north-west of Wick Farm fields, three little plots were created, one owned by John Bailey, another by the Nunn family and a third by Andrew Mackason. Further north, between the Windsor road and the park boundary, were more cottages, some set in meadowland.

To the north of Wick Heath lay several closes, some with dwellings. Most of these were part of larger land holdings, which had been held by Egham yeoman families for generations.[87] In such an idyllic spot, on the banks of the stream, the hamlet of Wick was a desirable location. Like Virginia, however, it lay dangerously close to the boundary of Windsor Great Park.

Chapter Two

The First Lake at Virginia Water and Life on The Great Western Road: 1746-76

The boggy valley of the Virginia stream that ran through the southern end of Windsor Great Park was an ideal setting for a style of landscaping coming into fashion in the first half of the 18th century: broad parkland adorned with trees and stretches of water that appeared to be natural but was in fact the result of studied artifice. Wide acres and a natural supply of water were the prerequisites and the area near Virginia had these in abundance.

The Virginia stream ran from west to east and was joined by another little watercourse flowing in from the north. Near its juncture stood a moated manor house, built in the 1240s for Henry III as a family residence and hunting lodge.[1] By the beginning of the 17th century the water in the northern stream was controlled by the construction of little causeways to create ponds that conserved fish and provided drinking water for livestock. There was another large pond and a watering place near the main road.

When William Augustus, Duke of Cumberland, second son of George II, was made Ranger of Windsor Great Park, he seized the opportunity to transform the existing river into a great artificial lake and the nondescript land into picturesque valleys and hills. The rangership was one of the many honours heaped on the duke as a result of his victory over the Scots, led by Charles Edward Stuart, the Young Pretender, at Culloden in 1746. As captain-general of his father's army Cumberland was acclaimed as a hero, having secured the throne for the protestant Hanoverian line. George II, to commemorate his son's victory, ordered an obelisk, crowned by a rising sun, to be raised in Windsor Great Park. The site chosen for this monument was the south-eastern corner of the park, to the north-west of the hamlet of Wick near Southbrooks or, as it was sometimes called, Sowsbrooks. The obelisk was set on an eminence, known as Hurst Hill, and below it, to embellish the view, a pond was dug, fed from one of the many streams in the area. Adorned by a bridge originally designed by the architect Henry Flitcroft, it became known as Obelisk Pond.[2] An inscription was added to the obelisk in

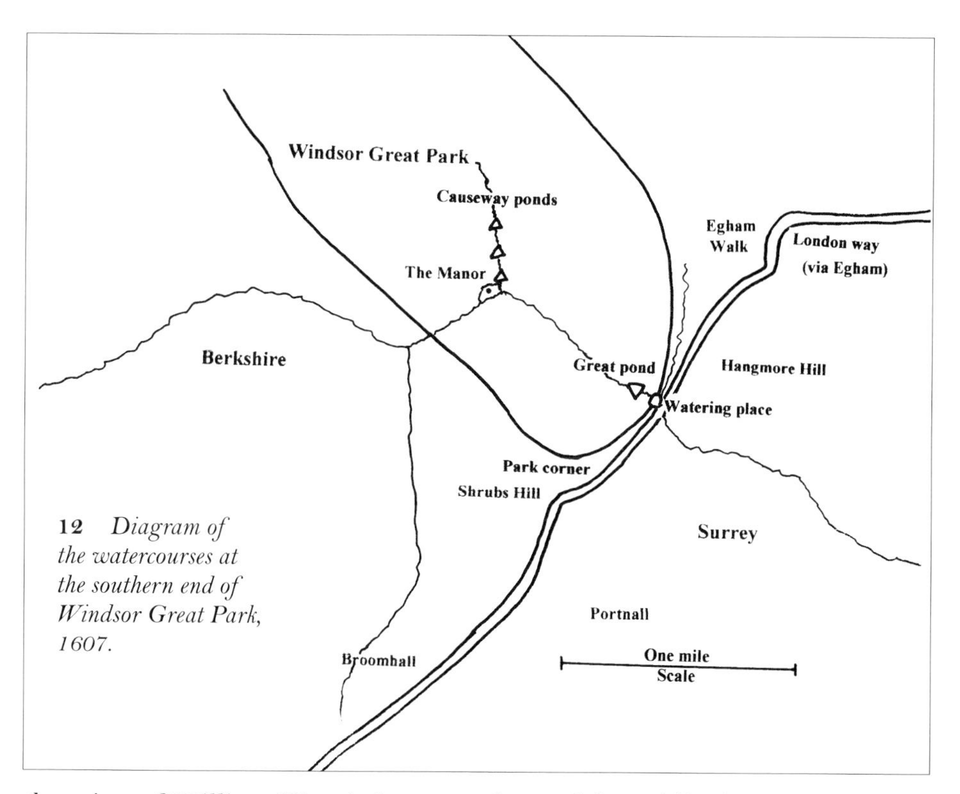

12 *Diagram of the watercourses at the southern end of Windsor Great Park, 1607.*

the reign of William IV to inform members of the public that it was erected by George II and 'commemorated the services of his son, William, Duke of Cumberland, the success of his arms and the gratitude of his father'.

The duke came to live at Great Lodge, the ranger's official residence in the park. His first task was to plan with his architects and advisors how to carry out improvements at his new home and design a garden to include a 'Great Lake', embellished with a temple, grotto and bridges. These peaceful plans, however, were interrupted in 1747 by a recall to arms: the War of the Austrian Succession was still dragging on in Europe. Cumberland faced Marshall Saxe of France at Laffelt in the Netherlands and outmanoeuvred the larger force. He was, however, forced to retreat when his allies failed him and he returned to England with his reputation as a soldier somewhat tarnished.

He had from then on ample time to concentrate on the larger work at Virginia. He commissioned John Vardy, architect and surveyor, to draw up a plan of the existing landscape. The resulting map[3] shows clearly the 'Virginy Brooke', the gate into the park of the same name and the half-dozen or so habitations that made up the hamlet of Virginia in 1750. Virginia House was still in existence, while further north lay the cluster of buildings round the farmhouse that was the heart of the hamlet of Wick. Vardy's plan shows the owner of Wick Farm as James Richards. When the latter died in 1750 the estate passed to his daughter, Elizabeth. John Vardy was so taken

13 *A View of His Highness The Duke of Cumberland's Lodge in Windsor Great Park, 1750,* The Gentleman's Magazine *Nov. 1765.*

with the area while surveying it—or was impressed by its potential for appreciation—that he acquired a copyhold estate, formerly held by Henry Strode, whose generosity had provided Egham with a charity school and almshouses. The large estate included a house and 11 acres at Wick and remained in the Vardy family until 1803.[4]

The first task for Cumberland's landscape designers was to dam up the Virginia River and to this end a pondhead or dam was built at the eastern end to impede the flow of water and force it to collect in the low-lying areas. The process was accelerated by the valley being dug out and the scene enhanced by the creation of mounds and hillocks, adorned by plantations of trees. Those privileged to visit the scene were fascinated by the scale and power of it all as well as by the prettiness of such details as the grotto and the little bridges.[5]

Cumberland was extremely loyal to his brothers-in-arms and with him at Windsor, as he had been in Scotland and the Netherlands, was his draughtsman, Thomas Sandby. Instead of mapping and depicting battle areas as he had done in the

14 *Bob Dun, one of the Duke of Cumberland's gardeners at the Great Lodge,* c.*1755,* *Paul Sandby—'A most facetious fellow' was written on the back.*

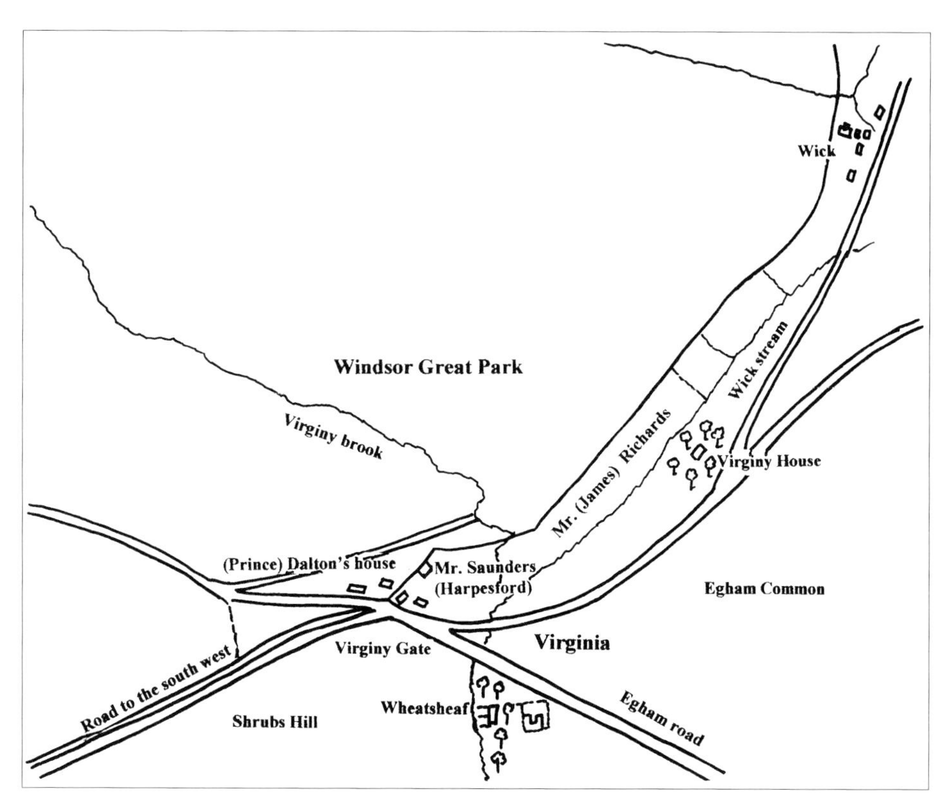

15 *Diagram of the southern end of Windsor Great Park—detail from The Plan of Windsor Great Park, 1750, John Vardy.*

16 *Cascade and grotto at Virginia Water, after Paul Sandby.*

17 *The Great Bridge over the Virginia River,* c.*1754, Paul and Thomas Sandby.*

war zones, Sandby was engaged, while staying at Windsor, to record the developments in the park. Thomas was later joined by his brother, Paul, the watercolourist. Together they created an artistic and topographically accurate picture of the transformations taking place at the southern end of the park. In 1754 a series of engraved prints, 'Eight Views of Windsor', were published depicting some of the wonders, including the single-span, Chinese-style bridge that crossed the water near Blacknest Gate.[6]

The Duke of Cumberland's entourage in the park soon became acquainted with the local gentry. In 1751 a cricket match was arranged between the duke's eleven, who emerged the victors, and a side led by Sir John Elwell,[7] the young Member of Parliament for Guildford, who owned land in Egham and Wick.[8] This gentlemanly exchange between town and Crown was a far cry from the violent confrontations of the previous century.

John Rocque's surveys of Surrey and Berkshire, published in 1752, show the lake not yet constructed and the river marked as Virginia Water, the name the lake acquired. Many labourers would be required to carry out this grand design. Tradition has it that Cumberland used his soldiers for the work.[9] Certainly there were soldiers quartered in Egham parish immediately before the Battle of Culloden: five baptisms of soldiers' children and the deaths of two soldiers and a soldier's child were recorded in the parish registers between November 1745 and April 1746. There are, however, no such entries for the succeeding nine years when most of the work at the lake would have been done. Between July 1755 and July 1757 the parish registers reveal that there were once more soldiers in Egham, the men of Colonel Choldmondley's Dragoons. Two children born to his soldiers were baptised and another child and two soldiers buried. In May 1757 Sir Robert

Riches' Dragoons were also in the vicinity, two children being baptised that month. By then the majority of Cumberland's soldiers would have been disbanded or engaged in conflicts in the colonies. Of the disbanded men it is not impossible that some of them had heard of their old commander's great project at Windsor and sought employment with him.

For the men from the several small communities round the park, the opportunity of finding new employment so near to home was a godsend. More births than deaths were recorded in Egham in 1725 and the population had risen to 1,200.[10] The wage offered by the Duke of Cumberland of between 9d. and 1s. 6d. a day for casual work was more than welcome. The duke seemed also to understand the perennial dilemma faced by the agricultural worker: at harvest there was too much work to be done while in winter there were few opportunities to earn a crust and avoid dependency on parish dole.[11] Dr Richard Pococke, visiting the works at Virginia Water in August 1754, reported that the duke carried on no improvements at harvest time, but employed a great number of men in the winter.[12]

Even before he became Ranger of Windsor Great Park, Cumberland was a lover of the hunt and in 1743 had appointed Prince Dalton to be his huntsman and gamekeeper in Windsor Forest. With such a significant Christian name, Dalton was more than likely born into a family of royal servants. In 1746 he was living with his wife, Mary, in East Hampstead, Berkshire, deep in the heart of the forest. There his son was baptised less than a month after the great victory at Culloden and named William Prince after the conquering hero who was also Dalton's employer.[13]

Cumberland was clearly anxious for his chief gamekeeper to be established nearer his great new project and, during the 1740s, repair work was carried out at the lodge near Virginia Gate.[14] The Dalton family had moved in by February 1751 when their daughter, Margaret, was baptised in Egham parish church. John Vardy marked the site of Dalton's lodge on his plan; it lay within the pales of the park and near the main road. It was a good position from which to observe those coming into the park and Dalton soon became the scourge of local poachers.

The cost of landscaping the southern end of the park came from Duke William of Cumberland's own privy purse and there are many examples of his consideration for his workmen.[15] His sister, the Princess Amelia, rebuked him on one occasion for his generosity in employing so many men. He replied that they needed him even if he did not need them.[16] His munificence was recalled in his obituary: his loss would be sorely felt in the neighbourhood where he had employed so many men.[17]

To add to the pleasure of the royal family and enhance the visual delights of the lake, a small fleet of boats was brought to the landlocked park. The hulk, from which the duke created a fantastic Chinese-style vessel known as the Mandarin yacht, came down the River Thames to the *Bells of Ouseley* inn at Old Windsor and thence overland to Virginia Water.[18] This provided an exciting

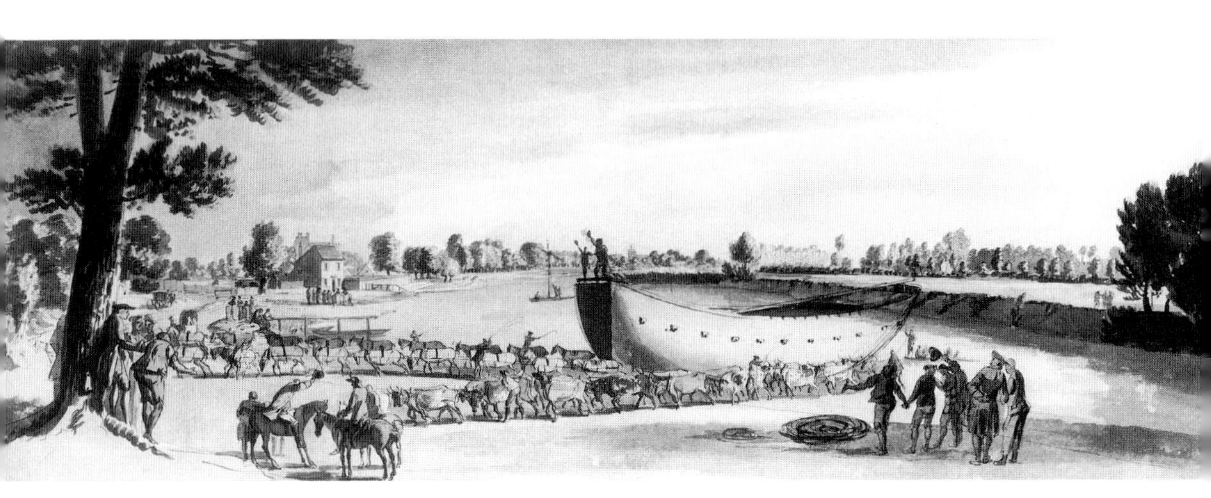

18 *The removal of a hulk from the Thames at Old Windsor, 1749, Paul Sandby.*

free spectacle for the local populace as the hulk was dragged ashore by teams of oxen. There must have been even greater suspense, as the hulk was drawn up the steep hill to Englefield Green and along the lanes to the lake.

Other materials and artefacts were brought to the park by more conventional methods. In July 1753 it was reported to the trustees of the Bedfont & Bagshot Turnpike Trust, meeting at the *King's Head* inn in Egham, that the Duke of Cumberland's wagons had gone through the turnpike overweight, presumably at Staines bridge. The keeper, doubtless for fear of losing his job, did not insist on immediate payment. The Clerk to the Trustees, Henry Brumbridge, was ordered to call on Andrew Ford, the duke's steward, to collect the penalty for passing the turnpike overweight. By the following December the duke had agreed to pay the £16 fine, but the money was not reported as received until March 1754.[19]

Most of the work at Virginia Water in the 1750s took place within the bounds of the royal park and was to the advantage of local people. It provided them with work, and travellers, stopping on the road to catch a glimpse of the wonders, brought custom to the *Wheatsheaf* inn. Two of the duke's plans, however, involved the acquisition of land outside the park. He wanted to build observation towers at each end of the lake so that the royal family might view the prospect as a whole and see its place in the surrounding countryside. The land in question, at Shrubs Hill and Hangmore Hill, appeared to be part of Egham Common, waste of the manor of Egham, land where commoners traditionally had the right to graze animals, gather wood, berries, nuts, furze and fern and even cut turf or peat. The area was far from the gaze of the steward of the manor and even the officials of the Egham Parish vestry, the local authority of the time, who supervised such matters. The poorer inhabitants used the common as their own, with or without official consent, and it made an important contribution to their survival.

Egham parish, stretching from Staines bridge in the east to Broomhall in the west, was extensive. It included vast swathes of common land—1,986 acres when the parish was surveyed in 1790. It was not surprising then that when representatives of the Duke of Cumberland asked permission of the Egham vestry to take the land at Shrubs Hill and Hangmore Hill into the park, it was readily given. The officers of the vestry, local gentry and yeomen led by the vicar, resolved that for a rent of five guineas a year, payable to the Overseers of the Poor, the land would pass to the duke.[20] Money in hand was more useful to meet the needs of the deserving poor than acres of scrubby land. Moreover, the gentry and tradesmen would have to contribute less in poor rates.

The Duke of Cumberland may, however, have paid rent for land at Shrubs Hill that was already part of Windsor Great Park. The fact that the road from Virginia to Reading separated it from the rest of the estate[21] may have helped to make it indistinguishable from the common heath land around it. The site for the tower at Shrubs Hill was shown marked with a cross on Rocque's map of 1752 and a triangular viewpoint, the Belvedere, was built there. The land at Hangmore Hill, opposite the cascade, was left undisturbed for a longer period. By 1760 Thomas Sandby had produced a plan for a simple, rectangular, red-brick tower with a spiral staircase to a central viewpoint and then to the roof. This building later became known as the Clockcase and Sandby's design shows a clock in place halfway up the tower.[22] F.T. Rawlins reported 100 years later that it had been Cumberland's own wish that a clock should be placed in the building, 'that the park-keepers and labourers employed hereabouts, might hear the hours strike, and thus regulate the day's labour', but it was never installed. Much as Cumberland cared about his workmen, his intention in planning a tower on Hangmore Hill had little to do with labourers' timekeeping. The building

19 *'His Royal Highness The Duke of Cumberland's Viewpoint on Shrubs Hill', 1777: engraving from a watercolour by P. Sandby.*

of the brick tower was delayed—other projects had priority. Landscaping and laying out the plantations had begun by 1764 but it is likely that by the death of William, Duke of Cumberland, a year later, the building had only just begun.[23] Around the tower a circular plantation of about 14 acres was 'Inclosed from the Common'.[24] Despite the decision of their vestry, local people found it hard to accept that this isolated patch was no longer theirs but had become a detached piece of Windsor Great Park. They continued to use it much as before, even after the plantations were laid out and the building in place. Usually the trespass was harmless, for such purposes as the gathering of dead wood—but not always.

By the 1760s the hamlet of Virginia was prospering in a small way from the improvements in Windsor Great Park, from its location on a turnpike road and from the presence of the *Wheatsheaf* inn. In 1763 this prosperity was undermined by changes initiated by the trustees of the turnpike trust. In that year the Bedfont & Bagshot Turnpike Trust was divided by a new Act of Parliament (3 George III cap.47) into two districts: the section from the 20th milestone on Egham Hill to the Basingstone became the Western District.

This more specific responsibility seemed to give the trust a new lease of life in the area. The most influential men in Egham parish were sworn in at the first trustees' meeting held on 7 May at the *Red Lion*, Bagshot: William Edgell of Milton Place, Richard Wyatt, who had succeeded his father at Luddington House, the Rev. Thomas Beighton, Francis Bartholomew, the younger of Rusham House, John Jebb of Portnall Park, Virginia Water, and Thomas Foster of Trotsworth, also in Virginia Water. Chief among them was Sir John Elwell,[25] who had just established himself in his fine new Gothic villa, Elvill's, at Englefield Green. It was built by Stiff Leadbetter, carpenter and builder of Eton, between 1758 and 1763 for £5,100.[26]

At the first business meeting held a fortnight later they were joined by Hugh Stevenson, the Egham surgeon and friend of Richard Wyatt and Thomas Sandby, and by Charles Buckworth of Bishopsgate. There was much to organise. New toll collectors for the Western District were appointed at a wage of 11s. a week. More labourers would be required and paid 8s. weekly, their foreman receiving 10s. Local farmers were approached about lending teams for a payment of 8s. a day. Finally new tools were ordered—pickaxes and wheelbarrows from Timothy Gates, the Egham blacksmith. The surveyor, shown in earlier minutes to have received a salary of £60 per annum, was granted an increase of seven guineas because of the extra work he would have to do. It was estimated that £1,000 would be required 'for Carrying on the Road'. Sir John Elwell and Richard Wyatt were among those prepared to lend money to the trust for this purpose at an interest rate of 4.5 per cent.[27]

By July 1763 the trustees' plans had become more ambitious: they were no longer merely repairing the existing turnpike road but 'Carrying on the Work of the New Road'. The initial £1,000 required had been secured and the surveyor could have whatever he needed for the work. There was

20 *Elvill's, the house of Sir John Elwell at Englefield Green, 1784.*

no discussion on the desirability of such a road in the minutes; no plans were mentioned until July 1765, when a Mr Hawkins was paid £112 for his civility in lending his plan for the turnpike road. The site of the new road seemed, however, to be so well known to the trustees by July 1763 that it was feasible to make an alteration to it: 'The new Road which was to be Carried on the Back Side of the Ground opposite the Red Lion Alehouse Westward from Shrubs Hill in a direct Line ... shall be Brought down to the Red Lion Alehouse into the Old Road.'[28] The new turnpike road would therefore run from the 20th milestone on Egham Hill, past Windsor Great Park in a straight line further south than the previous route to join the old road at the *Red Lion* at Shrubs Hill.

By this time it would seem that William, Duke of Cumberland, had become impatient with the liberties taken by local people. Their presence in the park, on whatever pretence, was prejudicial to the breeding of game there. They were forbidden in future to 'strole about therein' for such purposes as bird-nesting or wooding.[29] The removal of a public road away from the pales of the park would help to make unlawful entry more difficult, at least for strangers. Only an army of gamekeepers could keep determined locals out.

Fortunately for the duke's wishes and the smooth management of turnpike affairs, most of the land required for the new road ran through waste or common land of the royal manor of Egham. The men with most influence at the manor court and in the parish vestry were also trustees of the turnpike. Their agreement could be taken as read: the trustees gained a new road and

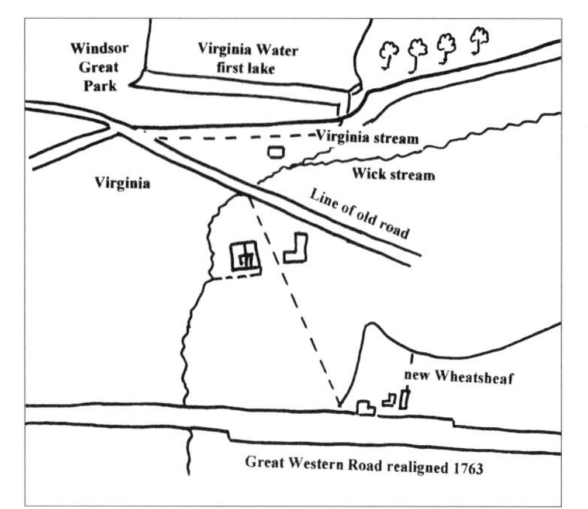

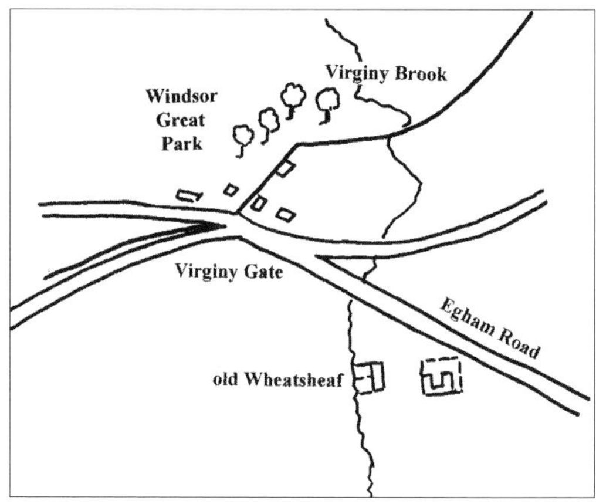

21 *Diagrams comparing the lines of the old and new turnpike roads at Virginia Water.*

the duke more privacy. There is no mention in the turnpike minutes of a need to buy land from the two private owners of wasteland in the line of the road. Neither Mrs Elizabeth Wentworth nor the Child family lived in the vicinity and their rights seem to have been overlooked.

By early 1764 it was clear that the chief financial provider for the creation of a new road was the Earl of Albemarle. Sums of money were regularly received from him, amounting to £1,000 by August 1764. From among the trustees at that time, Richard Wyatt had contributed £700 and the Rev. Edward Cooper of Windlesham £200.[30] George Keppel, 3rd Earl of Albemarle, was not a trustee of the turnpike trust and attended no meetings. He was, however, part of the trusted entourage that attended William, Duke of Cumberland, in war and peace, in Scotland, in the Netherlands, in London and at Windsor. Albemarle, then Lord Bury, had served with distinction at the battles of Fontenoy in 1745 and at Culloden a year later. Indeed, he had been chosen to carry the news of the victory over Charles Edward Stuart to London.[31]

During the Seven Years' War (1756-63) Albemarle's military expertise was not forgotten and in March 1762, with the duke's encouragement, he led an expedition against Cuba. The capture of Havana six months later was a military and financial triumph for Albemarle,[32] and Egham celebrated the victory with the lighting of bonfires. Albemarle returned to England on the cessation of hostilities with France and Spain in 1763 a very rich man.[33]

In times of peace Albemarle served the duke as lord of the bedchamber with rooms at Great Lodge. In 1759 he had been appointed Deputy Lieutenant of Windsor Forest and Ranger and Keeper of Bagshot Walk.[34] When he returned to Windsor after the Cuban adventure he found the Egham gentry, with whom the Cumberland set was not unacquainted, in almost sole control of that section of the turnpike road that touched the boundaries of Windsor Great Park. One thousand pounds was a small but invaluable investment if it ensured that the turnpike road was diverted away from the duke's improvements at Virginia Water.

The trustees moved quickly. By October 1763, bills were coming in thick and fast for the supply of bricks and lime to be used in the building of the new bridge over the Virginia stream. This was the major engineering challenge of the new road and was being dealt with first. A carpenter, John Smith, and a mason, Charles Munden, were paid for work at the new bridge at Virginia Water.[35] From February 1764 the surveyor presented regular bills for the teams and labourers employed on the road. He was always in need of more money for material as well as labour. Intensive work by craftsmen and labourers continued until the autumn of 1765. By the following summer the new road must have been finished, for the mason, Charles Munden, was paid 5s. to re-mark each milestone and paint the letters black. As well as the Earl of Albemarle's contribution of £1,000, Richard Wyatt and the Rev. Edward Cooper had each loaned a total of £800 for the project.[36]

Ironically William, Duke of Cumberland, did not live to see the new road completed. He died suddenly in October 1765 and was succeeded in his title and as Ranger of the Great Park by his nephew, Henry Frederick. It was fortunate that Thomas Sandby remained at Little Lodge as Deputy Ranger to provide continuity and supervision. Royal interest in the area waned: the excitement of the early days of the project was over. Henry was, moreover, in the 1770s, *persona non grata* at court because of his secret and unsuitable marriage.[37]

With the new road almost finished it became more difficult to attract the trustees to meetings, which often had to be abandoned. The authorisation of routine repairs was of little interest and it was only possible to hold one meeting in 1766. In an attempt to remedy this, new trustees were appointed in 1768, including Edward Bulkeley of Englefield Green, Thomas Sandby, to represent the duke, the Rev. William Robert Jones of Egham Wick and Thomas Burton,[38] innkeeper of Egham and aspiring landowner. Thomas Sandby was, by then, also a parishioner of Egham. As well as enjoying his lodgings at the Deputy Ranger's house in the park, he held, copyhold of the manor of Egham, a cottage and more than three acres of land fronting onto the wide expanse of pre-enclosure Englefield Green. Two neighbouring cottages were held by William Delves, described as a servant to William, Duke of Cumberland.[39] It is not likely that Sandby often resided at Englefield Green but the ownership of property provided an investment and a useful access to Egham society.

The hamlet of Virginia was isolated by the realignment of the road. Previously its cottages had been located on either side of a busy thoroughfare. After 1766 the hamlet became a backwater, its inn no longer so easily accessible from the Great Western Road. The hamlet of Wick, on the other hand, had not been affected by the new road, but there was a small realignment between neighbours. In 1761 Andrew Mackason negotiated

22 *Englefield Green near Egham, the cottage owned by Thomas Sandby and after 1798 by his son-in-law, T.P. Sandby, Paul Sandby.*

with Elizabeth Richards, the owner of Wick Farm, to acquire a tiny piece of land—only four roods—in order to tidy their respective entrances.[40]

In January 1768 Elizabeth married the Rev. William Robert Jones by special licence at Egham church, and the manor of Wick was settled on them both in trust. The Rev. Jones was a lecturer at Egham's parish church. Lecturers were appointed separately from the vicar to preach a certain number of sermons a year and financed by voluntary subscriptions from parishioners. Usually they were more puritan in their theology than the established clergy.[41] Jones was also the schoolmaster of Henry Strode's Charity School in Egham, where he conducted his duties conscientiously, while his wife, Elizabeth, busied herself with nursing the almsmen and women in the care of the charity.[42]

During 1767 and 1769 the Rev. Jones was acting as curate as well as lecturer, conducting weddings, possibly when Egham's much loved vicar, Thomas Beighton, 'the friend, the comfort of the sick and poor', was absent.[43] Indeed, in 1770 Jones described himself as curate and continued to act in this capacity after Beighton died in 1771. The Rev. James Liptrott was appointed to the living in the December of that year, but seems to have played little part in the spiritual life of the parish and only succeeded in antagonising his parish officers. He resigned from Egham, taking the neighbouring parish of Thorpe, but was reinstated to Egham, recording in a new baptismal register that he came to reside at the vicarage on 30 September 1773.[44]

That there was antagonism between the pleasure-loving vicar and the dutiful curate is suggested by the fact that Jones retained an old baptismal register for a while and made this entry in it: '10th Oct, 1773 The Rev. Wm Robert Jones, Curate and Lecturer, was in possession of this Book.' Liptrott held the living, however, and both men continued to live and work in the parish for many years, doubtless appealing to different factions in the church.

23 *Parish church of St John the Baptist, Egham, 1804.*

In the years after Duke William of Cumberland's death, wind and weather took their toll of the adornments round the lake in Windsor Great Park. In March 1768 Thomas Sandby wrote to the Commissioners of the Treasury listing repairs urgently needed. The palings were insufficient to keep the game in the park; the stone on the Cumberland obelisk was worn and its fence faded; the summerhouse on the moated island and the temple on China Island needed attention and the bridges by the cascade and the High Bridge over Virginia Water required repairing and repainting. As so often the keepers' lodges were barely habitable. Sandby estimated that to implement all these works would cost more than £11,000. His plea was reinforced two months later by no less a personage than the Duke of Gloucester, who declared through an intermediary that the bridges and ridings in the area were dangerous.[45]

Worse was to come. On 1 September 1768 a great storm swept across south-east England, causing flooding in London and Middlesex. At Virginia Water the pondhead at the lake was damaged and a surge of water swelled the banks of the River Redbourne. Mrs Mary Delany, the diarist, who had been privileged to visit the lake, described in a letter to a friend her difficult

24 *Henry Strode's Charity School and Almshouses, 1812.*

journey out of London and reported newspaper accounts that 'The Virginia Water broke head and is entirely gone, fish and all, and a house in its way carried off as clear as if no house had ever been built there.'[46] The hamlet of Virginia must have suffered severely in this deluge; most likely one of its houses was carried away. Indeed, Virginia House itself does not feature on any later 18th-century maps. The Annual Register recorded that there had even been several deaths by drowning. If this report was correct the fatalities did not occur locally, for there are no burials listed in the Egham or Thorpe parish registers for the first week of September. The memory of the disaster was long-lasting and widespread. As far away as Chertsey, people were outraged, claiming to have been nearly drowned by the flood.[47]

The first meeting of the Bedfont & Bagshot Turnpike Trust to be held after the collapse of the pondhead at Virginia Water was chaired by Thomas Sandby, but no mention of the storm was recorded. Damage must nevertheless have been done to the road, for in the February of the following year Edward Browne, the bricklayer, was paid £15 8s. 6d. for work at the bridge at Virginia Water 'per the Inundation of the Pond head bursting'. It was not revealed if the Crown paid the trustees for this damage, caused by the overflowing of the royal lake.[48]

There was, however, a silver lining even to such a heavy storm cloud for one person in Virginia. The deluge enabled John Atkins, proprietor of the *Wheatsheaf* inn, to rectify the damage done to his business two years earlier by the building of the new turnpike. He took full advantage of the opportunity afforded him by the lack of royal presence and the isolated nature of the hamlet to assart a piece of land from Egham Common. On it he built a new *Wheatsheaf* where an inn would profit him most—directly on the new main road. Both the breaking of the dam at Virginia Water and the construction of a new inn soon afterwards remained vivid in the popular imagination. Fifty-six years later three old men, John North of Portnall Farm, William Hutton of Egham and Thomas Tily of Bishopgate Heath, perfectly remembered 'the breaking of the Pond Head at Virginia Water'

25 *Design for a new pondhead at Virginia Water with the* Wheatsheaf *and Clockcase Tower,* c.*1782, Thomas Sandby.*

and Atkins building himself a new *Wheatsheaf*.[49] In 1771 Daniel Patterson published *A New and Accurate Description of all the Direct and Principal Cross roads in Great Britain.* In it he described the new *Wheatsheaf* inn, three-and-a-quarter miles from Egham, as the '*New England inn*', repeating the same fiction as Ogilby's map, compiled a century earlier.

The storm and the lack of enthusiasm for more work at Virginia Water were also to the advantage of the neighbourhood poachers and the magistrate was kept informed. Richard Wyatt, who had grown up at Luddington House, became a magistrate in 1767 and in this capacity kept detailed notes of the cases that came before him. Two years earlier he had married Pricilla Edgell, whose family resided at Milton Place.[50]

In November 1773 William Try, Keeper of the Purlieus of Windsor Forest, appeared to sue for his rightful share of the fine levied on a miscreant he had arrested. The man in question was Richard Wapshott, accused of keeping a greyhound for the purpose of killing game. Although not actually found poaching he was still fined for the offence, being unqualified by birth or position to keep hunting dogs or ferrets.[51]

In the November of the following year Prince Dalton, the gamekeeper at Virginia Gate, still in royal service, heard a gunshot near the park. He found Edward Rockall, a carpenter, and Edward May, a labourer, both of Egham, hunting with a lurcher dog and carrying guns. He warned them off. It made no difference that the men had not entered the park or killed the king's game. Like Wapshott they were not entitled to keep ferrets or hunting dogs or to carry guns or snares or any other device for catching game. Only the owners of parks and warrens, or of property worth £100 a year and their heirs might do so.[52]

A few days later Dalton found a whole crowd of men in a wood inside the park. Two of them he knew, a man named Tarrant and Richard Trundall, both Egham labourers. He told them to leave the park but Tarrant refused. When the other men got outside they met up with Rockall and May and returned. There was an exchange of words and Tarrant swore that if they were molested he would give the gamekeeper 'such a dressing as he never had in his life before'. Surprisingly he was the only one punished—fined the usual £5 for the admitted game offence—and no further mention was made of the threats. The local magistrate was, as previously, tolerant of forest misdemeanours.[53]

Dalton was busy that month. Only a day after dealing with May and Rockall he apprehended John Hopkins, a victualler of Egham, for using a lurcher and a gun in pursuit of game. Hopkins admitted the offence and paid the fine.[54] Though a mild punishment compared to death or transportation, the £5 fine was a hefty sum to find—the equivalent of 10 weeks' pay for a labourer. One has to conclude that poaching was worth the risk. A considerable number of local men were clearly involved, several of them known to the keeper by name, presumably because they were old offenders.

The gamekeeper could not patrol his entire walk at one time: perhaps an occasional purge was enough to warn the poachers off. It does not appear, however, that these men were being punished with the severity the 'Black Act' had demanded. The poachers for their part admitted the offence and paid the fine readily enough, being doubtless all the more determined not to be caught next time. Indeed, only a few weeks after May and Rockall had been caught with dog and guns near the park they were suspected of stealing a ferret with a bell round its neck from a stable in Egham.[55] Poaching by whatever means would clearly continue.

The turnpike road as well as the park attracted criminals. Cattle and horse thieves used the road network to facilitate their felonies but there was also more serious crime. Travellers in the Egham area suffered like other road users from the unwanted attentions of highwaymen. As early as 1673 John Aubrey, the antiquary, on his travels in Surrey, had described the road at Shrubs Hill, near Windsor Park, as 'the high Western Road so infamous for frequent Robberies'.[56]

The heyday of the highwayman was to come in the 18th century, with the improvement of the roads and greater mobility among the population. The road westwards from Virginia, passing over a lonely and isolated section of Bagshot Heath, had an evil reputation. According to G.M. Hughes, the *Broomhall Hutt*, a public house further west along the road from Shrubs Hill, was a favourite haunt of highwaymen, with whom the landlord and his ostler were said to be in league. Honest innkeepers, in an attempt to protect their businesses, banded together to employ horsemen to deter robberies. One such was possibly John Kunnison, working incognito as 'a London rider' while travelling as a linen-draper.[57] According to the statement made before Richard Wyatt by Thomas Luff, the victualler at the *Broomhall Hutt*, Mr Kunnison had arrived at the inn late in the afternoon of 17 January 1774. As the saddlebags were taken off the horse, the linen-draper asked if there were rogues about. Other customers were in the house at the time but 10 minutes after the last one left, Kunnison called for his horse and bags and also departed. It was 5 p.m. and dark.[58] His riderless horse was found the next day but of the linen-draper there was no trace. Later that month Kunnison's brother, Robert, arrived at the inn to investigate his brother's disappearance. He accused Luff and his servants of robbing his brother but no charges were brought.[59]

26 *Crossing Bagshot Heath, adapted from a drawing by Hugh Thompson.*

Another frightening incident took place near the *Broomhall Hutt* one afternoon in early December of the same year. Daniel Harvey, a driver of common post chaises, was conveying three ladies along the main road. Suddenly a man ordered him to stop and spoke to the women: 'Pray, ladies, don't be frightened. I am in distress and money I must have.' They gave him two or three guineas and, as the highwayman turned away, he gave the driver 1s. Just then the Taunton stagecoach approached and the women reported their loss.[60] A few weeks later, the same Daniel Harvey, this time driving two different ladies, was again stopped by the same person. Again the highwayman told them not to be afraid and reiterated his tale of personal distress. The ladies pleaded poverty but in the end gave him 3s. 6d.[61]

All this came to light at the end of January 1775 when Edward Turner, yeoman, and Thomas Swayne, victualler, both of Chertsey, were stopped and robbed on St Ann's Hill, Chertsey, by a man on horseback. Thomas Swayne had some 2s. in silver taken. Three days later the two men, having heard that there was a suspicious character on the road, set off in pursuit and apprehended a man, whom they believed to be the highwayman, at the *Red Lion* at Shrubs Hill. The chaise driver identified the man, by then known to be Robert Goodchild, a distiller of St Olave's, Southwark, as the person who had robbed his passengers previously. He also claimed that the mare belonging to the suspect was the one used in the robberies on the post chaises.[62]

Robert Goodchild was committed to the Kingston Assizes where on 3 April 1775 he was charged on six counts of highway robbery. The victims and informants questioned by Richard Wyatt were among the witnesses. Goodchild was acquitted on one count but convicted and sentenced to death for robbing a Mr Thomas Ellison of £13 4s. 7d.[63]

27 *The* Red Lion *inn, Shrubs Hill,* c.*1890, photograph by William End.*

Even Windsor Great Park itself was not safe; Sir Edward Blackett reported in a letter that a carriage had been stopped by a highwayman in broad daylight in the Long Walk 'almost under His Majesty's nose'. No date is given but Sir Edward lived at Thorpe Lee in the 1770s and 1780s.[64]

As well as enduring such threatening encounters, anyone driving on the turnpike roads in the 18th century was subject to numerous restrictions governing the number of horses he might use and the size of wheels on his vehicle. These regulations were designed to protect the road from excessive wear and save the trustees excessive costs for repairs.

The greatest damage to the roads was done by heavy wagons and the turnpike trustees were empowered to charge the owners of excessively bulky loads an overweight penalty fee. In May 1752, therefore, a machine for weighing carts and wagons near the turnpike gate between Staines and Egham was commissioned and by December was in use. The gatekeepers were paid an extra guinea for their trouble in weighing the wagons and their wages increased from 11s. to 13s. a week. Ironically some of the first wagons to be fined for going through the turnpike overweight had belonged to William, Duke of Cumberland.[65]

A number of Acts were also passed in the 18th century to regulate the vehicles using the turnpike roads. Several of these regulations were concerned with the relationship between horsepower and the width of wheels. A four-wheeled wagon with narrow wheels could only be drawn by a maximum of four horses. If the wheels were as wide as 9in (approx. 23cm) the wagon could

28 *A View from Egham Hill, Paul Sandby.*

be drawn by as many as eight horses. A two-wheeled wagon was proportionally allowed three or five horses. Any member of the public could arrest the driver of any wagon infringing this law and take him before a magistrate. As the penalty sometimes involved the forfeiture of the extra horses to the informer it was a profitable occupation to hang about on Egham Hill where the incline often tempted drivers to add extra horsepower to their vehicles.[66]

On 9 November 1771 Richard Pocock of Eton and Henry Crook of Abingdon, both bargemen, testified before Richard Wyatt that at 3 a.m. that morning they had seen a four-wheeled carriage with narrow wheels on the turnpike road travelling with six horses and carrying three sticks of timber. The informants, as good citizens, had taken it upon themselves to remove two of the horses and deliver them to Thomas Plim, Egham's constable. In this case the informants settled for a small sum of money from the owner in lieu of the confiscated horses.[67] Two more bargemen, William Pocock of Eton and Robert Taylor of Cookham, together with two or three others unidentified, were on the road looking out for traffic offenders in June 1773. They stopped a wagon on its way to Salisbury, measured two of its wheels, one of which was found to be less than 9in. They then uncoupled two of the eight horses forthwith and delivered them to the constable at Egham.[68] The drivers of the wagon protested that one of the wheels had broken to pieces on the road. They had tried to find a replacement but the only wheel available was of less than 9in. They had pleaded with the informants not to take the horses but to no avail. Fortunately for the wagoners, the magistrate, Richard Wyatt, was uncertain of the interpretation of the law in this case and did not allow the bargemen to keep the confiscated horses on this occasion.[69]

The vagaries of life on the road continued and poaching flourished but Duke William of Cumberland's grand project at the southern end of Windsor Great Park fell further into dereliction in the 1770s, with little royal interest or money to maintain its beauties.

Chapter Three

The Cost of Restoring 'an Ancient Piece of Water': 1778-1803

It was not until the late 1770s, when George III, Queen Charlotte and their growing family were spending more time out of the capital, that the lake and its environs once more became the subject of royal interest. It soon became known that the king was 'desirous of restoring an ancient Piece of Water which flowed through or over Part of Windsor Great Park, the Head of which, by Means of a late Flood, was broken down'.[1] Plans being drawn up by Thomas Sandby were more ambitious than before and necessitated extending the boundaries of the park to the south and east. The diversion of the turnpike road in 1763 had created space for the park to extend in a southerly direction while to the east the Wick stream, which joined the Virginia river near the old pondhead, would form a new branch of the lake. The king was represented in the new enterprise by John Pitt, the Surveyor General of Woods & Forests. As this was a publicly funded project he had to keep in close touch with his colleagues at the Treasury who had the power to veto any particular extravagance.

Many acres of land belonging to the parish and to private individuals at Virginia and Wick would have to be acquired if this ambitious scheme was to succeed. As early as June 1778 there must have been word of the king's interest in the area for that month, in a lease drawn up between the Child family and their tenant, the husbandman Hugh Gregory Staples, he agreed to give up all claim to the land 'as lays toward Windsor Great Park' in return for a reduction in rent.[2] By 1781 negotiations were well under way.

The land to the south-east of the old pondhead and along the Wick stream was the most crucial to acquire. An Act of Parliament would be required to take over land held in trust but in the immediate vicinity lay several small pieces of privately owned property. Closest to the pondhead was a one-acre piece of meadowland, known as Harpesford, which had been the site of a mill in medieval times. The owners were William Child of St Giles, Middlesex, a coachbuilder, his wife, Thomasine Strong Child, and his sister-

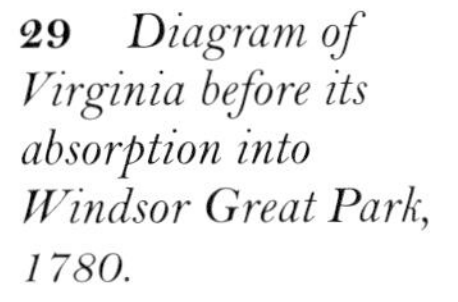

29 *Diagram of Virginia before its absorption into Windsor Great Park, 1780.*

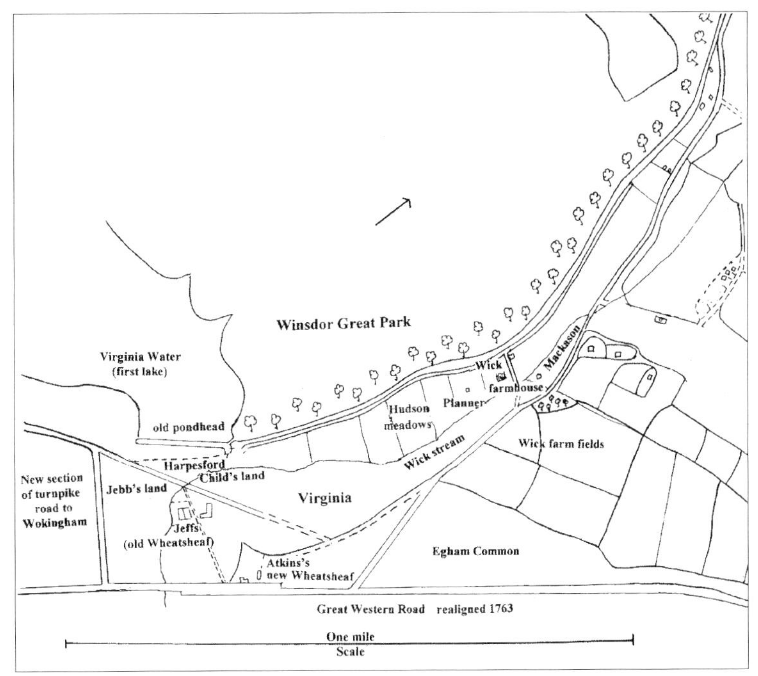

in-law, Charlotte Gilbert. The land was copyhold of the manor of Broomhall in the right of Thomasine and Charlotte, the heiresses at law. The Child family appeared before the manor court in October 1781 to signify their agreement to surrendering the land to the lords of the manor, the President and Scholars of St John's College, Cambridge. At this time, however, the wheels of feudal tenure turned very slowly and John Pitt was not finally admitted as the holder of the land for the king until 1785 when the new dam was well under construction (Appendix II).[3]

The Childs also owned more than 100 acres of freehold land in the vicinity, mainly unenclosed furze and heath. Fourteen acres adjoined the copyhold land and was required by John Pitt. The matter was agreed in October 1781 with the Childs receiving £100 for their land.[4] Having to sell to the Crown seems to have encouraged the Childs to get rid of the rest of their freehold land in Virginia Water; it was known as Child's Waste, was not of high market value at that time and parts still provided Egham commoners with rights of pasture. The Childs found a ready buyer in their neighbour, the Rev. John Jebb, Dean of Cashel in Ireland.[5] He was in the process of acquiring and enclosing various pieces of heath land to add to his estate at nearby Portnall.

Some meadowland belonging to John Jebb himself lay in the line of the proposed new lake and was required for the enlargement. This purchase was concluded in November 1781, Jebb being ready to surrender a few acres to the Crown. Two acres of his land had already had been taken into Windsor Great Park and 'now formed part of the head of water there'.[6]

Near the Childs' Harpesford acre was a property owned by Elizabeth Nunn and her sister, Sarah Jeffs. They were the daughters and granddaughters of royal servants, the nieces and also part heiresses of Baptist Nunn, the fanatical enemy of the forest 'Blacks' (see Chapter 1). Sarah was also married to a park keeper, Robert Jeffs. They had inherited the Virginia Water property from their cousin, Robert, who had, in turn, inherited it from Baptist Nunn in 1742. It had formerly been the *Wheatsheaf* inn but John Atkins, the previous occupier, had moved on to better premises since then. The old inn was a substantial building with stables, buildings, garden and yard but had since become a tenement in the occupation of Ambrose Phillips. Elizabeth Nunn and the Jeffs received £260 in payment from the Crown.[7] That signalled the end for the remaining houses in Virginia: they would soon disappear under the enlarged lake. The only surviving building was the new *Wheatsheaf*, built on the new section of the turnpike road after the great storm of 1768 and John Atkins, the licensee, stubbornly held onto it despite determined efforts from the Office of Woods & Forests to acquire it.

An Act of Parliament, the Pitt Estate Act, was required for the Crown to take over 43 acres of waste of the manor of Egham, as well as Wick Farm, an adjoining small property and some meadowland, all held in trust. On 11 November 1781 a notice was read after Divine Service in Egham's parish church explaining the king's wishes. Four days later the vestry met to discuss the proposal. In return for transferring the land to the Crown and for the loss of common rights on the 43 acres, the parish would accept an annual rent of three guineas to be paid to the Overseers of the Poor. The authors of the Act were confident that Egham had enough wasteland to satisfy all its commoners; it would hardly miss the 43 acres. The land in question was already staked out, from the hamlet of Egham Wick in the east, via the corner of the *Wheatsheaf* garden, to the Belvedere Plantation in the west. The Act also reiterated the responsibility undertaken by the late William, Duke of Cumberland, when he enclosed two pieces of the waste of the manor of Egham in 1746 to pay five guineas annually to the Overseers of the Poor.

The Act received its first reading and its royal assent in 1782. The Atwicks and the Rolfes, who in a previous century had objected to any extension of royal influence, had been replaced by landowners who identified more closely with their royal neighbours. Richard Wyatt, who had become the largest landholder in Egham, being head lessee of the manor of Egham and, in right of his wife, head lessee of the sub-manor of Milton, was on friendly terms with the Windsor Great Park set, in particular with Thomas Sandby. The Wyatts had moved into Milton Place, the capital messuage of the manor of Milton, which became a focus for the social and artistic life of the area. Wyatt collected pictures and supported such artists as John Opie and John Thomas Smith, who, with Thomas and Paul Sandby, were frequent visitors to the house.[8] With Thomas Sandby, the vicar, James Liptrott, the

30 *Egham looking north, showing the* Red Lion *inn, 1830, Edward Hassell—The inn is on the left: the inn garden on the right.*

physician and surgeon, Hugh Stevenson, and other local worthies, Wyatt was a member of a dining club that met fortnightly at the *Red Lion* inn in Egham.[9]

Richard Wyatt was also acquainted with George III. J.T. Smith reported that, while on one of his painting expeditions in Windsor, he had met the king, who enquired where he was staying. On hearing of his connection with Milton Place His Majesty remarked that Wyatt was a good man, adding, 'I have a high regard for him and all his family'.[10]

The largest landholding to be taken into the park was Wick Farm, sometimes known as the manor of Wick. The property was held in trust for the Rev. William Robert Jones and his wife, Elizabeth, who had inherited it from her father, James Richards. Agreement was reached in 1782 with some small pieces of copyhold land being surrendered to John Pitt a year later.[11]

The manor of Wick consisted of more than 100 acres. The manor or farmhouse, shown in the 1788 plan, stood with barns, stables and outhouses in orchards and gardens on the banks of the Wick stream. Most of its fields, however, lay to the east of the Windsor road and stretched down to the Great Western Road (Appendix III). Its soil was fertile enough to support arable cultivation, with some meadows, such as Rushy Brooks and Black Brook Close, where the ground was more boggy.[12] The farm must have provided employment for a number of farm workers, who would have lived nearby.

Only a small part of Wick Farm, that lying along Wick stream and nearest to the park pales, was initially required for the enlargement of the lake. As this included the house and water meadows and was, from an owner's point of view, the most desirable part of the farm, William and Elizabeth Jones wanted no piecemeal settlement but compensation for the loss of the entire estate. John Pitt at first found this very unreasonable but eventually agreed to pay them £2,500 for the whole farm, in the hope of selling off the land that was not required at some future date.[13]

The other properties immediately required at Wick also lay in the proposed path of the new branch of the lake. They were much smaller than Wick Farm. Adjoining the farmhouse to the south-west was a modest estate of two cottages with an orchard. It had been left in trust by Francis Gibbons, yeoman and baker of Egham, to Thomas Ashby, mealman of Staines, for the benefit of Gibbons's wife, Hester, and his younger son, John, who was only five years old, in 1782. After the death of Francis, Hester married Benjamin Planner, brickmaker and considerable property holder in Egham. He was also recently widowed and had, moreover, five children under 16 at home in need of care. John's mother, stepfather and trustee negotiated the legalities concerning the Wick property on his behalf.[14] Instead of money for the cottages they agreed to accept two other pieces of land, called Great and Little Hides, nearly fourteen acres in all, two of the more easterly fields of Wick Farm. The land was said to be worth £250, much more than the value of the original cottages. In fact, the Act concluded that this exchange 'was greatly for the Benefit of the said John Gibbons, the Infant', for the cottages of his original inheritance were in great decay.

The agreement took a long time to complete. As late as 1791, with the work of digging out the Wick branch of the lake well underway, Planner was still collecting rents from tenants living in his stepson's cottage. When the Office of Woods & Forests suggested it was time he gave them notice he replied, somewhat impudently, that he would continue to accommodate John Perkins, who had once worked Wick Farm's fields, 'till such time as he can suit himself better'.[15] The sale of the cottage with an orchard near the farmhouse on the north side of the lane leading to the Wick was more speedily agreed. It was owned by the influential Mackason family and occupied by the farm labourer John North, who would have to find a home elsewhere. The land passed to the Crown in 1782 for £155.[16]

Nearer Virginia lay some meadowland belonging to Atwick Hudson and his wife, Elizabeth. It included the right to pasture cattle and dig peat on the common. Hudson was a cooper and descended, on his mother's side, from a long line of Egham yeomen, the Atwicks. He had inherited the land from his brother, Robert, but 'legal estate and interest still rested' in his trustee, Francis Bartholomew of Rusham. Hudson was ordered to produce the documents that proved his claim to ownership and was paid £282 10s. Bartholomew received 10s.[17]

Royal personages were not exempt from the purchase of land. At the extreme western end of the new extension a small piece of land was required from the Belvedere Plantation, then held by Henry, Duke of Cumberland. A house with a garden had previously stood on the spot and adjoining was another 'pightle' of ground. This land would be needed in the realigning of the turnpike road to Wokingham, which joined the Great Western Road near the *Wheatsheaf* inn. A small section of the Wokingham road was in the way of the new lake and would have to be replaced. The new road would be only 205 yards longer than the old and made up at His Majesty's expense.[18] In the space between the old Wokingham road and the new, a house was built and named Virginia Lodge. Designed by Thomas Sandby, its elegant proportions and prime location above the cascade were much to be envied; it was a fitting residence for the new, gentlemanly office of the king's Head Gamekeeper.[19]

In all, the acquisition of more than 230 acres of land and nine properties belonging to the parish of Egham and its parishioners was required to realise George III's dream of restoring an ancient waterway. The park had swallowed up what was left of the hamlet of Virginia and the heart of Egham Wick. According to F.T. Rawlins, writing 75 years later, the remains of the old inn could still be seen halfway across the lake when the water was drawn off.[20]

With the land to the immediate south-east of the old pondhead in the hands of the Surveyor of Woods & Forests by 1782, the old *Wheatsheaf* and the house at Harpesford could be demolished, the area cleared and work begin on the construction of a stronger and, if possible, storm-proof dam. The Treasury, mindful of the events of 1768, insisted that the extended lake and its new pondhead should be built 'in a substantial and workmanlike manner'. Thomas Sandby had already produced numerous designs for the pondhead but the weather conditions of the early 1780s were extremely unfavourable

31 *Virginia waterfall and back of the huntsman's house, 1822, John Hassell.*

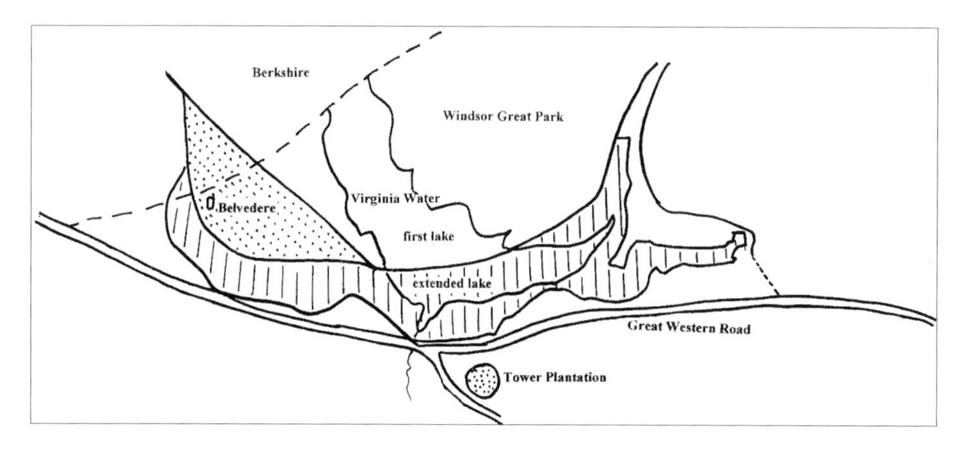

32 *Diagram showing land taken into Windsor Great Park, by William, Duke of Cumberland,* c.*1750, by George III,* c.*1785.*

for such an ambitious engineering project. Excessive rain in the summer of 1783, followed by frosts and sudden thaws in the winter and spring, had washed away the retaining soil and the construction collapsed.[21] The failure of several attempts to build a dam earned Sandby the soubriquet of 'Tommy Sandbank', the title of a satirical poem by George Huddesford, another of the Milton Place circle. Once more, it would seem, the countryside around Virginia Water was threatened with inundation. According to Huddesford, Trumps Mill, two miles downstream, received more water than it could cope with:

> Trumps Mill in the bottom was never supplied,
> Since first it went round with so plenteous a tide:
> Yet the Miller he wished that our Head-maker's skill
> Less water had sent and more grist to his mill.[22]

This is a fine comic image but for the miller an erratic water supply was no laughing matter. An excessive amount of water surging down the valley of the River Redbourne was no joke for the farmers of Thorpe either. Eight landowners sued the Crown for compensation amounting to £19 16s. 6d. when there was a sudden overflow of Virginia Water in October 1789. Henry Brumbridge must have suffered the most damage, receiving more than £10, while the lowest claim, from Richard Roseblade, was for 7s. 6d. They did not receive payment from the Foreman of the Works until 1792.[23]

Many people still remembered the breaking of the old pondhead in 1768 and alarm at a great body of water once more pent up at Virginia Water stretched beyond Thorpe to Chertsey. Its inhabitants had been promised that when the new pondhead was made, consideration would be given to their requirements, that not too much water would be released in wet weather and that an occasional supply would be let down in the dry seasons. Robert Porter, brewer of Chertsey, whose business would also suffer from erratic waterpower, was not sanguine about such promises. He wrote: 'This might be merely verbal or perhaps only thrown out to quiet the apprehensions of the people.'[24]

Not surprisingly the Treasury ordered the foundations of the pondhead to be made deeper and broader: the men had to dig more than 22ft deep and to widen the base to between 180 and 250ft. This meant that nearly double the quantity of material was required, with the resultant increase in cost having to be declared to the paymasters at the Treasury. Whenever possible, raw materials found on site were used. There was, of course, no shortage of sand and gravel in the area. Pockets of clay were more difficult to find; when the pit nearest the pondhead ran out, clay had to be carted three-quarters of a mile from the next available source. There was an abundance of timber in the park and of woodsmen able to supply any quantity of oak and beech. The number of labourers required in simply carting materials was considerable. There was also need for a few specialist craftsmen: metal workers to make cast-iron pipes, bolts and cramps for the cascade and bridge, masons to shape and fix the stones, carpenters to turn the trees into kerbs, sleepers, planks and piles, and bricklayers, who had their own kiln at Blacknest bridge.[25]

The dam would be finished with an impressively high cascade and more heavy labouring work was involved in digging up and carting the massive heath stones to create this feature. Bagshot Heath stones are indigenous to the Virginia Water area and an old pensioner of the Crown, John Tiley, told William Menzies, Deputy Surveyor of the Park in 1864, that the labourers used to watch for patches that turned brown in dry weather and then dig out the stones. There were few carts strong enough to carry the large stones needed for the cascade. Tiley explained that 'alder newly cut bore the strain best'.[26]

John Thomas Smith, the artist and gossip known as 'Rainy Day' Smith, then a guest of Richard Wyatt's at Milton Place, reported meeting Thomas Sandby at work on the cascade in 1785. Sandby was arranging stones to form

33 *Cascade and Hunter's Lodge, 1828, pencil drawing, William Delamotte.*

picturesque peaks and caverns at the head of the lake. Smith recounted the discovery of a stone of great size that would much enhance the impression of breadth in the composition, but it was too large to move. Sandby ordered it to be blown apart with gunpowder and was fortunate that it fell into two equal pieces that could be joined together at the cascade.[27]

John Pitt expected to have finished work on the pondhead by the summer of that year but progress was again bedevilled by floods. It remained incomplete at the time of his death in February 1787. Supervision of the work was undertaken by his deputy, Charles Cole, a builder and surveyor by profession, until John Robinson was appointed as Pitt's successor later in the year.[28] Cole rented Thomas Sandby's house at Englefield Green while he was working in the park and also acquired in his own right a small copyhold estate of about fourteen acres near Bakeham Farm.[29]

Not until October 1788 was the final penstock, or floodgate, in place so that a great sheet of water could form behind it. Attempts were then made to integrate the somewhat neglected red tower, later known as the Clockcase, that had been built on Hangmore Hill, with the rest of the park. From its windows and roof were extensive views of the surrounding countryside, with particularly fine glimpses of the lake and cascade. The problem was that in order to visit this viewpoint the royal family had to leave the park and cross a public road. Robinson proposed building an archway under the turnpike road to provide direct and private access to the amenity. This plan, however, never came to fruition and the isolated tower remained a cause for concern.[30]

It was not an easy task being Surveyor General of His Majesty's Woods & Forests in the 1780s. John Robinson was directly responsible to George III, whose pet project Virginia Water was; also involved were Henry, Duke of Cumberland and Ranger of the Park, who was by then spending more time at Windsor, and his deputy, Thomas Sandby. That there was contention

34 *Rowing boats at Virginia Water, 1825, John Thomas Serres.*

between the two factions is clear from the correspondence. In May 1788 there was disagreement about the exact positioning of the Wick bridge and the vistas that should lead to it. Robinson advised awaiting His Majesty's orders; Sandby was desirous of a meeting 'to settle on a plan for further operations'. A few months later Sandby wrote somewhat petulantly stating that he did not know how His Majesty wanted the cascade finished as he had not been informed. In order to avoid both irritation and expense he would not even attempt to start work on the bridge over the Wick stream until Robinson was present.[31]

Robinson on his part was reluctant to interfere with Sandby's designs but the problems continued to arise. Charles Cole complained in August 1789 that young beeches and oaks, planted on Robinson's orders above Wick bridge, had been cut down by men sent by Cumberland to mow there. Cole only persuaded the men to stop by promising to pay them for their lost time. The impropriety of the action had been pointed out to Cumberland's bailiff but Robinson was anxious what to tell the king, whose delicate state of health often made his reactions unpredictable. Only two months before Robinson had had to apologise for disturbing His Majesty's 'Quiet and Retirement' with too many reports.[32]

Robinson was no desk-bound administrator, having had experience as a land steward before he entered Parliament in 1764. He was extremely knowledgeable on horticultural matters and often sent his subordinates detailed instructions on day-to-day husbandry in the park. He could advise them of the distance to set between the drills in the planting of a hawthorn hedge and recommend just the right rake to disperse molehills or horse dung from the drives. Once the park nursery at Wick was established he insisted that a careful record of the number of beds and the number of plants in each was kept and a catalogue for identification retained on site.[33]

The daily organisation of the largely casual labour force was in the hands of the Foreman of the Works and between 1786 and 1789 Thomas Courtenay held this post. He was well aware of the friction that existed among his betters. In August 1788 he sent a long report to Robinson almost revelling in the rivalry when recounting a somewhat divisive conversation he had had with the monarch himself. Courtenay had had the honour to escort the king and his sons, the Prince of Wales and the Duke of Kent, around the project, at which the king expressed great satisfaction with what had been done. According to the foreman, George III went on to give the greatest praise and credit to Robinson while expressing 'animadversions' of Sandby and his designs, particularly of the cascade.[34]

Only a few weeks later the king was incapacitated by the illness that plagued him for much of his life. The king's absence provided an opportunity for a reassessment of the project at Virginia Water, which as usual was over-running its budget. Some of the more elaborate designs for the lake were shelved, including the building of a grotto near the cascade.[35]

This time the king's absence was short. To the delight of Courtenay and his men, the king's return to good health was announced the following spring and Courtenay was enthusiastic about celebrating his royal master's recovery in a suitable manner. He wrote to Robinson at the beginning of March 1789, expressing his relief that the best of kings had been restored to his people. He asked permission to take up a collection among his men in order for them to drink a loyal toast on the occasion. He also asked permission for them to organise other festive events: to fly a royal flag on the pondhead, to build a bonfire on the heath, to illuminate the *Wheatsheaf* and, most impertinent of all, 'to play the cascade for about half an hour'. At this time the water had only just reached its highest level and was only rarely allowed to flow over the waterfall as work had to continue at the pondhead and on the banks of the lake.[36] The Office of Woods & Forests was generous in its reply: five guineas were granted to be spent on drink and 1d. given to each labourer employed at the works. Courtenay was, however, instructed that he was on no account to run the water over the cascade except on the particular orders of the king.[37]

The foreman earned one and a half guineas (£1 11s. 6d) a week or 5s. 3d. per day, with the rate for an assistant foreman at 3s. 9d. a day. Labourers received from 1s. 6d to 2s. a day. Those with the unpleasant task of working in water might expect an extra 2d. a day and an allowance of beer. Men with some specialist skills such as thatching or sawing earned an extra 1s. or 2s. a week; those who had served their apprenticeships as carpenters or wheelwrights could earn 18s. a week. A master craftsman, such as a mason, could command 5s. a day.[38]

Such a project as the restoration of the southern end of Windsor Great Park was extremely labour intensive: scrubby common land as well as farm fields had to be transformed into an aesthetic landscape, the men having only the use of carts and wheelbarrows, picks and shovels. As in other agricultural enterprises the amount of work available for casual labourers depended on the seasons and the weather. Some tasks could obviously be done all the year round: these included carting and spreading gravel, levelling soil, digging new boundary ditches, removing old palings and fences and putting up new. In spring there were the essential routines of trenching, turfing and planting. In early summer as many as 136 men might be employed weeding, mowing and rolling the rides as well as watering the young trees and newly laid turf. During haymaking and harvest time, however, it was difficult to find suitable men to work in the park: 'Harvest here imploys all the Hands that are good for anything and worth having,' complained Charles Cole. Soldiers had to be brought in to take over such crucial assignments as backing the pondhead.[39]

Autumn was seed-gathering time. Even though many thousands of trees and shrubs were bought in, there was still need for as many native trees as possible to be cultivated. Acorns, haws, chestnuts and pinecones were carefully collected, then sorted, planted and nurtured at the Wick nursery.[40]

Winter was a different story: at the beginning of December 1788, 82 men had to be laid off, only 53 being kept on. 'I shall feel much Pain at discharging the poor men at this Time, but what can be done if there is not work to employ them?' wrote John Robinson. He was under pressure from the Treasury, at this time, not to begin any new works but to consolidate those already underway—the levelling of the Wick branch of the lake, the establishment of the nursery and, most important of all, the security of the pondhead. There were still fears about the safety of the new dam and its proximity to the main road. Thomas Courtenay was of the opinion that it would take a great deal of work to make it safe.[41]

The inclement weather continued throughout the month and added to the distress of the workmen. Later in that December Courtenay was ordered to reduce the workforce further because of frost.[42] Seasonal loss of employment was a common occurrence in the life of the casual agricultural labourer and forced many, however unwillingly, to seek dole from the parish to feed their families.

As well as apportioning the work and paying the men, the Foreman of the Works was responsible for maintaining discipline in the labour force. A disturbing incident occurred in April 1788 when a man was accused of causing a revolt among the labourers. Robinson advised Courtenay to take the accused and the witnesses to the local magistrate, who would 'do the Business'. It was expected that the man would be committed to the House of Correction for a month's hard labour.[43]

35 *The cascade at Virginia Water, immobile in frost, 1917.*

Accidents at work also had to be dealt with. In serious cases Hugh Stephenson, the Egham physician, was called out to treat the injured. He recalled in 1790 that he had made 10 such journeys to the park, for which he had received no recompense. One incident, described in detail, concerned Peter Smith, who had worked in the park for three years until he sustained a serious injury. On 27 March 1787 he fell down a bank of gravel and was admitted to St George's Hospital, where he was pronounced a cripple, 'unable to get his Bread'. Fortunately for him he had also served 22 years in the 41st and 11th Regiments of Foot and had been accepted as an Out Pensioner at the Chelsea Hospital. He was hopeful that the officers of the Crown might grant him the same allowance of 6d. or 4d. a day as received by other pensioners who could no longer support themselves.[44] After all, he had suffered his injury on His Majesty's service even if it was in Windsor Great Park and not on a battlefield.

During the early years of Courtenay's employment most of the work was concentrated around the new pondhead, where the hamlet of Virginia had once stood. The houses along the Wick stream remained intact; indeed Courtenay, as foreman, lived in one of them. By 1788, however, with work underway on the bridge and dam at Wick, their demolition was ordered. In March 1789, 52 men were employed, pulling down the barns, sheds and buildings, including 'my old home', as Courtenay rather wistfully wrote. The following week he had most of his workforce carting away the rubble so that the area could be cleared, ready for planting in the autumn.[45]

With his old home demolished, Courtenay had the inconvenience of having to live a good three miles from his work, and attempts were made to find him a more suitable residence. In May he reported that he had bought, on Robinson's behalf, a property at Harvest Corner called Dunton's Holdings for £340. Courtenay was anxious to get possession as soon as possible so as to start repairs that season but knew that legal procedures and the six months' notice for a sitting tenant to quit would cause inevitable delays. The occupier, he had heard, was 'an Old Singleman, Seemingly Civil and agreeable', who might leave earlier if a reasonable allowance were paid.[46]

It is possible that this feeling of insecurity was the last straw for a man already ill and becoming disillusioned with his job. Courtenay in the summer of 1789 was not a happy man: his reports of that time have a peevish tone. He complained when Robinson failed to get seed buckwheat delivered to him in good time for planting and at a shortage of garden tools and watering cans. In July he resigned, stating that his health was much impaired and his constitution broken as a result of 'the early Vexations and Slavish attendance of the three winters past'. Certainly his workload had increased since his arrival and he was only half a guinea a week better off. He planned to move to London where he hoped to find office work and even wondered if Robinson had such a position to offer. He left the *Wheatsheaf*, where he had been 'laid up', in August 1789.[47]

The buckwheat Courtenay had finally planted to provide winter feed for the game was eaten by hogs. John Robinson was determined to find out who was responsible and obviously suspected the Cumberland faction. In his opinion, 'Hogs are not fit things for a Park.'[48]

Despite these difficulties, work at Virginia Water continued. On Thomas Courtenay's resignation, William Maslin was brought in from the Berkshire side of the park to oversee the men at their habitual tasks of gathering seed, weeding, planting and laying and cleaning drives, while Charles Cole, John Robinson's deputy, provided continuity.[49] As the landscaping of the Wick branch progressed it became clear to Robinson that, to achieve its full potential, more land at Wick would have to be incorporated into the park. The Bagshot to Windsor road, which ran very close to the park pales from Virginia via Wick to Bishopsgate, was one of the problems. Part of the road, the piece that ran from the Great Western Road, near the *Wheatsheaf*, over Egham Common to Wick Farm, was already earmarked for acquisition by the Pitt Estate Act. A substitute for this section was already available in the form of a substantial track running across Wick Heath from further east along the main road, roughly on a line with the present Wick Road.[50]

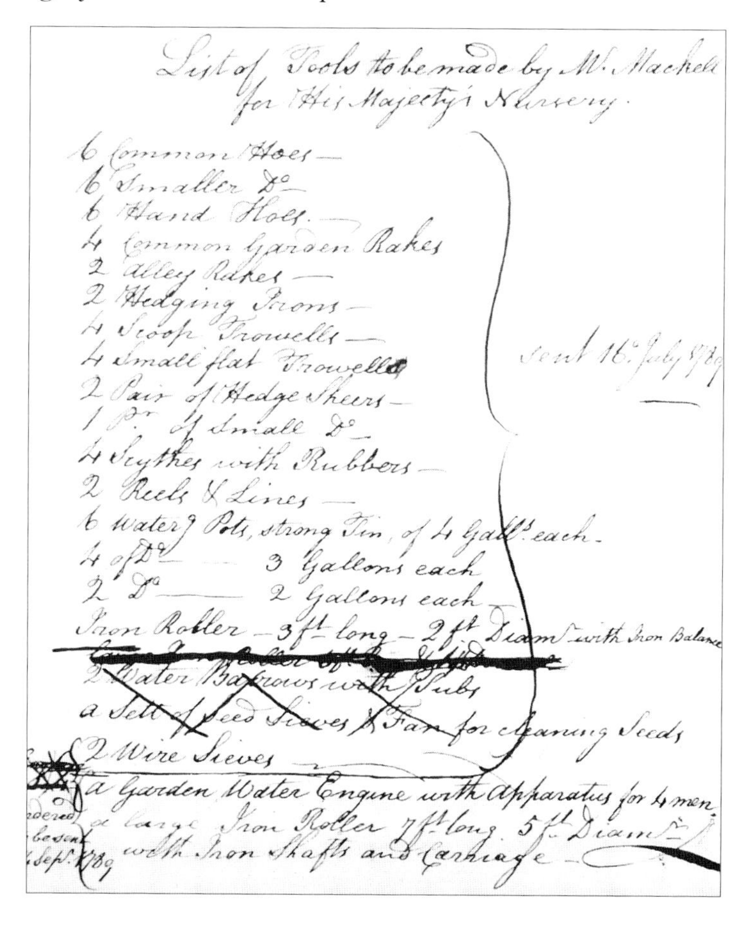
List of Tools to be made by Mr. Mackell
for His Majesty's Nursery.

6 Common Hoes —
6 Smaller Do
6 Hand Hoes. —
4 Common Garden Rakes
2 Alley Rakes —
2 Hedging Irons —
4 Scoop Trowells —
4 Small flat Trowells
2 Pair of Hedge Sheers —
1 Pr. of Small Do —
4 Scythes with Rubbers —
2 Reels & Lines —
6 Water Pots, strong Tin, of 4 Galls. each.
4 of Do — 3 Gallons each
2 Do — 2 Gallons each
Iron Roller — 3 ft. long — 2 ft. Diamr. with Iron Balance
2 Water Barrows with Tubs
a Sett of Seed Sieves & Fan for cleaning Seeds
2 Wire Sieves
a Garden Water Engine with Apparatus for 4 men
a large Iron Roller 7 ft. long 5 ft. Diamr.
with Iron Shafts and Carriage

sent 16th July 1789

Sept. 1789

36 *List of tools required for His Majesty's Nursery by the Foreman of the Works.*

The old road to Windsor was not, in any case, the best of thoroughfares. There was a steep hill from the end of Wick Farm down to Southbrooks and, being so near the Wick stream, the road was liable to flooding.

A radical new plan was therefore proposed to change the line of the Windsor road completely. The new road would run almost parallel to the old but much further east, through Englefield Green rather than the Wick. It would divert off the main road at a point on Egham Common, then sparsely populated but which would later become known, for obvious reasons, as the Bagshot Road. The road would run conveniently near the homes of those royal servants who had chosen to live in that desirable enclave around Englefield Green.

There was just one small 'nuisance'. Three cottages stood on the common by the lane precisely where the new road was to go. They were encroachments on the waste and owned by Richard Welbelove. The cottages were thought to be of very little value—except to the families concerned—and Robinson wanted them removed.[51]

The plan for the new road impressed the Egham magistrates, Richard Wyatt and the Rev. James Liptrott. The road would be built at His Majesty's expense and almost halve the distance between Virginia Water and the River Thames. It would provide an altogether more convenient route for the public, and the magistrates were only too pleased to order its implementation.[52]

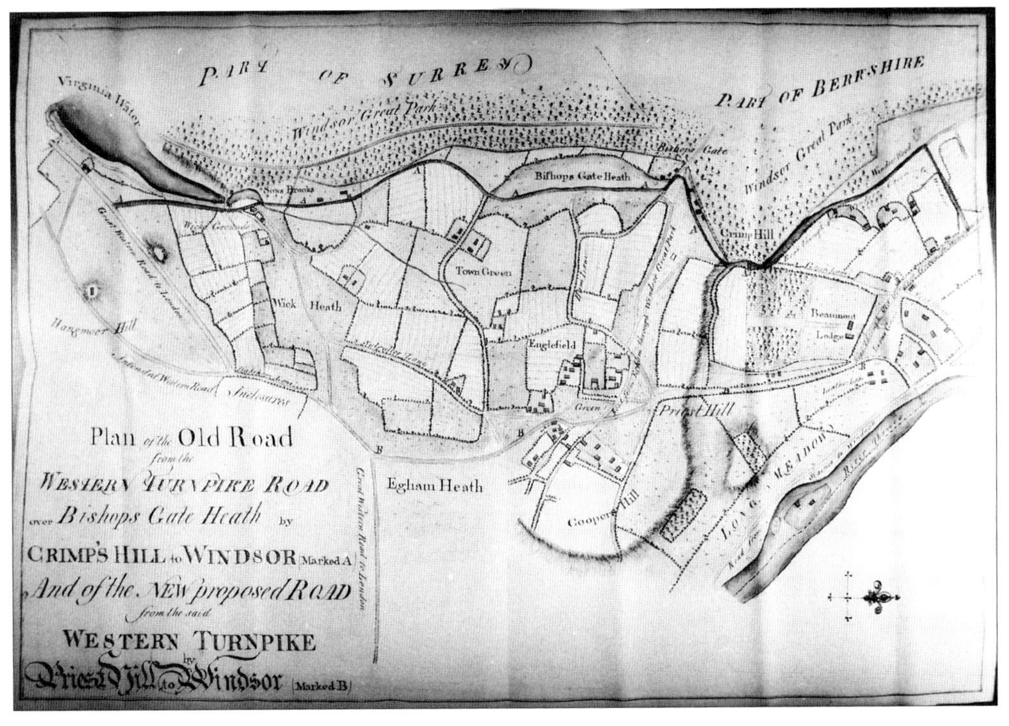

37 *Plan of Old and New Windsor Roads, 1789.*

For such technical tasks as road-laying Robinson brought in military aid. There were always regiments stationed at Windsor that could be called in at need. During the summer of 1789 the 23rd Regiment of Foot worked on the new Windsor road. This was not a cheap option for Robinson; in fact the soldiers probably cost more than labourers, requiring their bread money and coals for the guards at Windsor as well as pay for the work done. Each rod (5½ yds) of new road built cost 1s., or 2s. if the terrain was difficult: each yard of earth dug cost 3d. or 4d. One thousand five hundred and fifty loads of gravel would be required, costing 4d. a load, as well as ballast at 7d. a load. A quartermaster and five sergeants were needed to supervise the work. The entire bill for the three months' work came to £1,054 0s. 2d.[53] The Egham magistrates declared themselves satisfied with the new highway in February 1790, affirming that it was properly made and fit for travellers to use.[54]

At the same time as plans were being made for the new road, John Robinson drew up a list of cottages at Wick, in the vicinity of the old road, which would be desirable to absorb into the park. It was not so much the presence of the cottagers themselves that worried Robinson, though some of their tenements were clearly eyesores; it was rather the danger that the enhanced beauties of the park might attract purchasers who would want to develop the sites and thereby pose a threat to royal privacy.[55]

To the north of the new Wick branch of the lake, between the old Windsor road and the park pales, lay several properties—a desirable location even before the lake was extended. Here a widow, Henrietta Collins, held two cottages set in two acres of meadow. The cottage occupied by John King at Southbrooks had already been mentioned in the Pitt Estate Act for inclusion

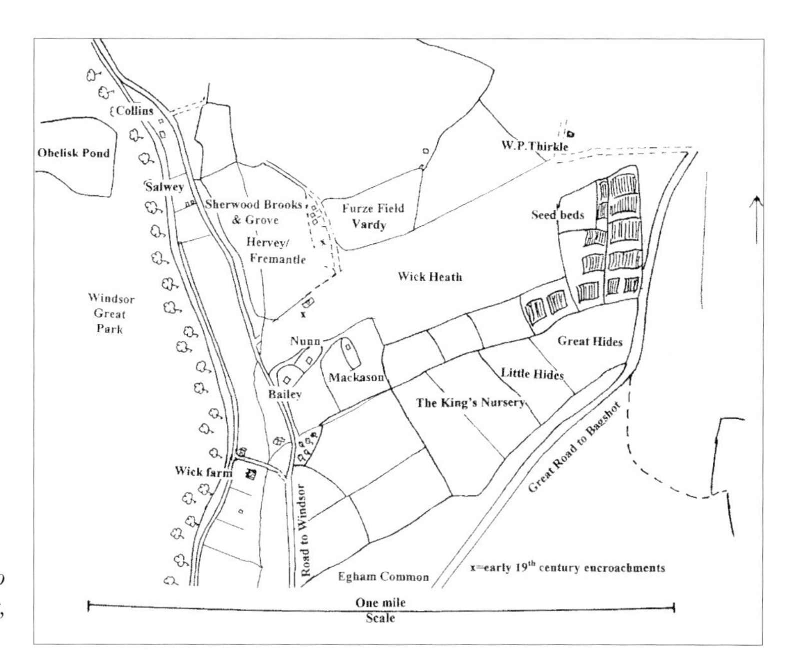

38 *Diagram of the hamlet of Wick showing properties about to be taken into Windsor Great Park, 1780–90.*

in the park. There was also the dwelling house, garden and extensive meadowland adjoining that was in the occupation of Mrs Salway. These had been granted by William, Duke of Cumberland, to a loyal servant and were held as an encroachment of the manor. Robinson noted in his minutes that of all the properties it was the only decent tenement.[56]

Further south, to the east of the old road, were more expendable tenements. One pair of cottages was copyhold of the manor of Egham and held by Elizabeth Nunn who, with her sister, Sarah Jeffs, had already sold one property at Virginia, its land to be flooded in the extended lake. The cottages were worth £6 a year to her and occupied by tenants, Payne and Thomas Dalton. Negotiations dragged on for many years until in 1799 the previous owner of a neighbouring tenement, Andrew Mackason, wrote to the Office of Woods & Forests on her behalf. He stated that she was a single woman in her 70s, and having just lost an annuity of £10 from the late Henry, Duke of Cumberland, her income was 'scarce sufficient to support Nature'. He reminded their lordships that Elizabeth Nunn's family had been keepers in Windsor Great Park for four generations 'in King William's time and ever have the most respectable Character'. Mackason begged them to be generous.[57]

The going rate for a cottage, so far as the Crown was concerned, was 200 guineas. All these properties, as well as the Welbeloves' cottages, were copyhold of the manor of Egham, though some occupiers claimed to have freehold tenure. It was necessary, therefore, to consult the head lessee of the manor, Richard Wyatt, to clarify these points and gain his consent. The Crown also required a three-acre field adjoining Wick Farm on its north-eastern corner near the Great Western Road. This was worked by Joseph Slark, a neighbouring farmer, already a tenant of the Crown. Presumably the transfer was reasonably straightforward, for the 1802 plan of the manor of Egham records it as taken from Slack's (*sic*) farm. Wyatt, like his tenants, was promised fair market value for all the land to be enclosed.[58]

As Richard Wyatt's lease from the Crown extended until 1804, he was entitled to receive compensation for his lost rents. Negotiations were entered into and Robinson suggested a sum of £260 per annum, to be reduced to £200 if paid immediately.[59]

Two pieces of freehold land were also required: these were close to the north-west corner of the main fields of Wick Farm, to the east of the old road. One was a small site owned by John Bailey, occupied by Richard Blay and worth £7 a year in rent. As late as 1798 the Crown was still not in possession of the property and its legal officers were worried that undue influence was being exerted on the Baileys to sell to persons unknown who would extort an exorbitant price from the Treasury.[60]

The other property adjoining Wick Farm's fields also belonged to the Mackason family, by then considerable landowners in Egham. For their three-and-a-half acres of pastureland with a tenement, the generous sum of

£525 was offered. The Crown was largely open-handed in its dealings with the owners; indeed the more worldly-wise took advantage of the situation. In stark contrast to the delays in buying Elizabeth Nunn's and John Bailey's tenements, the purchase of the Mackason land was completed in 1793. That the business was concluded so speedily may have been because Andrew Mackason kept John Robinson constantly informed of the many other buyers that were waiting to acquire it. In particular he reported that a 'Gentleman of the Law from Town has been with me twice and have Employed others to purchase it'. Mackason added that, of course, he had refused all offers, awaiting only His Majesty's pleasure![61]

With the acquisition of all these small properties as well as the farm, the pasture by the stream and 28 acres of Wick Heath, most of the land to the south of present Wick Road had been absorbed into Windsor Great Park. All that was left of the hamlet of Wick were a few encroachments on Wick Heath and two tenements in Swell Gutter Lane. The tenements belonged to Nathan Thirkle, an Egham yeoman, and after his death in January 1791 they came into the hands of his son, William Pinnock Thirkle, who built himself a house on the site.[62] At about the same time James Frost, a bailiff in royal service, saw an opportunity to acquire land at Wick. On a small piece of wasteland, known as Little Common, right up against the park pales, he made an encroachment and on it built four cottages, which he rented out. In 1792 he was admitted by Court Baron of the manor of Egham to about three-and-a-half acres of copyhold land, called Birchen Close, adjoining Little Common. Anthony White, one of Frost's tenants, later testified that he and the other tenants often took in and enclosed further small pieces of common land for their own use.[63]

In 1785 the most easterly of Wick Farm's fields were to have been put up for auction but the idea was abandoned at the last minute and the land designated the park's nursery ground, where seeds would be sown and saplings nurtured for use in the new plantations. Robinson was of the opinion that the soil was good for the purpose. Some of the labourers were already at work there in the autumn of 1788. Others were collecting pinecones, seeds and berries for planting before the birds took the best of them. By the following spring up to 77 men were employed barrowing, trenching, turfing and planting at the nursery. William Faden's Plan of Windsor Forest, made between 1788 and 1791, shows seed beds laid out at the eastern end of the site and a little plantation at the western end.[64]

Robinson was also anxious to acquire some 16 acres of land known as Sherwood Brooks and Grove. They lay to the north-west of the heath, near the pales of the park, and belonged to Mrs Selina Mary Hervey, the heiress of Sir John Elwell of 'Elvill's', Englefield Green, and the widow of Sir Lionel Felton Hervey. It was not generally known that Mrs Hervey's land was needed in order to avoid a zigzag on the park boundary. In Robinson's opinion the ground was very rough and worth only £30 or £35 an acre.[65]

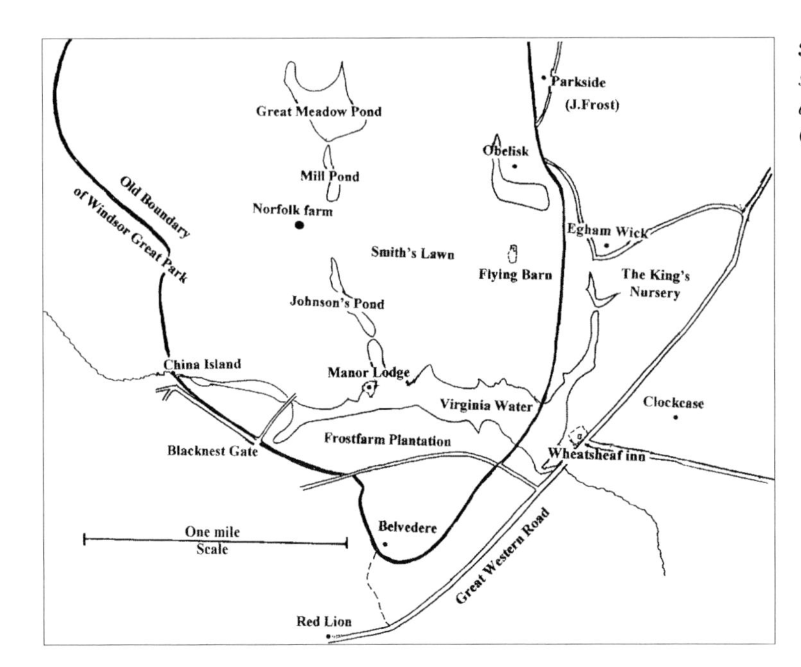

39 *Diagram showing the southern end of Windsor Great Park, 1790.*

There seemed no great rush to secure it, however, and it did not come into Crown possession until the mid-19th century, when there were more road realignments at Wick.[66]

By the end of the 1780s the plans for enlarging the park to the south and east were well underway. When Henry, Duke of Cumberland, died in 1790, George III himself took over the rangership and with it the opportunity to implement another of his enthusiasms, a passion for agricultural improvement. The king looked for help and advice to one of the country's leading land agents, Nathaniel Kent. While on government service in the Netherlands, Kent had studied that country's system of husbandry and, on his return to England, recommended its practice to his own countrymen. In the development of agricultural science he was ahead of his time.[67]

The Flemish system of cultivation, first copied in East Anglia, involved growing crops on an alternating or rotating pattern. The method finally evolved at Windsor to best suit its soil was 'a regular four course shift' of crops: barley, clover, wheat and turnips. Great emphasis was put on improving the fertility of the soil and Kent recommended folding sheep on young clover for the sake of the wheat crop to follow. He always tried to find his raw materials near at hand and ordered chalk to be brought from Windsor Home Park and burnt in the farm's own kiln to produce lime; this was either strewn directly on the fields or mixed with dung or the 'Sediment of Ponds' to create an excellent compost.[68]

Nathaniel Kent was unusual not only in his approach to agriculture but also in his attitude to the men who worked for him. One of the first tasks he set himself on his arrival at Windsor in March 1791 was to make 'a general

Muster of the Artificers and Labourers' already on the pay list. This, however, was no mere list. The workers' ages were included so that the harder work could be apportioned to the stronger and more active men. Their places of residence were also taken into consideration when setting tasks to avoid unnecessary walking in the morning and evening to and from work. The size of their families and their lengths of service to the Crown were also of importance in judging who was entitled 'to any little indulgencies or confidence' (Appendix IV).[69]

While a few men came in from Berkshire and the majority of the single men lived in the garden complex at Great Lodge, most of the married workers lived on the south-east boundary of the park. John Burcher, a carpenter, aged 71, lived at Bishopsgate and had worked for the Crown for 35 years. His son, George, aged 33, was a joiner and had gone into royal service at the age of thirteen. Coming from Wick was another father-and-son team; Daniel Chase, aged 47 with 13 years' service, worked on the rides in the park, while his son, George, at the tender age of 12, was a weeder and already had three years' service to his credit. Weeding was also done by women, such as Mary Finch, aged 50, from the Wick, whose husband, James, was also a park labourer. Between them this couple had worked for the Crown for 50 years. The only other woman on the list was Elizabeth Jackson, also aged 50, a widow who had worked for six years to support her four children.[70]

Nathaniel Kent's remit was to establish two new agricultural units in Windsor Great Park: Norfolk Farm was established to the south and west of Great Lodge to the north of Virginia Water while Flemish (or Gloucester) Farm lay in the north-west of the park. Their very names proclaimed their origins and philosophy. In some ways they were a challenge to the original concept of a park and it was important that the gamekeepers were informed of the new boundaries as fences and hurdles were put up to keep the deer out of the agricultural areas. On the other hand farm workers had to be equally watchful to see that stray pigs and 'shabby' horses did not damage park lawns.[71]

As Kent and his partners could only visit Windsor periodically they appointed Joseph Frost, who was already bailiff at Great Lodge, to be the superintendent of the project. As he had no direct experience of the Flemish system he was sent to Norfolk in September 1791 'to make observation upon the Husbandry of that County'. He came back, he claimed, with a 'good Opinion of its effectiveness',[72] though he remained a grievous thorn in Kent's side.[73]

Kent was a great believer in using oxen at the plough and Frost was dispatched to fairs as far away as Abergavenny, Ross and Hereford to buy oxen and other cattle. This was a task of some responsibility as he often bought hundreds of pounds' worth of stock. Invariably his expenses for the journey were only a fraction of the cost of foddering the animals he had purchased and driving them back to Windsor.[74] Toll keepers had a precise scale of charges for the movement of stock on their roads. At each turnpike gate on the Great Western Road, for example, each drove of 20 oxen or cows cost 10d., while a similar drove of smaller animals, such as calves, pigs or sheep, cost half as much.[75] Frost's purchases, however, were not always satisfactory and in April 1792 he was ordered to leave the buying of the Herefordshire stock to Kent or his partners. They needed Frost on site to keep the impetus of the project going and left him detailed instructions to be put in hand before their next visit. Kent was also concerned about the traditional practice of allowing a quantity of hay to certain employees. He considered it liable to abuse and suggested that instead each man be given enough meadowland on which to keep a horse or whatever cattle he chose.[76]

One of the first labouring tasks in the newly designated agricultural areas was to clear the infestation of fern and rushes although, even in farmland, a few ferns were kept around trees in some places 'for picturesque Patches'. The greatest economy was practised, especially in the resiting and reconstruction of old farm buildings. The discarded fern, as well as fallen wood from the park, was used to fuel the farm's own brick kiln, and George Dalby, the bricklayer, had need of extra hands. Butler, the painter, also had his hands full and passed one unusual task over to a man called James Brimmell. He was instructed to paint old tiles to look like slates; it was noted with approval that he was a tractable man who readily entered into 'the Spirit of the Business'.[77]

With all the activity in park and farm John Burcher, the foreman carpenter, one of the Crown's key workmen earning £80 a year, was in great demand.[78] In fact Kent had to select two of the most skilful labourers to help him. George III was closely involved in all Kent's proposals and often walked the farms with him, discussing the project. One of the king's suggestions was the making of a moveable barn, to be constructed of wood and thatched with reed, which Burcher built in a month in the summer of 1792. This small building later became the home of a park worker. The king was especially interested in ideas that improved the welfare of the workforce and in 1793 designed a cottage for Bradley, a park labourer at Flemish Farm. Burcher's son, presumably George, was employed with Lawrence, a bricklayer, to build it. Kent thoroughly agreed with His Majesty that the provision of such model cottages was an example that other landowners might do well to emulate.[79]

After a few months at Windsor, Kent felt he knew the men well enough to reorganise the establishment and encourage flexibility. The labourers began work at 7 a.m., had breaks for breakfast and dinner and finished at 5 p.m.—a total of nine hours. Any time lost was accounted for by a deduction of 2d. an hour. The casual workers, who carried out such tasks as clearing fields or turning muck heaps, received about 1s. 6d. per day. Women and boys continued to do the backbreaking work of planting and weeding for a much lower rate, while the boys also had the endless grind of keeping birds off the crops.[80]

40 *Norfolk and Suffolk ploughs used in Windsor Great Park from* A General View of the Agriculture of Berkshire with Observations on the Manner of its Improvement *by William Pearce, 1794.*

By September 1791 it was clear that much remained to be done. In order to improve the marshy, low-lying areas, a team of specialist drainers and ditchers was brought in from Essex. At the end of their first season Kent was delighted with the improvement they had made and admired their industry and skill.[81]

With more sheep being introduced, Richard Daphne, a shepherd, journeyed from Wiltshire with his family to help improve the king's flocks. The east side of the boathouse was converted into a cottage for their use. Suffolk horses and Suffolk and Norfolk ploughs were transported from East Anglia, while skilled ploughmen to use the new equipment travelled in from Norwich. More elaborate tools were ordered: an iron roller from Scotland and a scarifying machine to loosen the soil, together with an expert to explain its use.[82]

For annual tasks, such as sheep-shearing, teams came in from neighbouring farms. In June 1792, for example, William Johnson, the tenant farmer of Trumps Farm, some two miles south-east of the lake, charged 10s. a hundred to shear 950 royal sheep. By tradition on these occasions the men were also supplied with bread, meat and beer. Harvesting also required extra hands and teams reaped the crops at differential rates: 1s. 6d. to 2s. an acre for oats, 2s. to 3s. for barley and beans and, for the most valuable product, wheat, 6s. 6d. to 12s. an acre. That year the men who raised the first corn stack at Norfolk farm received a gratuity of 2s. 6d., while in other years harvest suppers were held for the estate workers.[83]

William Johnson, like other local farmers and tradesmen, found a valuable new commercial partnership in the park farms. Around the same time as he was shearing sheep in the park, he sold Frost 95 bushels of hayseed from his own store. Benjamin Planner, the brick-maker on Egham Hill, was a regular customer of the Crown, often buying large amounts of wood for his kilns and in turn supplying the royal farms with straw and hay from his own landholdings. He even played his part in helping to improve rough pieces of parkland. In December 1793 Planner was granted the use, free for two years, of two pieces of land near the stone bridge. In return he agreed to plough them in a husbandlike manner, grow corn on them and hand them back in 1796 for the planting of turnips.[84] Other neighbouring farmers provided extra feed for cattle as well as seed and stock: for example, in December 1791 Thomas Burton, one of the most up-and-coming landowners in the district, sold the Crown 14 loads of clover hay as well as seed rye and wheat. Other neighbours followed suit: Richard Hudson, tenant farmer of Callow Hill Farm, supplied turnips and a load of hay, and Joseph Slark, the tenant farmer of His Majesty's Crown Farm at Englefield Green, turnips, straw, seed rye and tares. There were undoubtedly opportunities for profiteering. Andrew Mackason, Egham's leading butcher and local landowner, sold eight store pigs to the Crown in July 1792 at the highly inflated price of 48s. each.[85]

Despite Joseph Frost's visit to Norfolk to learn its methods, relations between him and the men brought in from that county were not always harmonious. The Norfolk men found Frost unco-operative in preparing the fields adequately for ploughing; not enough lime had been produced and he was rebuked by Kent, who emphasised the importance of his work to the whole enterprise. Doubtless Frost promised to conform but Kent did not intend to rely on promises. He or one of his partners would visit every week at irregular and unannounced intervals to ensure that instructions were carried out.[86]

Frost did, however, win praise from Kent for his business acumen in always achieving a good price for the felled timber that was in abundant supply while the farm fields were being created. Frost also on one occasion detained several women who were stealing wood from the farm in a most barefaced manner. They were taken before the mayor of Windsor and some of them committed to Bridewell. They were, however, released after only a few hours' confinement, in what Kent believed to be mistaken motives of leniency.[87]

Kent expected a high standard not only from his supervisors but also from the workmen he employed. Absence, except in the case of illness, was not tolerated: the offender's pay would be docked and His Majesty informed. It was made clear that any man taking advantage of his position or ignoring his responsibilities would be removed from his post. On the morning of 30 May 1792 one pair of horses and a plough stood idle in the field, a silent rebuke to its absent driver. He was John Fisher, listed as a woodsman but, like others, taking his turn at ploughing. He had gone, it was reported, on 'an idle Frolick to London'. Needless to say he was summarily dismissed both as a punishment for his misdemeanour and also, more importantly, to set an example to others. On Egham Hill he had a wife and four children dependent on him.[88]

If irresponsibility at work resulted in dismissal there was no hope in September 1795 for Richard Rose, one of the ox drivers, when he was found guilty of selling wood out of the plantation and also of purloining seed corn. One of the Norfolk team, Thomas Gray, was the next to be in trouble: he was in his twenties, lived at Englefield Green and had worked in the park for about five years. Only a month after Rose's dismissal Gray was discharged, this time for repeatedly disobeying orders and refusing to acknowledge his fault.[89] It was not only young men who fell from grace. The following year William Gilkes, leader of one of the ox teams, was rash enough to use His Majesty's teams and labourers on his own business outside the park. He also was dismissed.[90]

Most of the men working on the royal farms, however, as in the park, were loyal and hardworking, aware that, especially under the leadership of Nathaniel Kent, they were fairly treated. There was praise and encouragement for promising workmen. In the winter of 1791, for example, George III lent four young horses of his own to be used for ploughing. Thomas Gooch, leader of the 1st Norfolk team, was given the honour of training and working these beasts, while Richard Tindall was selected to take over Gooch's team and use the iron plough. In Kent's opinion Tindall was a willing and active man, skilled at ploughing with two horses. Tindall was clearly a man of some initiative, having built a cottage on a small encroachment for himself and his family to the north of Wick Heath. He succeeded also in a major ambition of many of the men working in the park; he was able to secure employment for his sons. Richard junior and William served variously as carters, ploughmen or as ox drivers and were later joined by John, working as a 'Job boy'.[91]

By the autumn of 1794 Kent and his partners must have felt that the king's agricultural project in the park was well on its way to success. They had proved that poor soil could be made productive and looked forward to abundant harvests and profitable sales. A starlight walk on a surprise visit on 12 October, however, revealed examples of ill discipline among the men and too little will on the part of the supervisors to prevent it. Sylas Dornford, the assistant shepherd, as it was suspected, had failed to fold his sheep that night. He was ordered to be dismissed. A wagon had been left out in a potato field and Francis Watts, a bailiff, was reprimanded for allowing such a thing to happen. It was also discovered that the previous

41 *'Ye Gen'rous Britons Venerate the Plough', 1801, Valentine Green.*

night most of the labourers had left work at least an hour early and those in charge were told to enforce correct timekeeping. These incidents were symptomatic: tighter supervision was clearly needed. In future the sale of cattle going to slaughter would be closely regulated and no hay would be taken from the ricks except in the presence of Joseph Frost's clerk, Henry John Branch, who would weigh each delivery. Flagrant abuse had occurred in previous winters involving this valuable commodity and Kent hoped to make a 30 per cent saving.[92]

There was, however, no way of controlling the weather and for masters and men alike the severe winter of early 1795 was difficult. There was such a long-lasting snowfall in February that all outdoor work had to cease except the carrying of wood and chalk to and from Windsor. For the daily labourer no work meant no pay. Even when the thaw came conditions were hardly better. The resulting flood was the worst for 21 years and neither Kent nor his partners could reach Windsor. Most of the houses in Staines were 2ft deep in water and its inhabitants could only get about by boat. Ploughing had to wait until the end of the month.[93]

It was the right time for another of George III's charitable initiatives to come to fruition. He had ordered a mill to be built in the park to provide his workmen with subsidised flour and so cushion them from variations in the commercial price of bread. The site of the mill, to the north of Virginia Water, was decided by the end of 1793, the oaks for its construction chosen the following spring and it was scheduled for completion by the autumn. This was, however, too ambitious a timescale, even for the park's skilled carpenters, and it was not ready to run until April 1795.[94]

Inquiries were made in March into the details of each labourer's family so as to regulate a fair distribution of flour among them. On 7 April the mill turned for the first time and two days later tickets were given out to those labourers who wished to take part of their wages in 'meal'—a ground mixture of two-thirds wheat and one-third rye, sufficiently fine for making household bread. A single man was allowed 7lbs with the amount rising proportionately according to the size of each man's family. At a cost of only 15d. a stone the offer must have been a boon to the labourers' wives and mothers.[95]

The problems at haymaking and harvest times, when it was difficult to find the necessary extra labour, were the reverse of winter. In some seasons, Kent, like John Robinson in the park, had reluctantly to employ soldiers in the fields. He was, however, adamant that not only were the labourers cheaper than the soldiers, they also worked better.[96]

By the time of Nathaniel Kent's last report to the king in 1797, it was clear that the farms would not make a profit for the Crown. Kent had, however, much to be proud of at Windsor: through the enthusiastic patronage of George III, his agricultural theories and experiments had become more widely known and adopted. He had also created work and taught new skills to local men and their sons.

At much the same time that Nathanial Kent was appointed to supervise the creation of the royal farms, a Scot by the name of William Tough, was made Foreman of the Works to succeed Courtenay on the recommendation of John Robinson. He took up residence with his wife, Hannah, at the property purchased by Courtenay the previous year on behalf of the Crown, called Harvey's or Harvest Corner. The necessary repairs had still not been done but were scheduled for 20 March 1791. On that day, however, Isabella, the first of William and Hannah's 10 children, was born in the house and Charles Cole and his workmen had to postpone their visit.[97]

By the 1790s the heavy work at the cascade was almost finished but fine details needed attention. Robinson instructed Tough in the natural look the designers required: the stream flowing from the waterfall was not to run in a straight line and even the heath turf on its banks was to be laid in waves, 'following the Idea of Nature with little Irregularities'. A gang of men with 'an engine' kept the turf well watered.[98] Tough's main task was, however, to complete the landscaping of the Wick branch of the lake. The nursery, by then established on the fields of Wick Farm, was nurturing as many indigenous forest tree seedlings as possible, though Tough was less sanguine than Robinson had been about the quality of the soil. He wrote in 1791 that it was 'unaccountable', full of couch grass and weeds, and needed a great deal of ploughing, harrowing, raking and weeding. A massive programme of planting was underway, both of trees and shrubs bought in and those grown from seed; Tough reported in December 1791 that he had planted 6,000 trees, despite being hindered by frost and snow. Over a year later he was still employing men to sow acorns and to place haws and gorse seed on the banks of the plantations where they were to grow.[99]

As well as supervising the men at their various locations, Tough wrote almost daily letters to John Robinson, detailing the progress of the work, always concluding 'Your Dutyfull Servt'. A good working relationship was established between the Tory gentleman and his senior workman, with Robinson often dropping in on the Tough household. On one occasion Robinson left his watch on their parlour table and had to arrange for its return.[100]

At Wick many of the farm's landmarks were still recognisable and referred to by their old field names or owners. In the spring of 1794 the men were trenching in the Hop Ground near Mrs Salway's cottage and also planting over the old road. The latter exercise, Tough feared, was a waste of time for 'the Sheep is allways over that Ground and is Spoiling the trees that is Planted about there already'.[101] George III's enthusiasm for farming as well as for landscaping was sometimes difficult for his servants to reconcile. Part of a field near Wick bridge was still known as being formerly Mackasons, but by then was also called Courtenay's Orchard due to its being near the house once occupied by the previous foreman. As late as 1796 the purchase of all the area was not quite complete: negotiations were still underway with

42 *The Clockcase, 1822, John Hassell.*

Richard Wyatt, the head lessee of the manor of Egham, to acquire 'Slarke's Field', which adjoined the nursery ground.[102]

Rabbits continued to be a plague in the park as on any other agricultural estate, and in 1796 a man called Eves was appointed assistant warrener at a wage of 12s. a week, with a house provided and the right to keep the profits from selling the rabbits. A few months later he had the misfortune to be bitten by an adder and was laid up at home. William Tough, who was having trouble with vandals at the red tower, later known as the Clockcase, on Hangmore Hill, tried to solve two problems in one go. Repairs had been carried out on the building in the early 1790s when bricks of a special size had to be made at the park kiln. A chimney was also installed to make the building more suitable as a habitation. It was therefore suggested that Eves' bed should be brought to the red tower, where his presence might prove a deterrent to the 'Ill-Disposed Persons [who] have very much Broke the window in the Course of Last week'.[103]

Worse was to come at the tower. In 1799, despite the attendance of the nursery's water engine, a fire destroyed most of the wooden structure, the lead in the roof melted and part of the roof collapsed. Only the brickwork remained. Eves, the warrener, was able to rescue his furniture and the casements and doors from the building, which was clearly no longer habitable. Tough was very pessimistic about the future of the tower: the 'House ... is not fit for any Person to Live in as it is Likely to Tumble Down'.[104]

For the first years of William Tough's tenure of the foremanship, the gallons of water pent up in the lake were rarely allowed to flow over the cascade. This ensured that necessary work on the pondhead and along the banks of the lake could continue unhindered. Tough must have been delighted when he eventually saw the spectacle for himself and wrote in 1797: 'virginia water begun to Run over the Cascade yesterday morning and by the middle of the Day made a very fine cascad'.[105]

Sometimes as the foreman went about his daily tasks he, like his predecessor, encountered George III, who enjoyed viewing the progress of his project on the ground. In December 1795 the king found Tough and his men digging holes for the planting of trees on Manor Hill and dismounted to inspect their work. Several weeks later Tough reported another meeting with the king, who was 'very Much Pleased with the Manner we are Going on with'. In 1801 Tough wrote his most detailed account of a royal visit. The spelling and use of capitals has been copied faithfully from the original, as in other examples given, to give a flavour of the man and a hint of his accent.

> His Majesty and Family stoped at the Wheat Sheaf virginia water this morning and While Her Majesty and the Princess went into the Hous His Majesty and Prince Adolphus went on the Pond Head for a few minnuts. His Majesty told the Landlord at the Wheatsheaf that he thought the water Remarkably Pleasant.[106]

Tough conducted his financial transactions on behalf of the Crown from his pay table at the *Wheatsheaf* inn. There he paid his workforce and local tradesmen such as Benjamin Planner of Egham for fenceposts. The weekly accounts were sent to Robinson for scrutiny and usually accepted and paid without question. Occasionally Tough was rebuked: in 1791, for paying a bill without prior authorisation, and in 1795, for paying Jones, the smith, 6s. 6d. a day for himself and boy. This was more than double the amount the park carpenter earned and in Robinson's opinion Tough should not have paid such an exorbitant rate. The smith was not to be employed again on such terms.[107]

At the same time as the Windsor road was being diverted away from the park, plans were afoot for another diversion of the Great Western Road itself. The submersion of the hamlet of Virginia in the new lake had resulted in the park boundary being once more too close to the main road for royal liking. The Foreman of the Works had reported in 1789 that gentlemen had been stopping to admire the cascade as they rode by. To protect the new lake from prying eyes the turnpike road would have to be diverted again: from a point near the 20th milepost a detour would sweep south through the Clockcase plantation at Hangmore Hill then south-west to join the main road again at Shrubs Hill.[108]

The Great Western Road was controlled by the Bedfont & Bagshot Turnpike Trust and their approval for the diversion had to be sought. Accordingly, John Robinson presented himself to the meeting of the trust, held conveniently at the *Wheatsheaf* on 13 July 1789, to explain the

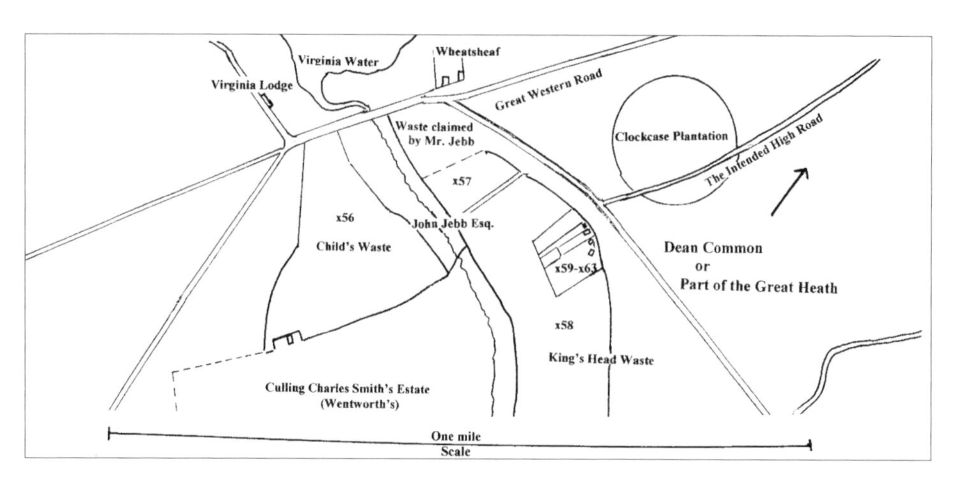

43 *Diagram showing the disputed wasteland and the proposed new high road, from The Plan of the Manor of Egham, 1805, Abraham and William Driver.*

proposition. After inspecting the site itself the trustees resolved to accept the Crown's offer of a new piece of road, to be built at His Majesty's expense. They noted that although the new road would be 122 yards longer than the old, cutting across Hangmore Hill would eliminate the steep climb that led to and from the bridge at Virginia Water. The Crown for its part promised that the road would be built to turnpike standards and that their workmen would make good any residual damage from the great storm of 1768, still well remembered.[109]

If the road were to be diverted, the new *Wheatsheaf* inn would have to go. Robinson was under no illusion that negotiating with John Atkins, its entrepreneurial licensee, would be easy. Robinson felt himself at a disadvantage. He believed the Crown had been imprudent to recognise Atkins' right to the land he held and knew the man would drive a hard bargain: ' ... he has raised his price from Time to Time; and I shall not be surprised if he should again increase it.' Atkins clearly had no desire to move his inn elsewhere. He had considerably improved his property since its initial construction: by 1783 it consisted of two acres of land, an orchard, two gardens, two barns and three stables as well as the house. 'Atkins Corner' was a centre of activity for the projects underway at Virginia Water, with the lake so close to his inn being an enormous asset to his business, and he knew more than most that Crown officials were under considerable pressure to turn the royal dream into reality at almost any cost.[110]

John Robinson had two proposals to put before the Turnpike Commissioners concerning the *Wheatsheaf*. The first was that the Crown should build Atkins an even better inn set in a large quantity of land on a site to be approved by the Commissioners. Alternatively negotiations could be based on two valuations of the inn and its goodwill made by independent assessors. In the meantime

Atkins presented his own claim for £3,500: £1,500 for the value of the house and £2,000 for the profit it might produce in 10 years.[111] Robinson expected to have to accept this—an exorbitant price compared to other purchases—but no agreement was ever reached. Atkins remained landlord of the *Wheatsheaf* until 1798, when he retired on the proceeds to live as a gentleman at Eton Wick. He leased the property, which by then included an acre of land on the opposite side of the main road, used as extra stabling, to Lawrence, Robert and William Sutton Porter, the Chertsey brewers, for 42 years at a yearly rent of £40.[112] The Crown would have to wait another 28 years before it acquired the *Wheatsheaf* at an even higher price.

When John Atkins gave up the license of the *Wheatsheaf*, William Tough was ordered to transfer his pay table to another place. He decided on a public house on Egham Hill, not named but most likely the *Pack Horse*. At the same time he took the opportunity to transfer the franchise for the hiring of horses for work in the park to the same establishment.[113]

When Thomas Sandby died in 1798 he had been involved for half a century in the extraordinary transformation of the landscape at Virginia Water. Most of the work was done: others would consolidate and complete the task. Some time later Joseph Frost moved into Lower Lodge, the Deputy Ranger's house, once used by Sandby, despite the fact that it was a residence far above his yeoman status. He was surprisingly allowed to remain there until the house was required for the Prince Regent,[114] enjoying not only his park salary but the income from his cottages.

At the same time as he was negotiating with John Atkins, Robinson tried to secure the rest of the land (about 170 acres) that lay between the intended road and the park. Most of the land involved was common or wasteland of the manor of Egham—experience showed that there would be no difficulty in acquiring such land from the parish. Some 26 acres, including 10 acres of unenclosed land, however, belonged to or were claimed by David Jebb, son of John Jebb, who had already demised some land to the Crown to be overflowed in the creation of the new lake. David had inherited a considerable landholding to the south of the lake and the main road, including the old estate of Portnall and several pieces of freehold wasteland. He also owned another property, Egham Park, on Tite Hill, Egham.[115] David Jebb seized the opportunity to strike an advantageous bargain with the Crown: in exchange for some of his unenclosed land near Virginia Water he would accept a similar acreage of Crown land near Egham Park. There were two difficulties here for park officials, who had hoped for a straightforward purchase. Firstly, Jebb's right to an unenclosed 10 acres was disputed by legal opinion, by the lessee of the manor and by the parish alike, and secondly the Crown jibbed at exchanging high-value farmland on Tite Hill, acre for acre, with poor-quality waste land.[116]

Nevertheless, even though no agreement had been signed, plans for the new road went ahead. The soldiers who would carry out the work were encamped on Wick Heath by 1791, as shown on William Faden's Plan, but Jebb would not allow them on his land. He reiterated his demands for a straight exchange and would not even allow the appointment of surveyors to make a fair valuation. Jebb's intransigence meant that the negotiations dragged on for years. By 1795 it looked as if agreement might have been reached, with the Crown changing the line of the road slightly to accommodate Jebb and conceding the need for a good oak fence to be built on his boundary—'not a post or open-paled fence'. On the Crown's side there was still concern about the ownership of the 10 acres. Several attempts at draft agreements were made but they were always obstructed by impediments and delays.[117]

Once again the Crown tried to press ahead: William Tough was sent onto Jebb's land in 1797 to stake out the south side of the new road, but Jebb objected to his presence and Tough had to remove the flag poles he had just put in. It strengthened Jebb's hand to know that the king himself was anxious for the exchange to take place and Jebb's next ploy was to demand that only an Act of Parliament could sanction the deal. The matter fell into abeyance once more until it was raised by Jebb in 1800 with a further objection. He claimed that his father had never been paid for the two acres of land taken into the park in 1782. He wanted compensation for that. He then changed tactics slightly in furthering his ambition to acquire the Crown land near his Egham house. He asked that when the manor was re-leased in four years' time he might be allowed to lease the said land directly, as it was of little value to anyone else.

In 1802 Jebb sold some of his Virginia Water land to Culling Charles Smith, informing him that if the Crown made no positive moves towards acquiring the 16 acres, Smith could have them. When no Act of Parliament materialised in the next two years Smith claimed the land. It may have been these legal exchanges with Smith that encouraged Jebb to compromise: he finally agreed to go to arbitration. However, Richard Wordsworth, solicitor for the Crown, was under no illusion that a deal was in sight. He warned the surveyors that they would have to measure the land with the utmost exactitude or Jebb would dispute their findings. A Deed of Agreement was reached in April 1803. Surveyors were appointed, titles to land proved and a petition for leave to present a Bill before parliament applied for in order to affect the exchange of land. Jebb took possession of his new land on Tite Hill in January 1805 and the Treasury presented him with a bill for £590 7s. 7d., the disparity of value between the exchanged lands.

In October of that year, with the bridge over Virginia Water in need of repair, the Commissioners of the Bagshot turnpike remembered that there was once a plan to rebuild part of the road and wrote to find out His Majesty's intentions. They had no wish to undertake an expensive project like enlarging a bridge when the Crown might do it for them. It might have been this correspondence that led General Harcourt, the Deputy Ranger, to report to the Treasury a year later that there was no longer any intention of building a new road. The 16 disputed acres were being farmed as part of Shrubs Hill Farm.[118]

Meanwhile, Jebb was in no hurry to settle his bill. It was not until 1807, when he was in the process of selling Egham Park, that he wrote to the Crown again. He complained that his purchaser had held back £1,200 of the purchase price because of the continuing dispute with the Crown. Jebb was of the opinion that as no Act of Parliament had ever been passed he was not liable. In fact Jebb never did pay: the account, with interest, was finally settled in 1813 by his purchaser, George Parry, who was wise enough to have held back part of the purchase price for such contingencies.[119]

The king's representatives in the park were vulnerable to local landowners, who were prepared to protract negotiations to their own advantage. The Crown either had to pay exorbitant prices for land or abandon cherished schemes. David Jebb and John Atkins profited from playing a waiting game. William Tough, on the other hand, was a conscientious man, aware not only of his duty to the Crown but of his responsibility to his men. In March 1800 he tried to gain an increase in wages for his labourers, suggesting that they should all receive a minimum of 2s. a day. He was also anxious to secure the services of a wheelwright or a carpenter and was prepared to offer between 19s. and 20s. a week for a skilled craftsman. It would appear that he succeeded in the latter aim in the light of an argument that later ensued with his brother, George.[120]

George Tough joined the Windsor Great Park staff at about this time as Foreman of the Nursery, at a wage of 16s. per week. He claimed that in

44 *The Wheelwright's Shop in Windsor Great Park, 1792, Paul Sandby.*

doing so he had halved his earnings but that John Robinson was so anxious to have him in the post that he had promised him a house. This proved a difficult promise to keep. George accused his brother of purloining the timber intended for his house and forcing him to live with his large family in one room in the wheelwright's house. According to his sponsor, George was an industrious and clever man, much oppressed by his brother.[121]

Unlike some in royal service, where nepotism was sometimes regarded as a virtue, William refused to do his brother special favours: 'it is not Consistent with my Duty to agree with his wishes.' If he were to have given his brother the house he wanted, William would have had no accommodation for the wheelwright whose services he urgently needed.[122]

John Robinson was only too aware of the pressing need to provide housing for his men, especially in view of this dispute. In 1802 he obtained a warrant from the Treasury to build three cottages at His Majesty's nursery at Wick for the use of the foreman and other workmen. The architect for the project, Mr Wyatt, however, recommended that only one house should be built on the site.[123]

George Tough eventually moved into the cottage at the nursery, where he once more proved himself a man of initiative. Adjoining the nursery he noticed some apparently uncultivated land; he enclosed it and made himself a productive little garden. In fact it was owned by the Planner family from the exchange transaction with the Crown in 1782, but had slipped through the records of both the Office of Woods & Forests and the Planner family.[124]

The nursery at Wick was often subject to theft and vandalism. During 1802 it was considered worthwhile to employ two labourers and to provide bed and bedding so that they could take turns at guarding the nursery. This practice was clearly not continued for in December 1803 there was serious loss and damage at the site: 'some evil disposed Person[s]' had stolen large quantities of forest tree seedlings, and thousands of 'Quick' or hawthorn seedlings had been cut down to about six inches from the ground to make them unfit for sale. This was serious enough for a poster to be displayed offering a reward for information that would lead to the apprehension of the villains. A lot of malicious energy had gone into the destruction of the hawthorn plants, reflecting no doubt the same mood of disaffection in a small section of the community that inspired the wanton vandalism often perpetrated against the tower and plantation at Hangmore Hill.[125]

The red tower, 'commonly called Callow Hill Clockcase', continued to cause concern. Only a few months before the incident at the nursery William Tough had reported serious damage to the building: bricks had been taken out of the corners and the doorway broken. He warned that the tower was greatly weakened and 'if not Repared and Properly Protected Will in Time fall into Ruins'. It would seem that nobody took any notice of his warnings and only when he repeated them some 10 months later was the building examined and an estimate made for repairs. Two years later the situation

45 *Poster advertising a reward for the apprehension of evil doers, 1803.*

BY ORDER OF

THE

Right Hon. Lord Glenbervie,

SURVEYOR-GENERAL OF HIS MAJESTY'S FORESTS, WOODS, PARKS, AND CHACES.

WHEREAS,

SOME evil-diſpoſed Perſon or Perſons, have at ſeveral different times pulled up and Stolen out of His MAJESTY'S NURSERY, at EGHAM-WICK, near Windſor Great Park, Quantities of FOREST TREE SEEDLINGS; and, particularly in the Night between the 2d and 3d of DECEMBER, 1803, did pull up, ſteal, and carry away from thence, a Quantity of One Year old SCOTCH FIR SEEDLINGS, One Year old HORNBEAMS, One Year old MOUNTAIN ASH, and Two Years old WEYMOUTH PINES, and about 5000 or 6000 Two Years old QUICK SEEDLINGS, which had been cut down to about Six Inches above Ground, for the purpoſe of rendering them unfit for Sale.

Now, in order to diſcover and bring to Juſtice ſuch Offenders, any Perſon who will give ſuch Information and Evidence as may be ſufficient to convict any one or more of them, ſhall receive from WM. TOUGH, Foreman of His Majeſty's Works in Windſor Great Park, and reſiding within the ſaid Nurſery, a REWARD of

FIVE GUINEAS

For every Perſon ſo convicted.

Likewiſe, the PARK PALE FENCE has at different times been broken down and carried away—*This is to give Notice*, that all Perſons found guilty of this Offence, will be proſecuted with the utmoſt rigour.

Wettons, Printers, Egham and Chertsey.

had still not improved: the tower was still broken down and defaced. Tough was anxious to affect some repairs himself for, in his opinion, it was a fine building.[126]

These outlying and detached areas of the park were the most difficult to manage. Knowle Grove, a mile and a half south-east from the lake and once 'a pleasurable wood for the chace', was often neglected. According to the Outranger, Colonel George Onslow of Ripley Green, it needed better fencing and he recommended that keepers should visit the grove on moonlit nights and early in the morning to deter poachers. This was, however, easier said than done. William Tough did his best, sending men there in March 1794 to repair fences at the request of a neighbouring farmer.[127]

Despite the responsibilities of the job and the long hours, Tough was thankful for the good fortune that had procured him such 'a Comfortable Subsistence'. In 1803, by then the father of eight children, he was doing well enough as a park employee to become a man of property. He bought a house and six acres of land near Wick nursery, copyhold of the manor of Egham. It was a small part of the estate once belonging to John Vardy, who had surveyed the area for William, Duke of Cumberland, in 1750.[128]

Chapter Four

Enclosure, Unrest and More Activity at the Lake: 1802-32

The early years of the 19th century were a time of consolidation at the lake. The extension and landscaping of the new vistas were virtually complete and a much smaller work force would be required for maintenance and repair. William Tough became Foreman of the Works in Windsor Great Park, a broader brief than before. George III's deteriorating health was causing increasing concern and there was no enthusiasm for new projects. While the king was taking the sea air at Weymouth in 1804 the lake was given a thorough clean. The water level was lowered and flags, rushes and weeds pulled up by their roots. Damage to the cascade because of a long period of dry weather was rectified. Tough regularly checked the rides and sometimes had to replace poor brickwork in the drains and arches that might trip up unwary riders or overturn carriages.[1]

In 1809 he made sure his workmen celebrated George III's Golden Jubilee in style. Food and drink were provided and a distribution of money made to the men and their families.[2] In Windsor guns were fired and church bells rung; an ox and a sheep were roasted, dinners given, buildings illuminated[3] and, to crown the day, Queen Charlotte invited 'all members of society' to a firework display on Frogmore meadows. The queen and her daughters often stayed at their 'cottage' at Frogmore in the summer, taking excursions round the lake and frequenting the Egham Races.[4]

At this time it would appear that there was a comparatively relaxed attitude to the local gentry enjoying the park. Edgell Wyatt, eldest son of Richard Wyatt of Milton Place, recorded in his diary of 1810 several occasions on which he rode or walked there, often in the company of his daughters, Maria and Louisa.[5]

With the park needing less attention, Crown officials could concentrate on the unsatisfactory state of the land outside the pales. Egham was a royal manor so the king had a direct interest in many of its estates as well as its open fields and common land. William Crosley, when surveying the parish of Egham in 1790, had noted the extensive nature of its commons and wasteland, much of which lay to the south-west of the town in the neighbourhood of Windsor Great Park.

A survey of the manor of Egham was ordered in 1802, which defined Crown ownership and identified encroachments and illegal enclosures. The task of surveying the manor was given to William and Abraham Driver. They listed numerous small assarts, mostly made by labouring men such as Richard Tindale and John Cheeseman, on Wick Heath. Such small encroachments were usually accepted by the manor and a quit rent charged. Richard Wyatt, head lessee of the manor of Egham, was tolerant of such behaviour, arguing that it was part of the manorial tradition.[6]

Some members of the gentry, like the Viscount Bulkeley at Englefield Green, had taken in small pieces of verge to add to their estates. The survey also noted some larger encroachments, particularly those made on the Great Heath or Egham Common, by local landowners. Thomas Burton, it was said, had enclosed some 10 acres of heath adjoining his land at Bakeham and was digging sand there. David Jebb, who had inherited all his father's lands in 1787, was accused of illegally enclosing no less than 82 acres of heathland.[7]

Many landowners had come to the conclusion that common usage of wasteland was uneconomic and that the time was ripe for enclosure. John Secker, steward of the manor of Egham, complained in 1806 that unofficial enclosure was already taking place, though 'it seldom happens that my permission is solicited'.[8]

The Crown, as lord of the manor of Egham, was obviously interested in any possible enclosure of land on its doorstep and informed John Secker in December 1805 that His Majesty had no objection if the landowners were

46 *Milton Place, Edgell Wyatt Edgell's house, 1822, John Hassell.*

in agreement. Indeed the Crown would profit greatly from a redistribution of common land and open fields. The realigning of the Great Western Road was once more raised and Secker reported that if the project were to go ahead, the king would expect to reserve, for His Majesty's exclusive enjoyment, 'such void spaces of Land which lies between the Park Pales and the new line of road'.[9]

In 1806 the officers of the parish of Egham had a very good reason to look to their common land to see if they could raise money from it. They were in considerable debt and wrote to the Crown to see if they could enclose or sell portions of the waste to relieve them of their 'Embarrassments'; that is, to discharge their debts and lower the Poor Rate. They rehearsed the usual arguments that the common land was of very little use to anyone in its current state and that certain landowners were prepared to pay good money to exploit its potential more profitably. John Fordyce, the Surveyor General, forwarded their request to the Treasury with the comments that he could not agree with such a partial enclosure and that in any case the Crown would be entitled to a share in the waste.[10] The matter was not proceeded with, there being no case in law for such a practice and not yet a large enough majority of the inhabitants in favour of full enclosure.

At court George III became more and more isolated in his illness and in February 1811 his eldest son, George, Prince of Wales, was proclaimed Prince Regent. Commissioners were appointed to administer Windsor Great Park on behalf of the king, while the Prince Regent busied himself with redesigning his houses in the park, Lower Lodge (later Royal Lodge), once the home of the Deputy Ranger, and Great Lodge (later Cumberland Lodge).[11]

Interest continued in the uses to which common land might more profitably be put. In 1812 the Crown received an application for a grant of 1,000 acres of wasteland in Egham, near the Great Western Road, from a man called Peter Schmidtmeyer. On it he proposed to settle superannuated and disabled British soldiers. The Crown did not wish to appear churlish and conceded that in theory it was a project 'well worthy of the Attention of a Humane and liberal Government'. The conflict with Napoleon was not yet over and men were still risking lives and limbs in the Peninsular War. It was doubtful, however, if ex-soldiers would be able to make such poor soil productive and more would need to be spent on the land than it was worth. The application was finally dismissed as 'a most wild, impractical and undigested Plan': the planting of Navy timber would be a better use for the land.[12] In the meantime poachers continued to use the common land as they pleased. John Secker and his gamekeeper, John Johnson, complained that the game was depleted by improper practice and threatened to prosecute anyone trespassing on the preserves of the manor.[13]

The animosity of the poorer inhabitants of Virginia Water towards enclosing common land showed itself clearly, as ever, in their treatment of the Crown plantation on Hangmore Hill. The red tower and its

47 *William Fremantle's house, 1822, John Hassell.*

surrounding trees were regularly vandalised. The ubiquitous John Secker wrote to the Commissioners for Woods & Forests in 1812, stating that the building was in such a dangerous state from 'the depredations and inroads of the Public' that he expected it to fall down and be carried away by the neighbouring poor inhabitants. He reported that even trees were being removed: 'anyone helps himself by stealth or otherwise'. He received the positive reply that the Prince Regent himself required the Clockcase to be repaired and maintained.[14] William Maslin was dispatched in early 1813 to Hangmore Hill to make an estimate for repairs. He concluded that new fencing would prove more expensive than replacing stolen trees and recommended that someone should live on-site to protect the property.[15] As usual at the Clockcase, nothing was done and the problem, for the moment, was overtaken by other events.

In 1813 the enclosure of Egham's commons, wastelands and open fields had started. Led by the Crown, as lord of the manor, and the lords of Egham's sub-manors, the required majority of the landed proprietors of the parish applied for the private Act of Parliament that would change the landscape. Prominent among them were William Fremantle and Viscount Bulkeley, residents of Englefield Green and close associates of the royal family. In 1797, on his return from military and civil service in Ireland, Fremantle had married Selina Mary, only daughter and heiress of Sir John Elwell and widow of Felton Lionel Hervey. Fremantle came to live with her in her late father's house, Elvill's (later Castle Hill) on Englefield Green. He entered English politics as the Member of Parliament for Harwich in 1806, proved himself an able Parliamentarian and became Secretary to the Treasury. Despite favouring such reforms as Catholic emancipation, he remained on close terms with George III and was a contemporary of the Prince Regent.[16]

48 *Viscount Bulkeley's house, 1822, John Hassell.*

Thomas James Warren, the Lord Viscount Bulkeley, and his wife, Harriott Elizabeth, were comparative newcomers to Englefield Green; she was descended from the Warren and Revell families of Fetcham in Surrey and his main estates were in Ireland.[17] Like the Fremantles they had *entrée* to the highest of court circles. Queen Charlotte and her daughters were frequently at Windsor, taking excursions in the neighbourhood and in the summer fishing and picnicking by the lake. To celebrate her birthday in January 1815, the queen gave a little party at Frogmore for members of her own family and a few favoured guests, including Viscount and Lady Bulkeley and Mrs Fremantle. The following year it was Lord Bulkeley's turn to entertain; Queen Charlotte, the Princesses Augusta and Elizabeth and the Dukes of York, Clarence and Cambridge, together with a select group of nobility, dined with Lord and Lady Bulkeley 'at their elegant villa at Englefield Green'. One hundred more guests joined them for a dress ball in the evening.[18]

Culling Charles Smith was another local landowner with royal connections. In 1801 he had purchased more than 200 acres of land in the vicinity of Virginia Water from David Jebb. There he built a crenellated mansion called Wentworth, which became his country seat.[19] His wife was Lady Ann, sister of the future Duke of Wellington and widow of the Hon. Henry Fitzroy; she was a Lady of the Bedchamber to the Duchess of York and rated high in the guest list at the Duke's birthday celebrations at Oatlands in 1802. Later her elder daughters moved in the same social circle as the Prince Regent's daughter, Princess Charlotte.[20] Like Bulkeley and Fremantle, Smith was in favour of enclosure.

These men were newcomers into Egham society but were on close terms with Edgell Wyatt, as the families exchanged visits and dined at each other's houses. Wyatt represented the old Egham gentry families and had succeeded his father, Richard Wyatt, at Milton Place in 1813 as head lessee of the manors of Egham and Milton. He adopted his mother's maiden name as a surname, becoming Edgell Wyatt Edgell by Royal Licence. Between 1813 and 1815, the crucial years for Egham enclosure, he was often absent from Egham on business or residing in Bristol or Bath for the sake of his wife Elizabeth's health. He made flying visits to London and Egham and managed at least one meeting with the Commissioners for Egham's Inclosure in September 1814.[21]

At the beginning of April 1814 the Egham Inclosure Bill was given its third reading in the House of Commons, the motion proposed by the Right Honourable William Henry Fremantle, resident of Englefield Green and by then MP for Buckingham. In the subsequent Act (54 Geo III cap. 153) the intractable nature of the common land was once more reported, its poor soil declared 'incapable of much improvement' and its open fields and meadows too inconveniently sited for effective cultivation. The sponsors of the Act made no bones about the fact that enclosure would be of great advantage to them. Three Commissioners for Inclosure, Sir William Gibbons, Thomas Denton and Abraham Purshouse Driver, were appointed; it was their task in the coming months to survey and distribute the common and open ground according to the value of the land already owned. For this they received a fee of four guineas a day.[22]

No time was wasted. In August and September 1814 meetings were called at either the *King's Head* or the *Catherine Wheel* inns in Egham for householders to state their claims to open land and common rights. A perambulation of the parish was also made. By the beginning of January 1815 objections could be heard.[23] Unfortunately the local newspaper did not report what was said at any of these meetings and no minutes have survived.

Once the Act was passed nothing could be taken from the commons without licence. This was disastrous for those who depended on turf, furze and fern for fuel. To solve this problem a Poor Allotment of about three hundred acres was established to provide fuel for cottagers paying a yearly rent of less than £6.[24]

49 *Culling Charles Smith's house, 1822, John Hassell.*

Some significant exceptions to enclosure were made in Egham. Runnymede was not enclosed because of the annual race meeting held there. Neither was Englefield Green, which was to be left open 'for the pleasure of the inhabitants and the ornament of their residences on the Green'. The court faction had received its reward for leading the move towards enclosure.[25]

John Secker, steward of the manor of Egham, reported that George III, in so far as he was able to express an opinion at that time, warmly approved of the proposed enclosure and had the most 'favourable disposition towards the Parish of Egham'. Yet another reward, this time for the whole parish of Egham, was about to be revealed. In the very month that William Fremantle had proposed the third reading of Egham's Inclosure Bill, April 1814, a vestry meeting was called to discuss the ruinous state of the town's medieval parish church. In attendance were all the supporters of enclosure, Fremantle himself, Viscount Bulkeley, Culling Charles Smith and the Rev. Thomas Bisse of Portnall Park in Virginia Water. Within two months any idea of repairing and extending the old church had been abandoned in favour of building a new one. Fremantle and Bulkeley sent a memorial to the government asking for support, pointing out that the Crown owned a considerable amount of property and a large number of houses in the manor. The proximity of Windsor Great Park had contributed towards an increase in population and improvements in the park had demanded sacrifices of the parish.[26]

The Crown, as the owner of one fifth of the parish of Egham, contributed £1,500, one fifth of the cost of building a new church. The money would be provided by the Surveyor General of Woods and considered as an indemnity to the parish for the wasteland enclosed into the park by the late William, Duke of Cumberland, and by George III. In return, six pews in the new church would be allocated to Crown tenants.[27] The gentlemen, farmers and tradesmen of the parish also came forward with their subscriptions. The list was headed by Lord Bulkeley, contributing 500 guineas. Edgell Wyatt Edgell, still residing in Bath at that time, gave 300 guineas. He was anxious that the labouring classes should be allocated sufficient seats in the new church, rather than the space being taken for pews for the rich that would, in all probability, only be used by their servants. Among the more humble subscribers to the church fund, contributing five guineas, was William Tough, the foreman responsible for the improvements in Windsor Great Park.[28]

Designs for the new church were drawn up and an architect, Henry Rhodes, employed in one of the departments of the Office of Woods, was appointed.[29] Thus the old parish church would be demolished at the same time as the landscape, especially in the west of the district, would undergo its most drastic change.

During the summer of 1815, as Wellington finally defeated Napoleon at Waterloo, the commissioners announced the line of the new carriageways, which would cross the commons, and also defined footpaths. Another responsibility of the commissioners was to sell some pieces of land in order

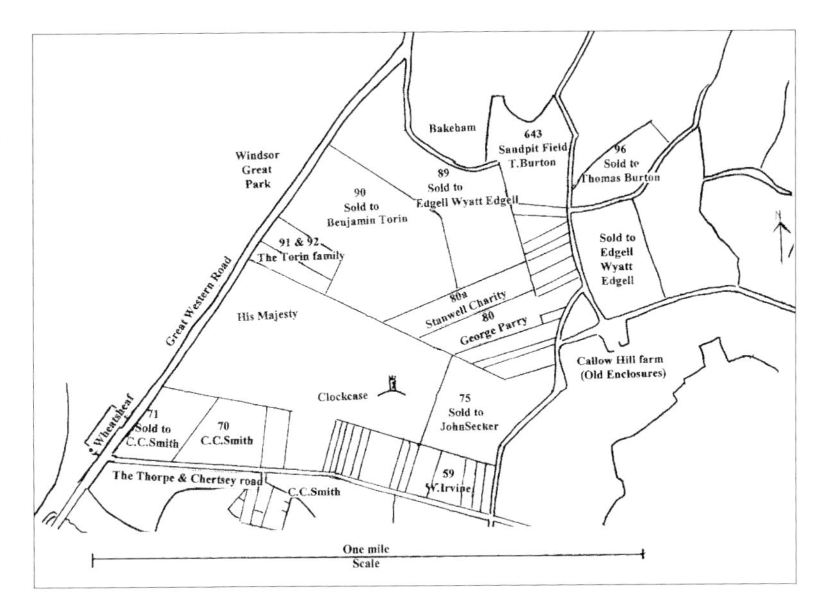

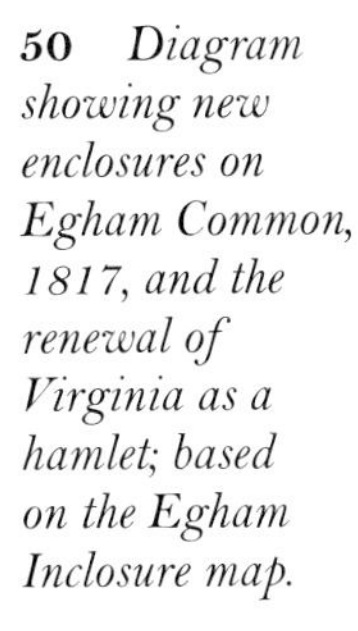
50 *Diagram showing new enclosures on Egham Common, 1817, and the renewal of Virginia as a hamlet; based on the Egham Inclosure map.*

to defray the expenses of enclosure; in July 1815 about eighty-five acres were on offer, much of it attractively 'contiguous to that delightful spot Virginia Water', while in February 1817 more valuable freehold wasteland was for sale, including 46 acres near the Clockcase. This arrangement enabled gentlemen such as John Secker of Windsor, a man very knowledgeable on Egham affairs, to acquire desirable freehold land in Virginia Water.[30]

From 19 April 1817 the commons and wastelands in the parish of Egham ceased to exist. The commissioners gave notice that any cattle, sheep, pigs or geese found on the land after that date would be impounded. Local inhabitants saw the world they had known being restructured before their eyes. They had been accustomed to an open landscape, too far from the centre of Egham to be closely supervised; by 1816 the new enclosures were staked out and road builders were throwing gravel swathes across the old common. A few sites, for example along the new Knowle Hill Road (present Callow Hill) and the Thorpe and Chertsey Road (present Christchurch Road), were reserved for the building of cottages and some artisans were able to buy small plots.[31]

During 1816 Egham's medieval church was demolished and the foundation stone for the new church laid on 9 April 1817. Viscount Bulkeley, William Fremantle, Edgell Wyatt Edgell, the Rev. Thomas Bisse, John Walley Gostling, the Vicar of Egham, together with the churchwardens and some other high subscribers, performed the ceremony in the presence of a large crowd. A collection of new coins in a vessel of oil was deposited with the stone.[32] The old church had gone with the old style of farming; the new church, Neo-Classical in style, was the symbol of a new order.

The road and church building, the digging of numerous ditches, the construction of many more fences and the creation of new plantations

51 *The parish church of St John the Baptist, Egham, rebuilt 1820.*

must have created a flurry of extra employment in the Egham area in the immediate aftermath of enclosure. Labourers were paid 2s. a day for such work as moving earth in preparation for the new churchyard. On exceptional occasions, beer was provided, at parish expense, for the workmen busy at the church.[33]

Enclosure also brought an inevitable drop in the number of small farms and agricultural jobs. In the longer term, however, the town's position on a main road and its proximity to London and the court at Windsor ensured the prosperity of the trading classes: for those living on the breadline in the poorer south and western corners of the parish the outlook was grim. While James Robinson kept the church wardens' accounts between 1816 and 1821, the parish boys and others in need could earn a few pence from killing vermin. A dead sparrow was worth a halfpenny, while a hedgehog, weasel or stoat rated a magnificent 4d.[34]

The fate and position of the Clockcase Plantation continued to be closely bound up with enclosure. Other gentlemen's estates would soon be taking their places on its boundaries and the presence of undesirables in the vicinity was to be deplored. In 1816 Secker again drew attention to the problem, suggesting that 'this trifling Property' be disposed of by auction, otherwise nothing would remain. This time the Crown acted speedily on Secker's advice: an auction was held on 28 May 1816 at the *Wheatsheaf* inn for the sale and removal of the bricks. Unfortunately there were no buyers: the bricks were too well cemented together for easy demolition.[35]

With the final stages of enclosure imminent, the Commissioners for Woods & Forests decided in 1817 to revert to William Maslin's suggestion for converting the Clockcase into a park worker's cottage. Plans were drawn up, showing considerable changes, including the removal of the top of the tower, but it all came to nothing because the Lords of the Treasury could see no point in repairing an apparently useless building.[36] By this time the Egham landowners who had been granted land on the common in the vicinity of the Clockcase were becoming impatient. They wanted to plant their own enclosures that season and were anxious to know when the Crown intended to make good its fences. Early in 1818 a bank was raised round the boundary of the Clockcase plantation, which by then had increased fourfold in size by the Crown's generous acquisitions under the Inclosure Act. Under pressure from the local worthies, the Office of Woods & Forests ordered an estimate from John Godfrey of Thorpe for making a more substantial bank round the property.[37]

By the end of 1819 even the patience of Crown officials seems to have been exhausted. William Maslin was instructed to value the property, including the Scotch firs and Spanish chestnuts growing on it, and application was made for permission to sell. On 22 April 1819 the Clockcase went under the hammer at the London Auction Mart and was sold for £1,500. The poster advertising the sale emphasised the beauty of the site and stated clearly that the property overlooked 'the Falls and Lakes of Virginia Water'.[38] It was a sale that the future George IV would bitterly regret.

The loss of Egham's common lands meant that there was less opportunity for foraging and scavenging in the neighbourhood, so more poachers were attracted to try their luck in Windsor Great Park. A notice appeared in the local newspaper in September 1818 warning trespassers off both the private and open plantations of the park. Poachers with guns and other devices had entered the royal preserves at night 'in the most daring and unlawful manner' and would be prosecuted with the utmost severity of the law. Even minor transgressions, like gathering chestnuts and hunting squirrels, which must have been customary on the commons, were not to be overlooked.[39] A few weeks later the newspaper was able to report a prosecution resulting from this proclamation. Two Egham labourers, William Emmett and Richard Hopwood, were found guilty of wilfully damaging a chestnut tree in Windsor Great Park and fined £5 each with costs. Other men had also been involved but charges against them were dropped on their promise of good behaviour.[40]

Thomas Denton produced the final Inclosure Award for Egham in 1817; he and the other commissioners had redistributed 2,266 acres of open fields, meadows and common land. Nearly 400 acres—almost a sixth—went to the Crown as by far the largest landowner in the parish. The Crown Award included considerable acreages at Virginia Water and all the common land at Wick.

In such a complex undertaking mistakes were obviously made. The 14 acres on the edge of Wick Farm, Great Hides and Little Hides, which had been given to the Planner family in 1780 at the time of the enlargement of the lake, were overlooked. No descendant of the Planners made claim to it

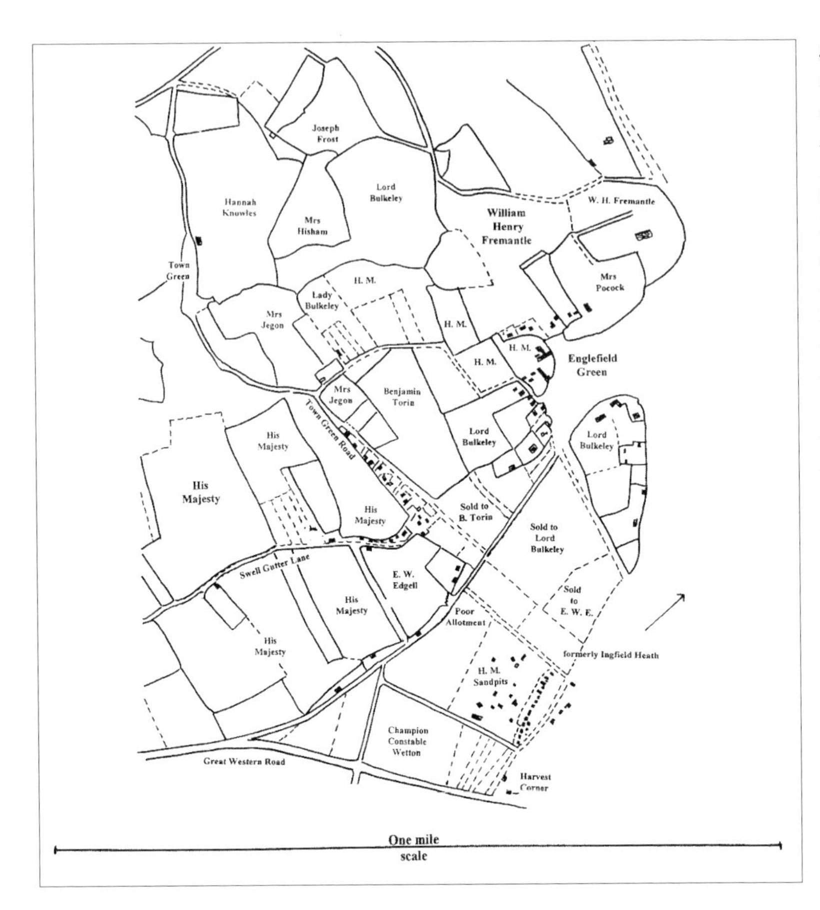

52 *Diagram showing old and new enclosures at Englefield Green, 1817, including the estates of Lord Bulkeley and William Fremantle and the growth of tenements in the Sandpits area, in Town Green Road (Bond Street) and Swell Gutter Lane (Blays Lane), based on the Egham Inclosure map.*

when the commissioners were asking for submissions in 1814 and it was sold to John Barnard.[41] Of the gentry who had favoured enclosure, Lord Viscount Bulkeley and Culling Charles Smith did very well. Bulkeley gained nearly twenty-four new acres, including 11 acres of Englefield Common, in the vicinity of his mansion, which had previously been set in a mere 33 acres of parkland. Smith acquired another 64 acres to adorn his more than 200-acre estate, Wentworth, while Mrs Selina Fremantle was granted a comparatively modest 20 acres to add to her 200 acres, located in different parts of Englefield Green and Wick.[42]

Some small land holders also seemed to prosper in the land shuffle following the Inclosure Award. At Wick, William Pinnock Thirkle arranged some judicious exchanges and acquired a neat little estate of about thirteen acres at the junction of Wick Road and Swell Gutter Lane. This he worked as a nursery and market garden and advertised the sale of such luxury produce as asparagus plants.[43] By 1819, however, he seemed to have overstretched himself, for he was unable to pay the mortgage. The holding was probably too small to prosper in a post-enclosure environment and he was forced to sell land, some of which had been in the Pinnock and Thirkle families for generations.[44]

53 *Parkside, Egham Wick, 1859, signed J.E.R.*

There was no attempt to sell the estate as a market garden: instead the desirability of its location was emphasised, especially its proximity to Windsor Great Park. There was great potential to improve the estate and in particular it would suit a gentleman interested in field sports. Fortunately for the Crown the smallholding was bought, not by a social-climbing outsider, but by Thomas Burton for the use of his eldest son, Brumbridge, and renamed Park Cottage. Thomas Burton owned the extensive Bakeham Farm on the opposite side of the Great Western Road from Thirkle's small holding. Burton had done conspicuously well out of enclosure, consolidating land and creating one of the largest estates in the parish: he had started life as the son of an Egham innkeeper.[45]

Joseph Frost, bailiff in Windsor Great Park, also profited from the available opportunities. He extended his land holdings at Wick to 44 acres, including the Little Common itself and land at Southbrooks. On the site of his four cottages he decided to build himself a house, which later became known as Parkside from its proximity to the park.

Encroachments had already been made on Wick Heath. The Plan of the Manor of Egham, surveyed by Abraham and William Driver in 1802, shows John Cheeseman, among others unnamed, as the occupants of three tenements alongside Sherwood Grove. John had come to Wick to work as a ploughman on the royal farms and had married Elizabeth Blay, the young widow of another park worker, Richard Blay. More tenements were built after enclosure and families like the Cheesemans became freeholders.[46] Richard Tindall, another park workman, was in the occupation of another assart to the north of the heath.

Enclosure was in the air not only in Egham but also throughout the parishes in the Thames Valley. Even Windsor Forest itself was under scrutiny. As in Egham, official irritation with a system that seemed not only out of date but out of control had been finding voice for some time. In 1798 Richard Wordsworth, a Crown solicitor, claimed he was 'tore to pieces at the incroachments daily made in Windsor Forest' and would like to exclude commoners from their traditional rights.[47] Commissioners appointed to enquire into the state of the forest found the timber neglected and the deer few in number. The due process of private Act of Parliament, claim and counter claim was set in motion and the Windsor Forest Award made known in January 1817.[48]

With the forest no longer dedicated to the nurturing and protecting of game, the remaining deer had to be driven out of the forest into Windsor Great Park. This scene was witnessed and recorded by Thomas Love Peacock, the satirical writer, who had attended school in Englefield Green and was, moreover, a close friend of the poet Percy Bysshe Shelley, who lived at Bishopsgate from 1815-16, in the early period of his relationship with Mary Godwin. Peacock described how the Royal Horse Guards drove hundreds of deer through the open pales of the park and what regret he felt that 'the life of the old scenes was gone'.[49]

In this time of upheaval, the radical journalist William Cobbett set out to expose the changes taking place in the English countryside. The improvements in Windsor Great Park and on the main road in the early 19th century had made the old forest land highly desirable from a residential point of view. In 1822 Cobbett reported a proliferation in the building of estates for those he scornfully called 'the stock-jobbing crew' on former wasteland near such villages as Sunningdale on the western side of the park.[50] This development was delayed at Virginia Water as the Crown had gained ownership of much of the old common land. The owners of the Portnall and Wentworth estates in the south-west of the area had also acquired pieces of common land to increase their landholdings even before enclosure, thus excluding outsiders.

The only developments at Virginia Water at that time were on a small scale. Two sites for future residences were allocated for sale on land next to the Clockcase Plantation. One plot was acquired by the London architect William Fuller Pocock and, by 1825, he had built a modest cottage on it, consisting of only four rooms and a wash-house. It was intended to give his family an experience of country ways during their holidays, 'away from the toils of London life'. The adjoining plot was bought by John Secker, legal adviser to the Crown and the manor of Egham: he built two gardeners' cottages on the site so that his men might start improving the soil and designing the pleasure park, but no mansion was, as yet, under construction.[51]

During the Regency, consolidation rather than innovation had been the theme in Windsor Great Park. Inevitably, when George IV succeeded to the throne on the death of his father in January 1820, there were significant changes. Even the first year of his reign did little to endear him to his subjects.

In June the king's estranged wife, Caroline, returned from exile in Europe to a triumphal welcome and he and his ministers, in a serious misjudgement of public opinion, brought her to trial for misconduct. As her reputation rose on a wave of popular sympathy so his sank.[52] With antagonism growing, Windsor Great Park was closed during the trial, new keys were ordered and access became strictly limited.[53]

Meanwhile, the workmen in the park were diverted by a somewhat farcical incident. The elephant keeper at the royal menagerie was accused of stealing the king's poultry and sending them to London on the Egham coach. A pair of the man's braces was found at the coach office and, facing such apparently clear evidence of guilt, he was dismissed from royal service. In a criminal court the most likely punishment would have been transportation.[54]

The charges against Queen Caroline were abandoned in mid-November and London exploded with joy, illuminating its windows in her honour.[55] George IV heard the news at Frogmore, Queen Charlotte's cottage in Windsor Great Park. In a dejected state he was consoled by food, drink and the singing of glees in the company of his sister, Augusta, and his trusty friend from Egham, William Fremantle.[56] The people of Egham, like those in many other towns and villages throughout the country, were anxious to join in Queen Caroline's celebrations. There was evidence, however, that pressure was put on the inhabitants to show loyalty to the king in this matter. An unknown correspondent, calling himself 'A Constant Reader' and significantly of Englefield Green, reported to the Windsor newspaper on 17 November that although it was rumoured that an illumination for the queen would be made in Egham, this had failed to materialise. The faithful inhabitants had apparently covered their windows, thanks to the efforts of the local magistrates and despite an offer of free beer to tempt them to disloyalty.

This view of events was challenged the following week. Another anonymous reader, this one styling himself 'Country Booby', alleged that, on the contrary, only nine of Egham's 200 households had failed to light up in thanksgiving for the queen's delivery. He was not suggesting that this was the start of a revolution, noting that the people of Egham had no disposition to riot; he merely wanted to put the matter straight. The editor, for his part, claimed to know the identity of 'Country Booby' and was ready to vouch for the veracity of his statements.[57]

The matter did not end there. Towards the end of November a meeting was called of the householders, gentlemen and nobility of Egham at the *Red Lion's* assembly rooms. William Fremantle moved a loyal address to the monarch and the constitution. It was somewhat extreme in its content, recalling the horrors of the French revolution and included a savage attack on 'a venal, corrupt and prostituted press'. He was voicing the government's fears that the mishandling of the queen's affair might lead to civil unrest. Culling Charles Smith, perhaps in an attempt to lighten the tone, suggested that there were black sheep in every profession, adding that he spoke as a farmer! William Fremantle's address was carried without dissent: Egham's upper classes had rallied to support their constitutional monarch.[58]

The lives of the town's poorer inhabitants, however, remained wretched. Agriculture was still in a state of depression and more able-bodied men were dependent on parish relief. In such circumstances crime also increased and more severe measures were introduced to prevent trespass on public or private property. A serious incident that occurred in Windsor Great Park, between Bishopsgate and Virginia Water, early in 1821, illustrates the desperation on both sides. It involved two Egham men, Joseph Chase and Martin Killick, and seven park keepers. Chase and Killick were found guilty of affray and sentenced to transportation for life, awaiting shipment to New South Wales on the hulk *Justitia* at Woolwich throughout the summer.[59] In a previous generation, men of the Chase family had been loyal servants of the Crown.

George IV retreated to his cottage in Windsor Great Park while the castle itself underwent refurbishment. He was obsessed with a desire for privacy and so fearful of intruders that his favourite outrider, Hudson, would check every thicket for trespassers.[60] During his regency, George had already revealed this obsessive tendency. Having no direct control over the park as a whole at that time, he had busied himself redesigning Great Lodge and the Royal Cottage. In November 1815 it was announced that the road through the park from Bishopsgate to the 23rd milestone on the Reading road would be replaced by a new thoroughfare that passed further from the royal residences. The prince and his guests could thereby enjoy greater privacy.[61]

As king, George IV tried to enjoy such seclusion whenever he could and Royal Cottage became a favourite residence. His summer-long attendance at Virginia Water, however, made it difficult for the men to carry out essential work. William Maslin had his labourers wheeling sand out of the lake at China Island in August 1824 and had sought permission to lower the water to expedite the task. The king, however, categorically refused his consent as he was in residence. The work would have to be carried out in the monarch's absence.[62]

Despite the king's obsession with privacy the local newspaper seemed to know his every move around the park that summer. It reported how, attended by his suite, he would ride around the lake and woodland drives in his pony phaeton, enjoy the diversion of angling, dine alfresco and return to Royal Cottage for the evening.[63] He was planning changes that would turn Virginia Water into a 'fairy scene'.[64]

Meanwhile, Culling Charles Smith of Wentworth was initiating improvements outside the park. It had been realised as early as 1782 that the turnpike road on either side of the bridge near the cascade was dangerously steep but nothing had been done to alleviate this because of George III's plan for the diversion of the whole stretch of road, which was later aborted.[65]

In August 1824, however, Smith, on behalf of the turnpike trustees, invited James MacAdam to oversee an ambitious road improvement.

Tons of earth were dug out of the hill and used to fill up the valley and a temporary road and bridge built. In May 1825 letters on the subject were exchanged between Culling Charles Smith and the Marquis of Conyngham, who had been appointed Constable of Windsor Castle and Steward of the Royal Household by George IV. The marquis was also the husband of Lady Elizabeth Conyngham, the close companion of the king in his final years. With the park the favourite home of the monarch in the second half of the 1820s, the Crown had a clear interest in plans for the improvement of the road and the bridge and a meeting was arranged with the king's architect, Jeffry Wyatville.[66]

George IV's passion for angling was well known and his first requirement at Virginia Water was the construction of a summerhouse from where he might fish and suitably entertain his guests. A Chinese-style fishing temple was built on the north bank of the lake, 'with painting and gilding and fantastic carving and swinging bells and flying dragons'.[67]

Other more monumental constructions were in the planning stage, all of them sited to the west of the cascade. The near-derelict stone bridge over the lake near Blacknest Gate would be rebuilt. The Belvedere, the viewpoint at Shrubs Hill, would be enlarged and converted into a miniature fort, complete with cannon. A collection of classical columns, languishing in the courtyard of the British Museum, having come originally from Leptis Magna near Tripoli, were to be conveyed by road and set up in the park to add interest to a rather dark corner of the lakeside under the Ascot road bridge.[68]

54 *View on Virginia Water, Patrick Nasmyth.*

55 *High Bridge over Virginia Water, detail from a plan in Brayley's* History of Surrey, *1850.*

56 *Ruins at Virginia Water, engraving after T. Allom.*

It was fortunate that the improvements to the turnpike road were on course. By February 1826 Culling Charles Smith and his neighbour, the Rev. Thomas Bisse of Portnall Park, had commissioned James Bedborough, stonemason, and George Lawrence, bricklayer, to build a new bridge across the stream at Virginia Water with foundations between six and 11ft in depth. The cost was an astounding £3,350. Such a sum could not come from turnpike income alone and bonds would need to be raised. In July the trustees were able to secure an Exchequer Bill Loan for £4,000 on the future tolls.[69] The estates of both Smith and Bisse adjoined the turnpike road and they would benefit from its improvement, as would the Crown.Work was to be completed by 12 August 1826, the month in which the first of the classical columns was brought by turnpike from London and set up at Virginia Water. Once more it seemed that the king's friends were in the right place at the right time.

The renewal of royal interest in Windsor Great Park, more road construction and the new buildings around the lake had once again brought valuable work opportunities to the area. In August 1826 the king celebrated his birthday in style at Windsor and invited all the men working at Windsor Castle and at Virginia Water, some 700 in all, to dine at various Windsor public houses. His 'happy and industrious workers' gathered at 1 p.m. on the castle's eastern terrace to cheer their benefactor. Another 115 workmen, brought down from London for tasks connected with the castle's refurbishment, enjoyed the same hospitality. Later that day the tradesmen working at the castle were entertained to a sumptuous meal at the *Swan Inn*, while in the evening the town was brilliantly illuminated.[70]

In order to guarantee his privacy at Virginia Water fully, George IV would need to acquire significant pieces of land outside the bounds of the park. The nearest of these to the lake was the *Wheatsheaf*, which had remained in private hands and, operating as an inn, gave customers a way in to the park. They were even allowed the privilege of walking on the pondhead and viewing the lake. The owner of the inn since 1808 had been Culling Charles Smith, who must have speculated that its future value would be much enhanced should the Crown ever try to buy it back. One of his tenant licensees was Robert Prince, who seemed to have been inspired by the old road directives to change the name of the establishment. He inscribed the words '*New England Inn*' on his inn sign but retained the image of the wheat sheaf at its centre. When Prince left the inn in 1818, however, his successor reverted to the original name.[71] Smith, meanwhile, had added an extra acre to the inn's extent under the Inclosure Award and was only too happy to sell it to the Crown in November 1824 for £5,000, having bought it from John Atkins for £1,500.[72] Smith must have assumed that the Crown would not wish to retain the licence, that the inn would be pulled down and its land absorbed into the park. He therefore entered into correspondence with officials about the possibility of transferring the licence to a new inn to be built on the opposite side of the road, on a piece of Smith's own land.[73]

The idea came to nothing. The *Wheatsheaf*, surprisingly, continued to operate as an inn but was under closer scrutiny from the Commissioners of Woods & Forests. Most of its land was taken into the park, leaving only about half an acre for outbuildings and stable yard, and clients were on no account to stray into the royal estate. Its licensee, George Baker, complained bitterly that the property had decreased in value.[74] The king, moreover, had his own plans for Smith's land immediately opposite the cascade. In order to avoid being overlooked, especially as improvements were in hand below the waterfall, George IV offered to lease 27 acres of Smith's Wentworth land, sited on either side of the River Redbourne as it flowed out of the lake. The financial settlement was generous: for 750 guineas Smith had only to fence off the required acres and ensure that they were reserved for the sole use of His Majesty. The lease would end with the death of the king.[75]

Next in the king's sights for acquisition was the Clockcase. Built as a viewpoint over the lake, it had been sold by the Crown in 1819. The new owner in 1824 was Henry Willmer, a London doctor, who had not 'the slightest wish or Intention to part with the Property'. He had spent thousands of pounds improving the estate, and his brother-in-law, William Fuller Pocock, an architect, had just bought the plot next to his.[76]

As the Crown became more insistent, Dr Willmer claimed to have received an offer of 10,000 guineas for the estate from a private individual: he himself valued the property at £12,500. The Office of Woods & Forests were not impressed with 'his fancy Price' and tried instead to appeal to his sense of duty. Willmer continued to affirm his loyalty to the king but remained a very unwilling vendor. The conveyance was finally drawn up in March 1826 with 'possession to be obtained without delay'. Dr Willmer had refused to accept less than £8,500. George IV's desire for privacy had overridden financial prudence.[77] William Willmer Pocock, Henry Willmer's nephew, who had observed some of the negotiations as a boy, was of the opinion that the deal had finally been made 'to quiet the susceptibilities of some of his [the king's] lady friends, who would not go on the lake with him until he had command of it'.[78]

Word had obviously got around that any land near the lake might prove to be extremely valuable if the king could be persuaded to buy. In September 1826 Thomas Stokes of Dartmouth Green, Blackheath, offered the Crown an estate

57 *Sign from the* Wheatsheaf *in the stableyard opposite the inn (detail from 'Virginia Water Lodge and the cascade from the Great Western road',* c.*1814).*

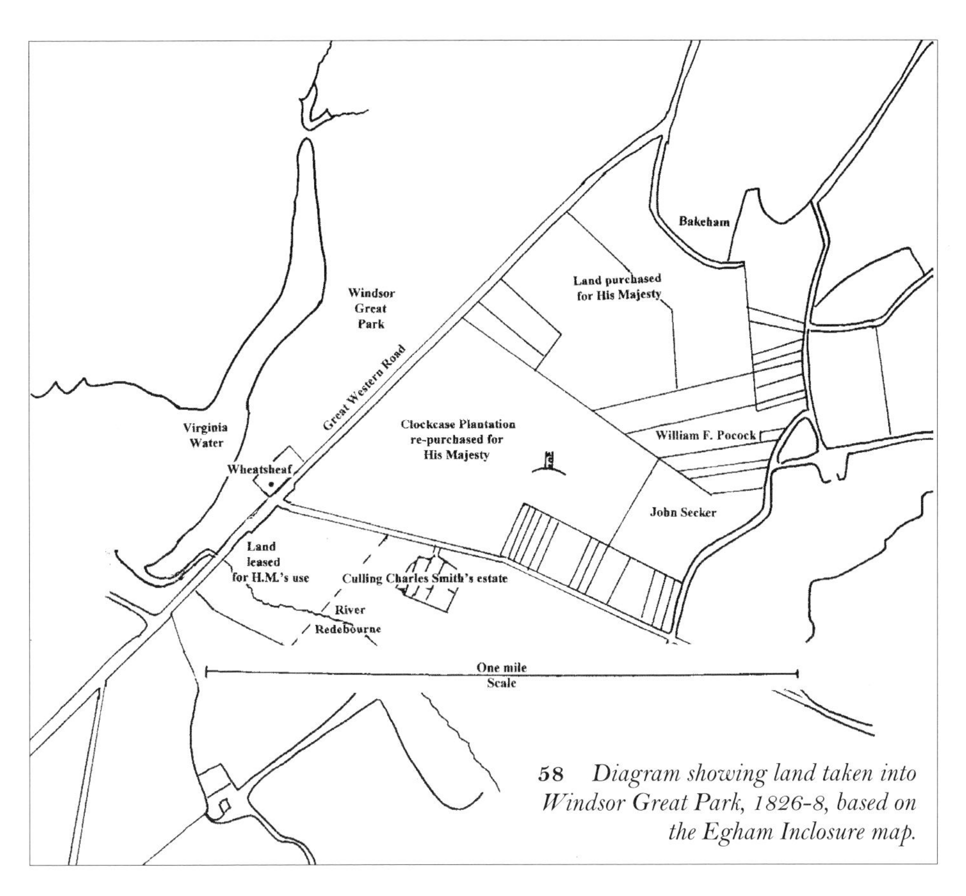

58 *Diagram showing land taken into Windsor Great Park, 1826-8, based on the Egham Inclosure map.*

59 *Clockcase Cottage, 1989, photograph by Dorothy Davis.*

of about sixty acres, adjoining the Clockcase. It had been acquired under the Inclosure Award by Edgell Wyatt Edgell and the Torin family of Englefield Green and then sold on. Stokes valued the land at 4,000 guineas, another vast over-valuation, though the Crown admitted it was a highly desirable acquisition. The parties finally agreed a price of £3,500. Those wealthy enough to have bought land in such a desirable location as Virginia Water were reaping fine rewards. Stokes, however, was still awaiting settlement in December 1826, despite the fact that Crown workmen were already busy on his land.[79]

For the king's part he had achieved his objective: the boundaries were protected and he could fish at Virginia Water without being observed. The cost of acquiring the new land was around £20,000. The king's extravagance did not go unopposed. Soon after becoming Prime Minister and First Lord of the Treasury, in January 1828 the Duke of Wellington objected to His Majesty applying for yet more money for plantations at Windsor. The budget for the Office of Woods & Forests for that year had already been allocated to finishing the London parks, a far more important project in the duke's opinion. 'I assure you', he wrote, 'that we have not a shilling.'[80] This decision had an immediate effect on work at Virginia Water: plans to deepen the lake at its western end at China Island were postponed. Wages had to be kept down and a newly appointed gatekeeper was to receive only the lowest rate of pay current in the neighbourhood.[81]

The large amount of money already spent at Virginia Water much enhanced the pleasure of George IV's drives around the lake, and he enjoyed inspecting the progress of his improvements, 'monuments to his eccentric taste and his expensive habits', according to one observer.[82] In June 1827 the king viewed the setting up of the ruined columns and inspected the new bridge, the boathouse and the fishing temple with its delightful parterres. It was clearly irksome to have to return to London even for a day. He liked to be out in his phaeton in the park, or in his closed carriage if the weather was inclement.[83]

Outside the park, the agricultural depression that had started at the end of the Napoleonic war showed no signs of abating. There was chronic unemployment and subsequent stagnation, if not actual decrease, in wages. In 1819 there had been some attempt to establish an annual agricultural show, which would reward working men who raised their families without recourse to parochial relief.[84] Nothing came of this high-minded aim, however, and the root causes of poverty were not tackled.

Poaching and scavenging became, more than ever, a way of life for many young men. In 1820 Charles Hackett was brought before the Chertsey magistrates on a charge of stealing timber from Knowle Grove, a piece of Crown woodland nearly two miles from Windsor Great Park but on Charles's doorstep. He knew the grove better than the keepers, as he had been brought up at nearby Knowle Hill, in a cottage assarted from the waste by his grandfather, Robert Hackett. Charles was fortunate on this occasion in court, for though the magistrates wished to press charges, they did not know which Act of Parliament to invoke and he was let off.[85] Two years later he was once more before a Surrey court, this time for stealing wood from a neighbour's timber yard, a charge he denied. One of Charles's younger brothers was called for his defence but admitted, under cross-examination, that six guns, a dark lantern and some poaching nets had been found in Charles's house. This evidence was probably more damning than the possible theft of wood and, as an old offender, Charles Hackett was sentenced to seven years' transportation.[86]

More honest men were forced to seek parish help. In Egham claimants had to present themselves at the Sunday morning vestry meeting, a walk of some two to three miles each way for the inhabitants of Virginia Water and Wick, hoping that the parish officials would be in a benevolent frame of mind. The main business of the Sunday vestry was to allocate dole, either in kind—a pair of shoes, a greatcoat, a shift, a shirt, calico to make garments—or as an addition to the weekly allowances—6d. here, 5s. there, even 'a whole pound note' to one family where the children were seriously ill with measles and scarlet fever.[87] There was a reluctance to grant unqualified relief to able-bodied men. One man was so desperate that he threatened to run away and leave his family dependent on the parish. He received 5s. from the Assistant Overseer to help him with his responsibilities. If possible such claimants were set to work on the parish roads in return for their pittance.[88]

Families also became dependent on others when the breadwinner was no longer able to work. By 1818 Richard Tindall, formerly a labourer in the park, had become chargeable to the parish. He lived with his wife on an encroachment at Wick. If the land was proved to be freehold it would have to be sold for the relief and maintenance of the old couple in the workhouse.[89] Elizabeth Welbelove, the owner of another pair of cottages at Wick, became a pauper in 1825 and the vestry ordered that the weekly rent from her tenants, her son Richard and James O'Brient, should be paid to the Overseers of the Poor for Elizabeth's keep in the workhouse. This decision was challenged but the answer was sharp and to the point: if Richard Welbelove refused to take his mother home and keep her himself, the overseers were entitled to the rent of her cottages and, failing that, to sell them to pay for Elizabeth's support. Nothing more was reported on the matter and the Welbelove family had to accept the fact that even the workhouse did not come free.[90]

William Thirkle also came to the notice of the Overseers. The one-time land-owning yeoman was reduced to begging for parish dole: in December 1825 he was offered a choice between an allowance of 3s. a week or the hospitality of the workhouse. His son, also William, was in no position to offer his father support for he too was in need, asking for help from the vestry to provide his family with shoes and clothing.[91] Only a month before, William Cobbett, riding on familiar ground on the Surrey, Sussex and Hampshire borders, was informed that the 'allowed' wage in the area, presumably the lowest amount a family might survive on, was 7d. a day for the man and 'a gallon loaf a week for the rest of the family'. In Cobbett's opinion, prisoners and 'the meanest foot soldier' were treated better.[92]

For those families on the Windsor Great Park establishment life was easier, but there was always the fear that death or infirmity might rob a family of its security. Fathers did what they could to secure jobs for their sons and it was no shame to speak up for oneself. In January 1821 William Tough, who had worked for more than 30 years to transform the landscape of Virginia Water, died aged sixty-four. Within a few days his brother, George, who still worked at the royal nursery, applied for promotion to his late brother's position. William must have died suddenly for his son, John, who was employed as one of the park men, was left for a while to manage his father's workers and their wages. In presenting the accounts he pointed out that no wages for his work had been included and he left it to the generosity of his superiors to grant him whatever was appropriate.[93]

Neither George nor John Tough succeeded to the post. Instead, William Maslin, who was foreman on the Berkshire side of the park, extended his responsibilities to Wick. As he lived near Bracknell, 10 miles away, it was clearly necessary to appoint an assistant. Another John Tough, this time George's son, a nurseryman, was proposed but Maslin would have none of it: 'As an assistant to me he is of no use', he wrote. Instead he put forward his own son, Charles, who was forthwith appointed to the post and given a house at Wick nursery from which to supervise the work at the eastern end of the lake.[94]

In 1828 Charles Maslin took over from his father and became Deputy Surveyor in the park at a salary of £200 with an extra £30 in lieu of fodder for cows. He went to live at Parkside, the house built by Joseph Frost, who had died the year before. Frost had held the land as a copyholder whereas Maslin was merely a tenant of the Crown.[95]

As poverty increased so did the poor rate. To keep the rates from rising too high troublesome paupers could be removed by the vestry proving their legal settlement elsewhere, while dependent children over the age of 12 could be put into service or apprenticeship, preferably outside the parish. If it cost too much to keep claimants in their own homes they could be ordered into the workhouse. Egham's purpose-built workhouse had been constructed in 1804 on a piece of land, granted by the Crown, at the eastern end of Egham Street and by 1827 was already too small.[96]

Some families were persistent in their requests. John Beauchamp, who lived near the Clockcase Plantation, was twice refused shoes for his children. In March 1829 he was out of work and desperate, having seven children to support, the youngest born the very day of his appeal. He was given 5s. The following year, with the employment situation no better, he was granted an allowance of 2s. 6d. a week for three months, a gesture that might pay his rent for the winter.[97]

60 *Egham's Parish Workhouse, 1824, John Hassell.*

The fairs held annually throughout the forest area provided some respite from the misery of subsistence. Amusements at the fair held at Englefield Green in May 1825 included donkey racing for a bridle, winding 15yds of string round a peg for a hat and playing cricket for ribands. Boys willing to make spectacles of themselves could scoff rolls spread with treacle in order to win a smock frock.[98]

The more socially conscious gentry were, however, concerned at the depths to which some of their poorer neighbours had sunk during the reign of George IV. Edgell Wyatt Edgell painted a most depressing picture of the depraved state to which men had been reduced by poverty. He described the people in the east of Egham parish as drunkards and likely sheep stealers, while those in the centre were ignorant and wild. The inhabitants in the west of the parish were, however, in the greatest need: they had little employment and some had suffered the extreme penalty of the law. He noted that the crimes they were supposed to have committed had mostly occurred in the neighbourhood of Windsor Great Park.[99]

Despite the increasing severity of the game laws, 'depredations and trespass' by 'numberless disorderly persons' in the park continued. In October 1825 a public notice announced that trees had been damaged and game disturbed and killed by poachers. As some of the men had entered the park on the pretext of gathering chestnuts and acorns or hunting squirrels, such practices would no longer be permitted by the Hon. the Earl Harcourt, the Deputy Ranger.[100] For many labourers, unable to find work to keep their families, poaching was a means of survival. The poacher was popularly regarded as the victim of unjust laws, even as a folk hero. In March 1828 the local paper described the fate of a young man called Field, previously employed on the alterations at Windsor Castle. He had been found guilty of poaching and hanged at Reading. Subsequently his body had been exhibited in a chandler's shop, his face on view, apparently showing no signs of his violent death and strewn with flowers.[101]

Wyatt Edgell feared that the poor might be led astray by dissenters. Even the grand new church in Egham could not accommodate all its inhabitants and many, like those in the vicinity of Virginia Water, lived too far away to attend regularly.[102] In August 1824 the vestry agreed that it would be desirable to build a chapel in one of the more vulnerable areas of the parish, either at the crossroads at Virginia Water or at the Sand Pits at Englefield Green.[103] The Sand Pits had once been part of Egham's common land, at Englefield Green near the turnpike road. Large amounts of sand were excavated after enclosure and in 1821 Earl Harcourt, acting on behalf of the king, gave permission for poor people to build cottages in the old pits.[104]

No benefactor came forward to build a chapel, either at Englefield Green or at Virginia Water, but it remained a popular belief among the ruling classes that good order could be re-established in society if only the backsliding poor could be brought back to the Church of England. For some this reflected true religious fervour; others were more pragmatic, seeing in the teaching of doctrine a means to produce a docile workforce that knew its place in society. It was Edgell Wyatt Edgell, genuinely concerned for the spiritual and material welfare of those who lived on the outskirts of the parish, who acted. In 1829 the vestry granted him permission to put down a deposit for the building of a chapel 'for the poor of this parish on the Heath'.[105]

A chapel was duly built at Rusham End, just to the south-west of Egham and near Edgell's own residence, Milton Place. With his neighbour, Mrs Catherine Irvine of Luddington House, he already maintained two schools in Stroude, between Egham and Virginia Water, conducted under the National Plan, according to the teachings of the Church of England, for about 80 to 90 poor children. There was a similar day school, catering for 40 to 50 children and supported by local contributions, at Shrubs Hill, which had developed into a hamlet after the Inclosure Award. In Egham itself the charity school, founded by Henry Strode in 1704, had been reorganised and enlarged to take in more poor pupils, but its trustees were unwilling to become involved with a parish National School.[106]

Englefield Green, with a population by then nearly the size of Egham and with 250 to 300 children, was worse off than any other part of the parish. It had only two or three small schools, run by private individuals and paid for by the poor families themselves. Some of the local gentry were in the habit of financing the poorer children, but only 60 to 70 children benefited from this.[107]

In December 1826 the Egham vestry met to draw up plans to ameliorate this state of affairs. The education of the poor was clearly a matter of significance in government circles and the meeting was chaired by the Rt. Hon. William Fremantle. He was still a member of parliament but had that

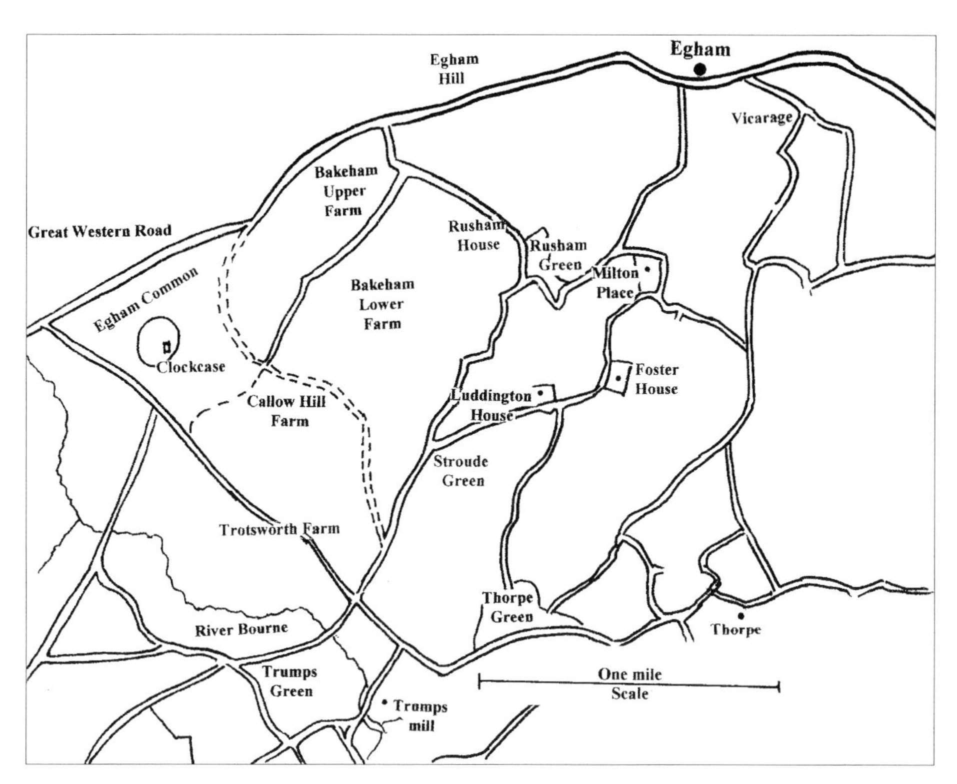

61 *Diagram showing gentry houses and communities to the south and south-west of Egham,* c.*1794, based on Ordnance Survey draft map.*

year been appointed Treasurer of the Royal Household to George IV.[108] The harshest criticism, doubtless led by Fremantle himself, was reserved for the 'opulent householders' of Englefield Green who had failed to notice the almost total lack of education available for the children of their poor neighbours. Immediate steps were taken to set up a school in the hamlet where 'the want is so manifest and the means are so evident for its support'. Within three weeks a quarter of an acre of Poor Allotment land near the Sand Pits at Englefield Green had been acquired and subscriptions raised for the building and maintenance of a National School. Fremantle petitioned His Majesty, who donated £50 towards building costs and £20 a year for the support of the Egham schools.[109]

The vestry was unwilling to propose a rate for the purpose of education, relying instead on the liberality of parishioners. This was possible at Englefield Green, where the richest and most influential landowners lived, but not elsewhere. The provision of education at Shrubs Hill, Stroude and Egham remained much as it was before and the children of Virginia Water had to wait another 17 years before their National School opened.

On Virginia Water's boundary with the parish of Thorpe, Trumps Mill was suffering from a more erratic water supply than usual because of George IV's enthusiasm for angling. Managing the level of water at the lake was not easy: it had to accommodate the diversions of the king and yet maintain a satisfactory flow of water in the river that served the neighbouring countryside. In 1828 and early in 1829 Thomas and George La Coste, proprietors of the mill, wrote to the Commissioners of His Majesty's Woods & Forests complaining of their financial loss but received no reply. In September they once more spelled out their grievances. The flow of water at Virginia Water was sometimes 'penned up' and on other occasions 'allowed to escape in such quantities as to materially interfere with and injure the mill'. They threatened to take legal action to enforce their claim, but all relevant official departments denied responsibility.[110]

It was important for the park workers to maintain a good stock of fish for the king's pleasure at Virginia Water. In March 1830 George IV expressed his concern that too many fish might be getting out of the lake and spoke to Charles Maslin, Deputy Surveyor, about the possibility of putting an iron grating across the stream at the waterfall to retain the fish. Maslin estimated that it would take six labourers six weeks to carry out the work, at a cost of £21 12s. From this it would appear that labourers employed in the park received a wage of 12s. a week at that time.[111] This was only a small increase on the 10s. to 12s. a week paid when George III began his improvements in 1780 but it was better than some employers offered. William Cobbett recorded meeting a hedge cutter in 1825 who received only 1s. 6d. a day.[112]

62 *Trumps Mill House, 2003, photograph by Alan Bostock.*

63 *George IV taking his favourite exercise near Sandpit Gate.*

The permanent jobs, such as those of keeper, were even more valuable and it was in the royal servant's interest as well as the king's to carry out his instructions to the letter. It was the keeper's task to protect His Majesty from unwanted visitors. When Robert Huish entered the park in an attempt to sketch Sandpit Gate Lodge in June 1830 he seemed surprised to be accosted by a keeper, William Portsmouth, who ordered him off the premises. Perhaps Huish was ignorant of the fact that only certain privileged artists were licensed to record the work in Windsor Great Park. Ironically George IV died that very month and the most fanciful period of construction and the time of tightest exclusion at Virginia Water was over.[113]

The accession of William IV in succession to his brother in June 1830 did nothing to relieve the tensions in society. Changes were, however, made in the park. William Fremantle, having been knighted by George IV in 1827, was appointed Deputy Ranger of Windsor Great Park by William IV. With the encouragement of the new king, Fremantle took on responsibilities not only for the game and its well-being but also for the workforce and its salaries. In a plan to improve the financial viability of the park, some labourers, carters, gatekeepers and carpenters were made redundant in October 1830.[114] It could not have happened at a worse time.

In the south-eastern counties of England some labouring men had reached breaking point. Disappointing harvests in 1829 and 1830 had exacerbated the suffering of families already subsisting on a diet of little more than bread. Riots began in Kent in August 1830 and soon spread south and west. They became known as the 'Captain Swing' riots after the assumed name often put at the foot of threatening letters. The incidents usually took the form of incendiary attacks on the property of gentlemen, farmers or clergymen. Windsor's local newspaper expressed its understanding of the plight of men 'farmed out at eight shillings a head' and warned that without hope, 'Hunger will be clamorous and starving men might grow desperate.'[115]

By November the violence had reached the edges of Windsor Great Park and one of its first Surrey victims was Sir William Fremantle. On the evening of 12 November flames were seen coming from a shed dangerously near a barn of hay on his estate at Englefield Green. His steward called both the Egham and the Staines fire engines and local men also came to the rescue with buckets of water to help in whatever way they could. The fire was eventually put out but one hayrick had caught alight and it took all the next day to make it safe. It had been William Fremantle's suggestion in 1827 that the parish should purchase a fire engine and the Fremantles had been the chief subscribers to the fund.[116] Other inhabitants of Egham would also have cause to be grateful for their foresight. The fire at the Fremantle estate was, without doubt, malicious and no accident. During the night some unknown person, possibly the arsonist himself, had cut the fire engine hose with a knife. It is likely that Sir William was specifically selected as a target because of his connections with the Crown estates and because of the redundancies he had recently made. The Crown was also regarded as being influential in determining the level of local wages. The whole community of gentlemen, farmers and tradesmen was alarmed, fearing they might be the victims of the next attack. A meeting of the vestry was called for the 16 November, attended by Sir William and everyone of significance in the parish, to decide what best to do to protect their properties from 'the nightly incendiary'. They clearly could not believe that their own poor and industrious labourers were to blame but put the responsibility more obliquely and anonymously on 'malicious and evil disposed persons

64 *William Fremantle's house at Englefield Green, 1828, pencil drawing, William Delamotte.*

excited by foreign emissaries'. The French Revolution was never far from the mind of the English establishment. Immediate action was necessary: the yeomanry was called up under Captain Richard Wyatt Edgell and inhabitants invited to join nightly foot or mounted patrols. Rewards of up to £100 were offered for a successful prosecution and special constables were sworn in. Egham, like the rest of the country, was dealing with the symptoms of the malady and not the cause. Fearing 'the destruction of social order and of [their] domestic security and comfort', they turned to repression rather than reform.[117]

On 25 November, despite a vigilant watch being kept, there was another malicious fire in Egham. A barn belonging to Thomas Burton of Bakeham Farm was discovered ablaze. It was about half a mile from his house but near some cottages and hayricks. Prompt action from the Egham fire engine and the 'effective exertions of the peasantry' confined the fire to the barn. This time the miscreant was observed, though still managed to escape. Once more the local gentry convinced themselves that, as the Egham labourers showed no outward sign of insubordination, the perpetrator must have been a foreign incendiary.[118] Whoever he was he was armed with significant local knowledge: Thomas Burton was not only a very large landowner but one of the parish's church wardens.

Encouraged by the local paper, some employers declared their intention to increase their labourers' wages or reduce their rents. A few weeks later, in a highly provocative statement, the newspaper pointed out that workers in Windsor Great Park received lower wages than other employees—'that is to say they do not receive a sufficient pittance to keep them from the parish pay table'.[119] This must have acted like a red rag to Sir William Fremantle in his new role of Deputy Ranger. The newspaper was forced to 'rectify a misrepresentation' and print a true picture of the wages and conditions enjoyed by park workers. This stated that all the men working under Sir William earned at least 15s. a week, out of which many were able to save 2s. to meet occasional want. They received half-pay when sick and a generous pension.[120] If this were true, no wonder secure positions in the park were jealously guarded and, if possible, passed down from father to son.

In the southern counties as a whole, the disturbances were ruthlessly put down by the local militia and the army; the ringleaders were arrested, tried, imprisoned or transported and a few executed. There were fewer incidents in Surrey than in neighbouring counties.[121] Spasmodic isolated attacks still occurred, however, in the next two years. On 2 October 1831 a barn and stable at the Clockcase were burnt down. William Willmer Pocock, then in his teens, witnessed the blaze while staying at his family's country retreat, Glenridge, which adjoined the Clockcase plantation. He later wrote: 'We [the children of the family] were forbidden to talk about it for fear of further mischief nearer home.'[122]

65 *The Keeper's Royal Lodge from the summit of the waterfall at Virginia Water.*

After two years of political turmoil the Reform Bill of 1832 was finally passed, extending the franchise more widely to the middle classes. In Egham the unrest continued. On 17 November that year two hayricks, the property of Benjamin Planner of Egham Hill, were set on fire. Once more the parish officers pledged their determination to discover the perpetrators of such an outrage and to preserve the peace of the parish. Once more a reward of £100 was offered for the conviction of the miscreant.[123]

Somewhat submerged in the political agitation of the time was one change in the administration of the park, initiated by William IV, that was universally praised. The southern and eastern banks of Virginia Water were opened to the public. In February 1833 *The Penny Magazine*, which sought to encourage and educate the poorer classes, celebrated the king's generosity and recommended a visit. The writer suggested 'a more circuitous route' than the entry by the *Wheatsheaf*. The persons at the gate of the keeper's lodge on the Ascot road, he claimed, would readily give admission to the lake, from whence 'a scene of great beauty soon bursts upon the view'.[124] George IV must have turned in his grave at this popular invasion.

Chapter Five

From Spade Husbandry to the Gentrification of Virginia Water and Egham Wick: 1831-1901

The Reform Bill of 1832 did little for the working classes or the destitute poor. The steep rise in population since 1801 meant that even more men were unemployed with only the parish to keep their families from starving. In 1831 the Egham vestry decided it could no longer afford to pay relief to able-bodied men and John Beauchamp's allowance was stopped. He and others like him either did what parish work was available for a minimal wage or went without. In November of that year John Beauchamp and Robert Pickett complained that they could not earn enough from trenching at the Poor Allotment at Virginia Water to keep their families. John was given a derisory 5d. and Robert 2s. with an order to grub out root wood for fuel for the parish workhouse at 3s. 6d. a stack. The following month John let it be known that the 7s. the parish paid him for a week's work was inadequate.[1]

There was clearly insufficient public work available to meet the needs of the unemployed and to justify paying them dole. In 1831, therefore, the vestry introduced a system they called 'spade husbandry', whereby local farmers provided land to be worked by the unemployed. Great care was to be taken 'to keep the digging price at something below farming prices'. Culling Charles Smith of Wentworth, in particular, applied himself to the scheme 'with zeal and ability'. Out-of-work labourers were sent to plant potatoes at Stoney Pits in Egham and at Trotsworth Farm and Shrubs Hill in Virginia Water. In the autumn the men harvested the potatoes, which were sold for poor relief or used in the parish workhouse.[2]

At the time the scheme was regarded as so successful that the vestry recommended other districts to consider it. Culling Charles Smith was much praised by his colleagues for 'the sympathy which he has thus felt and the desire shown to save this class of labourer'. It was resolved that he should receive £10 as a token of the approbation of the parish. More significantly for those still mindful of the Swing riots, it was agreed that Smith's initiative had been 'productive of a degree of good order most gratifying to observe'.[3]

There was still not enough work and the money paid for what was available was inadequate. Men who asked for an increase on 5d. a load for digging gravel were told to dig more gravel. The pits at Wellington Bridge over the River Bourne and near Virginia Water were constantly broken into and plundered. In June 1833 Edgell Wyatt Edgell offered the Crown woodland known as Knowle Grove to provide more parish work. That winter the unemployed were given spades and sent to Knowle Grove to grub out the roots of trees to provide fuel for the workhouse.[4] Virginia Water was in danger of becoming the parish's work camp.

At the Wick, where more of the established park workers lived, there was more security. Such men as James Perry, the warrener, J.D. Davis, the locksmith and George Turner, an under-gamekeeper, had tied cottages. George Wheeler, the fisherman, lived in the Flying Barn, converted into a dwelling with a permanent stand near the Obelisk Pond.[5]

George Tough and his sons continued to live and work at the royal nursery and had for a considerable time used the apparent waste land in its south-west corner as their own private garden. It had actually been granted to the Planner family in the land exchanges of the 1780s and subsequently forgotten by them. They had not even made a claim for it at the Inclosure enquiries and it had been sold to John Barnard, who had also neglected his acquisition. No one questioned their right to the land until 1833, when a member of the Planner family, Richard Smith Planner, a master hatter from Walworth Common in London, came to Wick to investigate his inheritance. To his surprise he found it enclosed and cropped with the Tough family's potatoes. He enquired to whom rent was paid and George replied that he paid none: 'only by the Swete of my Brow'. George further explained that he had worked the land without hindrance for nearly 30 years and no one knew who the owner was. Richard Smith Planner was able to prove his title to the land and immediately sold it to the Crown.[6]

Three years later George, then aged about seventy-five, was clearly concerned for his future and for that of his family when he could no longer work. He looked back with some bitterness on his 52 years and three months' 'servitude' with the government; he had not done as well as he had expected. He was anxious that his only son still living at home, also called George, should succeed him at the nursery. His chief motive seemed to have been to arouse pity and ensure some security of tenure for his wife and unmarried daughters on his decease. According to his father, George, then in his 22nd year, was strong and able to work but could not get employment, having 'no friend on earth nor the means of earning his bread'. Charles Maslin's response to this request can have brought no comfort to the family. He had no wish to employ George Tough's son and was, moreover, of the opinion that the Wick Nursery land was worn out and he would discontinue using it if anything happened to old George Tough.[7]

In October 1834 the Egham vestry reported to the Poor Law Commissioners that they had reduced the Poor Rate and hoped to diminish it still further by their stringent policies. These had been carried out, they claimed, without complaint from the poor, and despite the fact that neighbouring Windsor Great Park provided 'a great temptation to poaching and idleness'. Sir William Fremantle had been responsible for drawing up the report and the vestry was grateful for the help of this experienced politician.[8]

The Poor Law Amendment Act of 1834 put responsibility for the care of the poor in the hands of a group or union of parishes, run by boards of elected guardians. The Union workhouse that would serve the paupers of Egham and Windsor was built adjacent to the eastern pales of Windsor Great Park at Bears Rails, Old Windsor, well away from the centres of both communities.[9] It was unusual for towns in different counties to form one Union. Egham and Windsor were, however, united in their proximity to and dependence on a great royal estate.

The population of Egham had risen to over 4,000 by this time and yet there was still only one place for Church of England worship in the parish. Mrs Catherine Irvine of Luddington House, a widow whose husband, Walter, had made a fortune in Trinidad & Tobago, and her younger daughter, Christina, were about to change that. Under the Inclosure Award Walter Irvine had acquired several small pieces of land in the Virginia Water area. One of these, only half a mile from the lake, Mrs Irvine proposed to offer to the parish as the site for a church for the labouring poor. It was near the crossroads first proposed as a possible location for a chapel in 1824. Christina Irvine would provide an endowment of £2,000 for its maintenance. The

66 *Windsor Union Workhouse, Crimp Hill,* c.*1992, photograph by Dorothy Davis.*

initial meeting in March 1837 was for a select few and held at Benjamin Torin's house at Englefield Green, with Sir William Fremantle and Colonel Chaloner Bisse Challoner of Portnall Park in attendance. William Keith Douglas, the husband of Mrs Irvine's elder daughter, Elizabeth, explained the ladies' wishes. The conventions of the time did not allow them to speak for themselves at such a gathering.[10]

The benevolent offer was accepted unanimously. The church was planned to accommodate a congregation of 400, most of the seats would be free of pew rents and Miss Irvine herself would hold the patronage. The full vestry was informed, a subscription list opened and the offer of the architect, William Fuller Pocock of Glenridge, Callow Hill, to draw up building plans for the church was accepted. William IV and Queen Adelaide had been asked to head the list of subscribers but Sir William reported that the king was too ill to be disturbed. The task of eliciting subscriptions fell to the Rev. Thomas Page, curate of Egham, who was designated the first vicar of Virginia Water.[11] William IV died in June 1837 and was succeeded by his niece, the Princess Victoria.

Sir William was asked to submit a memorandum about the project to the new queen, reiterating the fact that Egham was a royal manor and that the new parish of Virginia Water would include part of Windsor Great Park. The moral benefit of the new church was emphasised, as it offered church accommodation 'to the poorer class of inhabitants' of the parish of Egham. By October 1837 over £1,400 had been raised and the building work entrusted to Northcrofts of Englefield Green, their tender being the lowest.[12]

Queen Victoria agreed to contribute £200 on condition that the church would accommodate any Crown officers or tenants living in the neighbourhood. The vestry was only too happy to comply and sent Her Majesty a loyal and humble address of thanks. The new church would confirm the pre-eminence of the Protestant establishment 'so essential for the security and happiness of the Empire'. So much money had been raised that it was possible to add a tower and spire to the original design and Miss Irvine was asked to divert some of the money for the endowment of the church into the building of a clergyman's house.[13]

On Monday 10 September 1838 many of the people involved in the project gathered at the *Wheatsheaf* inn to view the new church. Although most of the seats were to be free, the transept pews would be let out to the larger subscribers, Culling Charles Smith of Wentworth, Colonel Chaloner Bisse Challoner of Portnall Park, Mrs Irvine and Edgell Wyatt Edgell. The district allocated to the new church included the estates of Wentworth and Portnall, Trotsworth Farm and the hamlets of Shrubs Hill, Virginia Water, Callow Hill, Knowle Hill, Trumps Green and Stroude (Appendix V). The church was to be called Christ Church, Virginia Water.[14]

Thus the district as a whole became known as Virginia Water from the fact that Mrs Catherine Irvine donated a piece of land near the old hamlet of

67 *Christ Church, Virginia Water.*

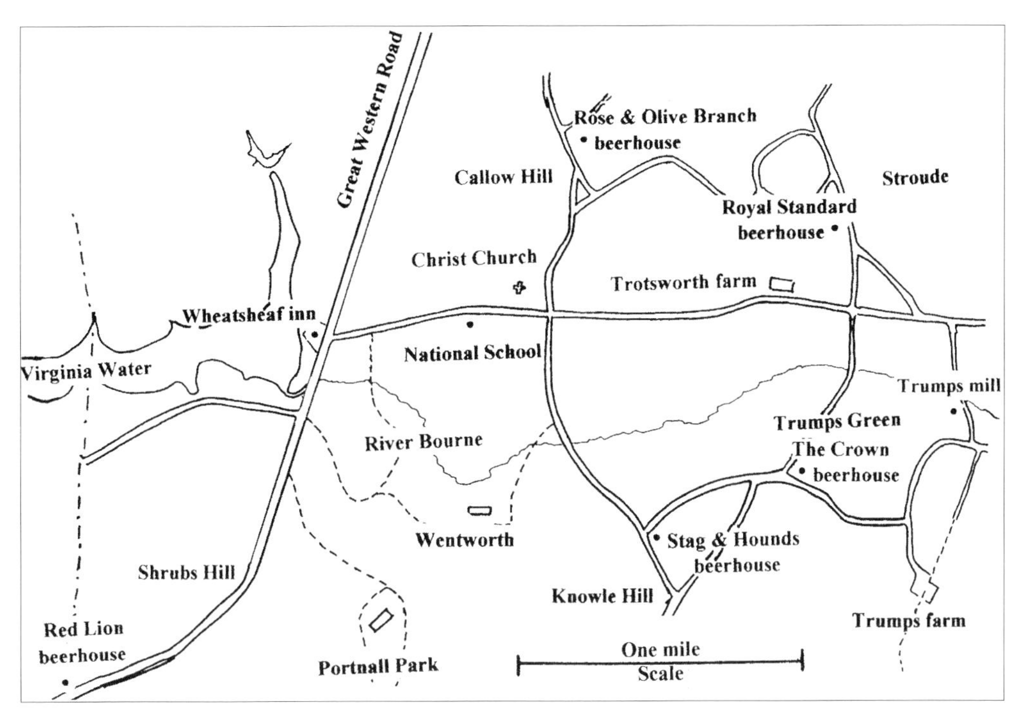

68 *Diagram showing the hamlets and estates that formed the parish of Virginia Water, 1838.*

Virginia for the building of a church. A small community, mainly consisting of labourers' families, had grown up there and, with the *Wheatsheaf* and a few cottages on the Wentworth estate, had adopted the name of the lake. Perhaps there remained a folk memory of the hamlet of Virginia that had once existed on the old turnpike at the edge of the park. Of the other hamlets in the new district, Shrubs Hill and Callow Hill had grown since enclosure and Knowle Hill from encroachments on the heath. Trumps Green and Stroude were older settlements, the former's known history dating back to the 17th century and the latter's to the Reformation.

Just before Consecration Day at the beginning of November 1838, a violent storm erupted and blew down two of the pinnacles that decorated the roof of the church, damaging tiling and plaster. The builder was ordered to remedy the damage immediately and Christ Church was consecrated by the Bishop of Winchester on the day appointed.[15]

In 1840 Queen Victoria married her cousin, Prince Albert of Saxe-Coburg-Gotha. On the wedding day itself, 10 February, all the park workers—some 120 men—were given 'a Holy day', with wages paid in full and a 5s. bonus to celebrate the occasion.[16] Soon after the marriage the queen granted her husband the Rangership of Windsor Great Park, a felicitous appointment for a prince who was fond of field sports and interested in the well-being of the estate and its workers.

Windsor Great Park continued to be a favourite place for recreation for the royal family in the early years of Queen Victoria's reign. On 26 August 1843 Prince Albert's 24th birthday was celebrated with a grand fête at Virginia Water. The queen, Prince Albert and their guests dined at the fishing temple, where the gardens had been brilliantly illuminated. The shrubs and bushes were festooned with lamps, the light reflected in the fountains. The public continued to be admitted to the lakeside and the bank opposite the fishing temple was packed with 10,000 people, it was claimed, who had come from miles around, including many from London, to enjoy a free spectacle.[17]

69 *Prince Albert's birthday fête from* The Pictorial Times.

70 *Virginia Water with Belvedere and ruins, 1845.*

At dusk the fireworks started: volleys of rockets and comets lit up the sky at the lake and at Fort Belvedere. The miniature frigates were illuminated from stem to stern and also discharged fireworks. During the evening the royal couple appeared on the balcony of the fishing temple to the cheers of the onlookers. A salute from a battery near the lake was returned by the cannon at Fort Belvedere.[18] The bombardier in charge of the proceedings at the viewpoint at this time was James Tait from Scotland, a Chelsea Pensioner and formerly a sergeant in the Royal Artillery who earned 2s. 6d. a day.[19]

With the new reign there had been administrative changes in Windsor Great Park. Lord Duncannon, Commissioner of Woods and Works, with economy in mind, decided to curb the powers acquired in the previous regime by Sir William Fremantle, the Deputy Ranger. Fremantle, not unnaturally, wished to retain all his authority, believing his way of working to be in the best interest of both his queen and country. By September 1837, however, with Duncannon having enlisted the backing of the Prime Minister, Lord Melbourne, Fremantle accepted the need to cede some of his responsibilities to the Deputy Surveyor, Charles Maslin. Implements and stock were transferred to Maslin and all workmen were to report to him. The Deputy Ranger retained his responsibility for all the game in the park and for the gatekeepers.[20]

Within a few years Sir William Fremantle suffered a more personal loss. His wife, Lady Selina, died in 1841 and the house at Englefield Green with its associated lands passed to relatives of the children of Selina's first marriage, the Hervey Bathhursts.[21] In the following year Sir William moved into the Deputy Ranger's official residence, Holly Grove, in the Cranbourne Walk area of the park,[22] and out of Egham society.

The former Fremantle land in Egham was sold and the Crown acquired Sherwood Brooks and Grove, an attractive piece of land at Wick with a stream running through to the lake. This was a move planned by John Robinson as early as 1792 but not put into practice until 1845, when Charles Maslin was authorised to take possession of the land. The public road to Bishopsgate that ran between the park and the new acquisition disappeared and four cottages had to be demolished. The Crown bore the whole cost of building a new road next to the Cheeseman and Welbelove tenements, causing what is even today a very sharp right-hand bend where Wick Road meets Wick Lane.[23]

By 1841 the new hamlet of Egham Wick had grown to 25 households, 16 of which were concentrated in the area of the original encroachment made by John Cheeseman and others. Most of the men listed in the census return were classed as agricultural labourers. For nine men and five teenage boys, three of them Welbeloves, the space was left blank and it is possible they were without work.[24]

Upon arriving in a district it was clearly a profitable move to acquire property as soon as possible, however small and insignificant an encroachment it might be. By 1841 the Cheeseman family owned three cottages, one occupied by John's widow, Elizabeth, her married daughter, Ann Cripps, and her family. The other two were occupied by John's sons, William and Thomas. The Welbelove family had managed to keep their cottages out of the hands of the vestry and had also prospered, being not only freehold cottagers but also the owners of the hamlet's beer house, which they rented out. The only women who had a trade were those who had no choice, the widows who kept themselves from pauperism by working as washerwomen.[25]

All the men with specific skills, such as gardeners, gamekeepers, warreners or nurserymen, were employed in the park, and most lived in

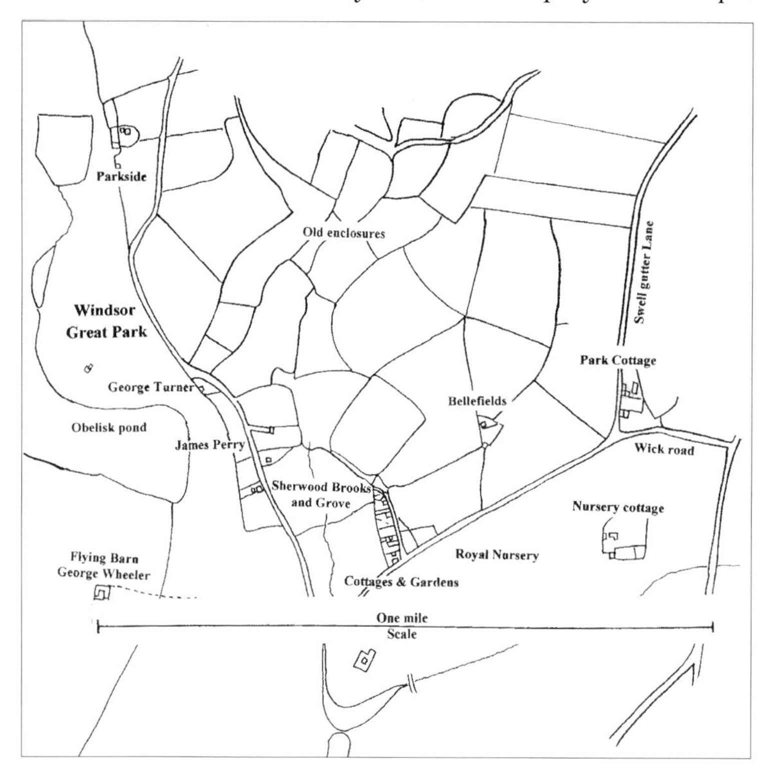

71 *Diagram showing the new hamlet of Wick in the mid-19th century, based on The Plan of the Parish of Egham, 1841.*

72 *Cottages at Egham Wick, 2003, photograph by Alan Bostock—The beer shop later became the Bailiwick and in 2006 is Edwinns Restaurant.*

tied cottages within the pales. George Tough was still working at the nursery at the age of 80 and living at a nursery cottage with his wife, their two unmarried daughters, Catherine and Isabella, and son, George, who had found work as an agricultural labourer. A nephew, John, also a nurseryman, lived nearby with his wife, Phoebe, and their seven children, one of whom, another John, aged only 15, had also been lucky enough to secure Crown employment as a fisherman. Apart from the Deputy Surveyor, Charles Maslin, residing at Parkside, only one other man living and working in the park at Egham Wick had any middle-class credentials: he was a Navy pensioner, John Smith, who was presumably one of the men responsible for the sea-worthiness and safety of the boats on the lake. Outside the park the only other gentleman in the hamlet was Brumbridge Burton, living at Park Cottage on the turnpike road, and styling himself a farmer, despite his family's affluence.[26]

At Virginia Water, Catherine and Christina Irvine remained true to their earlier vision of providing education for poor children, for included in the original fitments for the church were two benches for the schoolmistresses. Here the Sunday School was held where the children of Virginia Water's labouring poor learnt their catechism. It was the establishment's pious hope that thereby licentiousness, crime and ignorance might be banished from their lives. The Sunday School was a success and by 1843 the vicar, the Rev. Thomas Page, was able to report that 70 boys and 60 girls attended. There was only one proper schoolroom in the district, at Stroude, a mile and a half from the church, and a daily school at Shrubs Hill, which was too small and inconveniently situated to accommodate all the children from Virginia Water. Some of the older boys trudged all the way to Englefield Green, up to two or three miles, to acquire the rudiments of literacy. Mr Page sought to remedy this unsatisfactory state of affairs by setting up a National School connected

73 *Virginia Water National School, built 1843, line drawing.*

with his own church.[27] He planned to raise the money for the school, as he had for the church, by public subscription. It would not be easy: the district was poor and in a population of 800 there were only two wealthy families and three 'respectable' farmers to call on. Many of those who had subscribed to the church again dug into their pockets, and St George Caulfield, the new owner of Wentworth, gave a small piece of his land opposite the church for the site. The school opened on 4 December 1843, with 103 children on its register. They were taught by a master who earned £60 a year and lived with his wife in the adjoining schoolhouse. Only 10 months had passed since Mr Page had written his first enquiring letter to the National Society for Promoting the Education of the Poor in the Principles of the Established Church. Queen Victoria headed the list of subscribers, donating £50, while Prince Albert and the Dowager Queen Adelaide each gave £25.[28]

'Train up a child in the way he should go: and when he is old, he will not depart from it': this quotation from Proverbs headed the school's first account sheet and was the maxim that motivated its benefactors. A poor, dispersed community had gained a focus in the construction of a church and school; their location was not, however, in the centre of the hamlets they served but in a westerly corner of the new parish of Virginia Water.

The hamlet of Wick did not receive the direct benefit of its own church or school. Its children were within a mile of the Englefield Green National School but there was still a walk of more than two miles to Egham for the blessing of a church. When the church for the labouring poor was built at Virginia Water in 1838 the cluster of tenements at the Wick was within the boundary of the new parish, being south of the line between the obelisk and the crossroads at Bakeham Lane. Wick was not, however, one of the hamlets accredited to Christ Church and the distance to Virginia Water from Wick was only slightly less than to Egham. There was, however, for those in the know, a short cut to the church through the Clockcase Plantation from the main road near Wick.[29]

In 1847 the cost of all food, but particularly bread, was so high that many landowners in the vicinity increased their rates of pay. The Windsor Great Park labourers, still earning only 12s. a week, requested a rise in pay also and were supported in this by Charles Maslin. He believed that their wages were insufficient to keep them and their families from starvation and suggested an increase of 1s. to 2s. a week and a bonus of 10s.[30] There is clearly a discrepancy here in the Deputy Surveyor's department with the claims made by Sir William Fremantle in 1831 that all the men on his payroll received at least 15s. a week.

By 1849 both George Tough senior and his wife were dead, but their son, George, and his family as well as the daughters, Catherine and Isabella, earning their own keep from dressmaking, were still living in the old nursery cottage. It was, however, in such a dilapidated state that Charles Maslin did not think it was worth repairing and wanted to pull it down.[31]

Charles Maslin died in 1849 and, in keeping with family tradition, Charles's son, Wilby, then in his early twenties, had expectations of taking over the Deputy Surveyor's post. He was informed, however, that he was too young and a complete outsider was appointed. He was William Menzies, a graduate of Edinburgh University, who had studied forestry and engineering. Ironically he was much of an age with Wilby Maslin and lodged with the family at Parkside while finding his feet in his new job. Mrs Maslin, he wrote, made him most comfortable.[32]

Wilby had been appointed his father's assistant in 1847 at a salary of £125 a year and must have continued to act in that capacity with the new Deputy Surveyor for a while, as Menzies recorded the young man's helpful attitude. In March 1850, however, the Commissioners for Woods & Forests suggested that Wilby, being 'young, active and well acquainted with the management of Timber' should be transferred to the New Forest. When Wilby failed to take up the offer he was told his services would be dispensed with. He wrote to the Commissioners to express his distress at his dismissal, reminding them of his long family connection with Windsor Forest and Park. He had hoped for this to continue as his mother and sisters depended on him for support.[33]

In appointing such a young professional man as William Menzies to the post of Deputy Surveyor, the Commissioners were able to affect not only a change in policy but also to make further economies. Over the years Charles Maslin's salary had risen to £300 per annum. William Menzies' starting salary was only £200, though he would still receive the extra £30 in lieu of feed for a horse. In addition, by leaving the assistant's post vacant, a total saving of £195 per annum had been made.[34]

William Menzies' remit was to manage the park's timber, woods, plantations, roads, drains and fences diligently and economically. With no assistant to help him he had to rely more on the experience of the Foreman of Windsor Great Park, whose wage was raised accordingly. In 1848 Josiah

Lever had earned only 18s. a week whereas George Perkins, two years later, received 29s. Unlike Thomas Courtenay and William Tough, who supervised the works at Virginia Water at the end of the 18th century, the new foreman neither paid out nor received money. Such duties belonged to the Deputy Surveyor, who was also responsible for the large workforce.[35]

The Deputy Surveyor was granted an extra £70 a year to pay the wages of a clerk to help him in his administrative work. By 1851 Menzies had turned Parkside into a veritable Scots enclave with his 17-year-old cousin, Daniel Wishart, acting as his clerk and a middle-aged Scots housekeeper, Agnes Micklejohn, looking after them both.[36]

By 1848 the railroad and its revolutionary form of transport, the 'iron horse', had reached Staines, only five miles from Virginia Water. Long-distance coaches disappeared from the roads and turnpike tolls were drastically reduced. Land within reach of the rail stations increased in value and the Crown was well aware that estates around the park might be targeted by developers as they came on the market.[37] In 1850 a valuable plot of more than 40 acres, known as Bellefields and including a neat farmhouse, was up for sale. It fronted on Wick Road and was once part of Selina Fremantle's land holdings (see Figure 85). A representative of the Crown was dispatched to the auction mart, authorised to spend £1,100 on the purchase. The winning bid, however, for the bulk of the property was £1,200 although the Crown was able to acquire one lot of six-and-a-half acres for £250. This field had once been owned by William Tough, John Robinson's foreman at Virginia Water.[38] On this occasion the Crown had no need for concern, for James Gray, the new owner of the estate, was a farmer and continued to use it for agricultural purposes.

The 1851 Census Return reveals the hamlet of Egham Wick to be little different from 1841: its menfolk still worked as agricultural labourers or park employees, its widows as washerwomen. One of the park men, James Perry, aged 70, who had served as both warrener and under-gamekeeper, had earned the reward of long years of service to the Crown and had become an 'annuitant'. On the strength of his Crown pension he had bought a cottage on the old Cheeseman enclosure and, unlike many of his class, was able to live out his old age in independence.

It was not long before William Menzies, like his predecessors, became seriously concerned about the wages of the men he employed. In March 1852 he brought to the attention of his superiors the plight of George Richardson, one of the woodmen in the Virginia Water district. He earned less than the others, only 14s. a week, even though his district earned the highest revenue. Menzies asked for a rise for Richardson, and must have been reasonably pleased when the woodman's wage was increased to 15s. a week.[39] Two years later Menzies asked for a general increase in wages for his men. It was a familiar story: a very severe winter coupled with the complete failure of a particular crop—this time potatoes—had caused food prices to rise alarmingly. Many farmers had already raised wages but local proprietors were holding back, waiting for the Crown to take a lead. Menzies was emphatic in his support for his labourers. He refuted the suggestion that they spent their money in public houses: they simply could not keep their families on 12s. a week. Rent accounted for 2s. every week and the remaining 10s. could only buy 12 loaves made from inferior flour. Menzies pointed out that the rise in his yearly revenue was due to the skill of the woodmen and suggested a maximum wage for them of 18s. a week with a 14s. maximum for the labourers. The Treasury agreed his new pay scale and even maintained it for the next three years on his insistence.[40]

Another problem that faced Menzies was the continuing trespass at the Clockcase. On the whole he was tolerant of poor women who, out of necessity, gathered wood in this detached area of the park. The security of the plantation was somewhat improved when the Clockcase became the residence of under-gamekeepers, Thomas Foker living there throughout the 1850s. Woodmen visited the plantation periodically to manage the trees but it was impossible to police its 128 acres of woodland effectively. Menzies was fearful that any attempt to crack down on the practice of wood-gathering might lead to the plantation itself being fired.[41]

There were similar concerns about another isolated portion of Crown property at Knowle Grove, about a mile and a half south-east of the lake. It was, according to Menzies, a bad neighbourhood for gypsies and vagrants, being close to Chobham Common. Fencing and faggots were constantly stolen. On one occasion, when a woodman caught their donkeys in the wood, the gypsies attacked him and then moved the whole encampment off, long before a policeman could be brought from Egham.[42] The situation had worsened since 1856 when the railroad divided the grove in two and crossing gates also became subject to depredation. In 1861 the Crown decided that enough was enough and the Commissioners sold Knowle Grove to Marianne Catherine Cabrera, Countess of Morella, the then owner of nearby Wentworth.[43]

74 *Thomas Foker, Gamekeeper at the Clockcase, early 1860s.*

75 *Gipsies encamped on Chobham Common,* c.*1900, photograph by William End.*

In addition, there was always potential for trouble at the *Wheatsheaf* inn. In 1851 Menzies received complaints that disorderly people were entering a plantation near the lake. The innkeeper, William Loader, was charging the public to enter the park and employing two disreputable characters as guides. Menzies found them carrying beer out to his men.[44] Since the reign of William IV the public had been allowed to enter the park at the *Wheatsheaf* and walk along the southern and eastern banks of the lake without charge. Possibly because of this incident, Loader did not remain at the inn for much longer. The building and grounds were surveyed in 1852 and the *Wheatsheaf* described as a badly managed house, built haphazardly over different periods. The new occupier, Henry Jennings, was anxious to make improvements and did his best to run an orderly house, but there were always others ready to break the rules. In May 1852 a large party of between thirty and forty people attempted to carry out forms and tables from the inn in order to have a jollification on the banks of the lake. They had to be restrained by the keepers and the park constable.[45] As a result of this, clearer rules had to be drawn up for park visitors. They might enter at the *Wheatsheaf* or by the wicket gate at Blacknest. No gypsies, fortune tellers or vagrants were to be admitted and dogs only if led 'on strings'. Refreshments in small baskets were allowed but not vast picnic dinners.[46]

In November 1852 Jennings, still looking to improve the inn, wanted to build a water closet and run a drain from the *Wheatsheaf* into the stream. John Clutton, the Land Receiver for Surrey, found this idea objectionable, not because it would pollute the river but because it would damage the trees nearby. The building of a cesspit was suggested instead, so long as the mill owners and others downstream did not object. Some 10 years later Jennings, a man who liked to keep abreast of the latest technology, was involved in the installation of a ram pump to bring water from the lake to the inn's out-buildings.[47]

In the intervening years more building had taken place on the plots near the Clockcase Plantation. Glenridge, the simple summer retreat of the Pocock family, was enlarged and extended and, after William Fuller Pocock's death in 1849, became the country home of his second son, Thomas Willmer Pocock, a surgeon by profession but not in practice. He continued to improve the house in keeping with the needs of a mid-19th-century gentry family.[48]

The Crown did not find Thomas Pocock an easy neighbour. In 1854 he engaged in a long dispute with the officials of Woods & Forests about their claimed access to the Clockcase through his land. He complained also that the Crown's fences were inadequate and that unauthorised people regarded the Crown land as fair game for gathering fuel and litter for pigs. The Crown in its turn accused him of blocking off entrance gates and trespassing on the Clockcase Plantation in order to gain access to the Great Western Road. The matter came to a head with Pocock being threatened with prosecution and declaring in reply that such proceedings were 'more worthy to have proceeded from the Winter Palace of St Petersburg than from a government which professes to make justice and equity the law of its actions'. An agreement was finally drawn up in 1856 but the park's Deputy Surveyor, William Menzies, was still trying to resolve the problem of access a year later, complaining that Mr Pocock was only rarely at Glenridge.[49]

76 *Glenridge, Callow Hill, 1920s, once the home of the Pocock family.*

In the summer of 1853 Chobham Common, to the south of Virginia Water, was a centre of activity. With war against Russia inevitable, a camp was set up for the army to practice military manoeuvres in the surrounding open countryside: the common was crowded with pavilions and tents, canteens and stables, soldiers and spectators. Members of the royal family visited on several occasions, usually travelling by train to Staines or Windsor and thence by carriage.[50] One of the great set pieces of the camp was to be a mock battle on the north bank of the lake at Virginia Water. At the beginning of July sappers practised setting up a pontoon bridge across a narrow arm of the lake to the north of the *Wheatsheaf*. The bridge was made up of 15 rafts, constructed from metal cylinders in a wooden framework. The men involved in the operation, accompanied by their band, attended divine service at Christ Church, Virginia Water, on the following Sunday.[51]

From 9.30 a.m. on 5 July, Virginia Water was full of soldiers, 7,000 men in all, infantry, cavalry and artillery converging on the lake by various routes. The spectators from Chobham Common as well as local people were also on the move, vying with each other to get the best views from the southern and eastern banks of Virginia Water. The 'enemy', easily identified by their conspicuous white flannel jackets, took up position near the fishing temple and were engaged by troops guarding the Blacknest bridge at the west of the lake. Meanwhile the sappers set up their pontoon bridge at the eastern end of the lake, watched by Queen Victoria and Prince Albert in the queen's barge. Several companies of guards and riflemen immediately crossed the bridge to take the 'enemy' by surprise.[52]

When the batteries of artillery attempted to cross, however, the horses became restive on the unfamiliar surface. The sappers who were manning the sides of the bridge tried to calm the animals but one man was thrown into the water, taking six others with him. The soldiers driving the artillery

77 *The Pontoon on Virginia Water, 1853, Edward Armitage.*

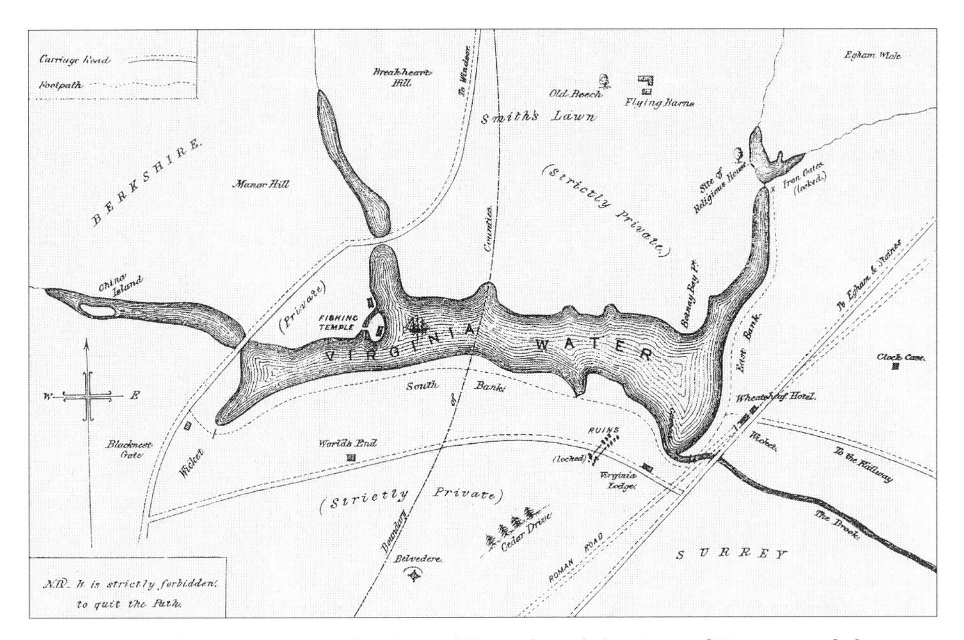

78 *Plan of Virginia Water showing public roads and the supposed Roman road, from Rawlin's* Notes on Virginia Water, *1866.*

vehicles showed considerable skill in keeping the horses and guns upright in the circumstances. The sappers were drenched but unhurt.[53]

Torrential rain had marred the manoeuvres on several days at the camp but on this occasion the weather was fine enough for the queen to ride to Smith's Lawn in an open barouche, where she took the salute.[54] Queen Victoria, even in her later years of isolation, never lost her affection for her soldiers and sailors and many more military reviews would be held in the park during her reign.[55]

The southern and eastern banks of Virginia Water continued to be a popular venue for local families to enjoy a picnic or an afternoon stroll.[56] Visitors were, however, forbidden to stray from the designated paths and plans were produced to distinguish the public areas from the private. One produced in the 1860s also showed the supposed line of the Roman road from Silchester to Staines.[57] A possible route had been surveyed in about 1835 by an officer of the Royal Military College at Sandhurst. He was particularly interested in a section of a park ride between Blacknest Gate and the lake that old labourers in the park told him never required repairing. He concluded that the ride was constructed on the surface of an old road.[58] He had almost certainly identified the old turnpike road that was realigned in 1763.

Prince Albert, as Ranger of Windsor Great Park, was concerned for the welfare of his workmen. In 1850 he founded the Royal Association for Improving the Conditions of Labourers and certificates and prizes were awarded annually to encourage independence and self-esteem. In particular he wished to see working men and their families decently housed within easy reach of the wage-earner's work.[59] To this end, he had a number of

ROYAL ASSOCIATION

FOR IMPROVING THE CONDITION OF LABOURERS AND OTHERS.

FOUNDED, IN 1850, BY HIS ROYAL HIGHNESS THE PRINCE CONSORT, K.G.

IN GRATEFUL REMEMBRANCE OF WHOM, THIS PORTRAIT IN LIEU OF H.R.H.'S VALUED AUTOGRAPH, IS

Presented to David Goddard, of Sunningdale,

who received a prize of £1. 0. 0,

in the Year 1862,

for Cleanliness and Tidiness in House and Person

By Order of the Committee,

Francis H Seymour

Chairman.

79 *Certificate from the Royal Association for Improving the Condition of Labourers.*

model cottages built. Four such cottages were built at Egham Wick in the 1850s on land newly acquired by the Crown and once owned by William Tough. In 1861 the families of two park labourers, a brickmaker and a butcher were in residence.[60]

The example of such enlightened employers as Prince Albert for the well-being of their employees had a beneficial effect on other landowners. In Egham, an attempt in 1819 to set up an annual agricultural show to reward 'diligence and fidelity in agricultural servants' had failed. In 1857, however, doubtless encouraged by the example of Prince Albert, who was created Prince Consort that year, the Egham Agricultural Association was

80 *David Goddard and family,* c.*1900, photograph by William End.*

established. Prizes were given annually, not only for such skills as ploughing, but also for long service, the neatest cottage and, inevitably, for bringing up the largest family without recourse to parish relief. The Prince Consort agreed to become a subscriber to the association.[61]

In 1856 railway stations were built at Egham and Virginia Water as the Staines, Wokingham and Woking Junction railway forged a link with the line from London to Reading and the West Country.[62] The coming of the railway made Henry Jennings even more ambitious to extend the *Wheatsheaf* to meet this new challenge. He was given permission to use part of the Clockcase woods opposite the inn to build a shelter to accommodate parties coming down from London on excursion trains. He wanted to extend his inn into a hotel but the Crown was sceptical: the *Wheatsheaf* was too far away from the new station to profit from rail traffic and there was no evidence that Jennings could attract a superior class of visitor. Despite its doubts the Crown offered a contribution of £250 for improvements, as did the brewer Nevile Reid of Chertsey.[63]

The new railway stations attracted City gentlemen to acquire land near the park on which to build desirable residences. By 1860 James Gray had sold his small farm and a bigger house, stable and plantation were under construction on the site. The new owner, John Giles Pilcher, a barrister, had not yet moved in; a farm bailiff was still living in the farmhouse to tend the remaining acres. It was, however, clear that Pilcher did not intend to farm: within three years he had sold off part of his estate from which another gentleman's estate was being carved, its acreage not yet decided. The owner of this second house on Bellefields was Adolphus Fredrick Govett, a member of the London Stock Exchange, who had previously lived at Rusham House, between Egham and Bakeham.[64] Brumbridge Burton of Park Cottage died in 1856 and his house and small estate, including two fields of Bakeham Farm, were first rented and then owned by Captain William Mills of the Royal Navy. It was during this period that the name of the house was changed to Park House in keeping with the growing gentility of the neighbourhood.[65]

81 *Bellefields, Wick Road, 1989, once the home of the Pilcher family.*

Bakeham Farm lay opposite Park House and was a large, complex agricultural area, stretching from the top of Egham Hill along the eastern side of the Great Western Road towards Virginia Water, and consisting of three units. The Crown owned Lower Bakeham Farm to the east with its own farmhouse and Upper Bakeham Farm to the west that had no residence, only farm buildings. Intermingled with the fields of Upper Bakeham Farm was the privately owned Bakeham House estate.[66] The management of this conglomeration had been successful during the early part of the 19th century when Brumbridge Burton's father, Thomas, had been the proprietor of Bakeham House. He had leased and worked the Crown lands with his own, until his death in 1831.[67] Bakeham House estate and the Crown lands suffered when the railway cut a swathe through their fields, separating the upper and lower farms. The land began to fall into decline and it became increasingly difficult for the Crown to find suitable lessees. By the 1860s Bakeham House estate was more a pleasure farm than a working unit.[68]

In 1861 the park's Head Gamekeeper, James Turner, retired and his house, Virginia Lodge, situated above the cascade, was no longer required as an official residence. Setting an unusual precedent for the time, Queen Victoria offered it as a home to Mrs Maria Jane Byng, the widow of Vice-Admiral the Hon. Henry Dilkes Byng and the mother of Beatrice, one of the queen's maids of honour. If the house was to be occupied by a lady of quality, improvements and extensions had to be made and these were carried out at royal expense.[69] In 1863 Beatrice married Henry Blundell Hollinshead Blundell, a captain in the Grenadier Guards, and they too made their home at the Lodge.[70] Mrs Byng's lease of Virginia Lodge was only to last for her lifetime and when she died in 1874 it returned to its intended use as a home for park employees. With the alterations carried out for Mrs Byng it was large enough to convert into three cottages, and these were occupied for the next 20 years by Jonathan Stevens, woodcutter, Thomas Wells, locksmith and Charles Prior, the park policeman.[71]

82 *Virginia Lodge from the Ascot Road,* c.*1910.*

The Prince Consort's tenure of the Rangership benefited the park and its workers, and his untimely death from typhoid fever on 14 December 1861 cast a shadow over the whole district. George Longhurst, son of the baker and grocer's at Sunninghill, went to Windsor the following day with his fiancée, Emily Cotterell, to hear a preacher at the Windsor theatre. George described it as 'an awful solemn evening Windsor being still as death'. Only the previous January the queen, with the Prince Consort and the Prince of Wales, had enjoyed the exhilaration of winter sports on the ice at Virginia Water as had a large number of her subjects, including the Longhurst family. Nearly every day for the six weeks the frost lasted there had been skating, sledging, curling matches and in the evening fireworks, enjoyed by prince and commoner alike.[72]

A few months after the death of the Prince Consort the local newspaper reported a touching little incident involving Queen Victoria, showing a side to her character not often seen in public. Her Majesty, accompanied by Princess Alice, was being driven from Windsor Castle through the park to Egham, when on the main road near the river the queen's attention was caught by the stock-in-trade of 'a poor Italian vendor of images'. With 'characteristic consideration and kindness of heart', she stopped and bought some of his wares. When the man realised who his customer was he was apparently 'completely overcome with emotion'.[73] For the most part, though, the queen sought solace for her grievous loss in the isolation of Osborne on the Isle of Wight and of Balmoral in Scotland. She returned to court life at London and Windsor only when duty called.

One such duty was the marriage of her eldest son, Edward, Prince of Wales, to Princess Alexandra of Denmark at St George's Chapel in 1863, when there was an attempt at rejoicing in the country, and at Virginia Water money was collected to enable the children of the National School to celebrate the event.[74] A holiday for the workers in Windsor Great Park was declared for the wedding day but William Menzies, the Deputy Surveyor, conscientious as ever, was concerned that the park would be left unprotected that day. In addition the queen ordered a donation of 2s. 6d. to be made to each single 'common labourer' and 5s. to each married man. It was agreed that this would be more acceptable to the workmen than a dinner. The upper servants were invited to a ball at Cumberland Lodge.[75]

The following winter was very severe. A soup kitchen had to be set up at the *Catherine Wheel* inn in Egham to alleviate the hardship caused to the most needy by the harsh weather. For those who lived above the breadline the icy conditions again provided relaxation and fun. Local ponds and lakes, covered in thick ice, became skating rinks: Virginia Water was, as usual, a popular venue. At the beginning of January 1864 the Prince of Wales invited a large party from town, including the London Skating Club, to join him at the lake. Their prowess at skating and ice hockey and particularly the skill and elegance of the ladies was much admired by the spectators. While the

83 *The 'Swiss Cottage', built on the site of the fishing temple in 1867.*

Princess of Wales watched from a sledge, a band played and a charcoal fire near the fishing temple burned brightly.[76] By this time the ornate fishing temple built by George IV was in need of repair and in 1867 was replaced by a new building resembling a Swiss chalet, but still often referred to by its old name.[77]

In 1864 William Menzies published his history of Windsor Great Park in which he recorded the additions made to the estate over the years, traced the lines of old roads and identified and dated the trees and plantations in his care. When the water level of the lake was lowered he was able to admire the craftsmanship of the 1750s pondhead.[78]

The book also reflects Menzies' easy relationship with his men. He often stopped and chatted with old pensioners and recorded their recollections of park and forest life. Thomas Tiley told him that as a boy he had seen the water flowing over the pondhead for the first time in 1790. Cottagers explained how their forebears had built huts of turf on forest land and how they hated the park keepers, some of whom led near-solitary lives, more in harmony with nature than with their fellow men.[79]

In November 1866 James Tait, the bombardier at Fort Belvedere, became ill and Queen Victoria visited her old and faithful servant, still in royal service at the age of seventy-eight.[80] When Tait died in early December he was succeeded by another old soldier. Robert Turner, a master-gunner in the Royal Artillery, had served with distinction in the Crimean War, gaining a medal at the Battle of Inkerman.[81] During his occupancy of the post he became a great favourite of local children. On Queen Victoria's birthday they were let out of school early and ran with all their might up to the

Belvedere in order to see Sergeant Turner, in full regimental uniform, firing the cannon. If they were lucky they were allowed to see the cups and saucers used by the queen when she took tea at the viewpoint.[82]

The number of men engaged in agriculture in the country had steadily declined by the mid-19th century, in contrast with the growing numbers in the manufacturing industries. Agricultural labourers were still among the lowest paid, averaging only 14s. a week in a table of wages of 1867. The improvements in working conditions achieved by factory workers in the 1870s could not be replicated in the countryside.[83]

The Crown seems to have decided by this time that farming Upper Bakeham Farm was uneconomic and that if one could not beat the developers it was more profitable to join them. In 1867 the Crown granted a building lease on a compact 23 acres of land, immediately south of Bakeham House, to Henry Thring, a Parliamentary Counsel and later Knight of the Order of the Bath, at an annual rent of £6 per acre.[84] A gardener was immediately in residence, transforming the small, hedged enclosures into pleasure grounds. The mansion, Alderhurst, was ready for occupation the following year.[85] When, therefore, the freehold Bakeham House estate came up for sale in March 1867, the Crown, having just granted one building lease, saw the advantage of acquiring more 'Remarkably Choice and Nicely-Timbered Building Sites'. The Crown was, however, not the only bidder interested in securing building land within easy reach of London.[86] According to the local paper they were beaten at the post by William Ventris Field QC, who bought the estate for £18,000.[87]

84 *Master-gunner Turner firing the cannon at the Belvedere,* c.*1900, photograph by William End.*

The Crown, undeterred, entered into negotiations with Field. Within two months John Clutton, Crown Receiver for Surrey, and Mr Field's surveyor had decided on a mutually advantageous division of the estate. Field would retain the main residence, Bakeham House, with all its outbuildings, together with another 48 acres of land to its north and east; for which he would pay £8,323 10s. The Crown would purchase the remaining 125 acres for £9,976 10s.[88]

Bakeham House was no grand residence. It was only of moderate size, according to the sale particulars, with cheerful family bedrooms and a drawing room on the same floor to catch the view. It was still in essence a Georgian farmhouse with its piggeries, cowhouse, dairy and salting house in close proximity to the residence.[89] It did not meet William Field's requirements and he chose a new site for his mansion a few hundred yards nearer Egham. He retained the name Bakeham House for his new home and let the old farmhouse out to tenants under the new name of Little St Anne's.[90]

In May 1872 there was more opportunity for land acquisition: the Park House estate, including Kitts Close and Bakeham Brooks, two remaining Bakeham fields opposite the house, came on the market. The Crown's representative was as usual at the auction and eventually purchased the two fields for a total of £3,500. The Crown had also hoped to buy another lot, a field in Wick Road adjoining Crown land, but was thwarted by Adolphus Fredrick Govett who added it to his adjacent landholding at Bellefields. The Park House estate had been advertised as being 'Particularly well adapted for the Erection of first class Residences' but the Crown's intervention made a rash of buildings unlikely.[91] Park House itself and the 13 acres around it were sold to Griffith Thomas, a solicitor. He, like William Field at Bakeham House, found the old Georgian building inconvenient and small by contemporary standards: he had it pulled down and built a new house for his family. On a stone plaque on the tower were engraved the initials GMT for Griffith and Martha Thomas.[92]

The possibility of leasing Crown land for building attracted local gentlemen as well as City of London men. In 1870 Henry William Coxen, who rented a comparatively small house on Egham Hill, took a Crown lease on a 10-acre field called Owen's Close, once part of Upper Bakeham Farm and fronting on the turnpike road. He put up two posts to indicate the approach to his future residence and was ordered by the Turnpike Commissioners to remove them. He countered by demanding the removal of the turnpike trust's sand and pump that obstructed his right of way.[93] By the end of 1871 Coxen and his young family were living in their new residence, which they called Bendemere.[94]

At about the same time John King Farlow, who had succeeded Govett as tenant at Rusham House, was looking for development opportunities. He acquired from the Crown some 28 acres of Bakeham land on the main road near the 20th milestone. His lease was for 99 years from 10 October 1870.

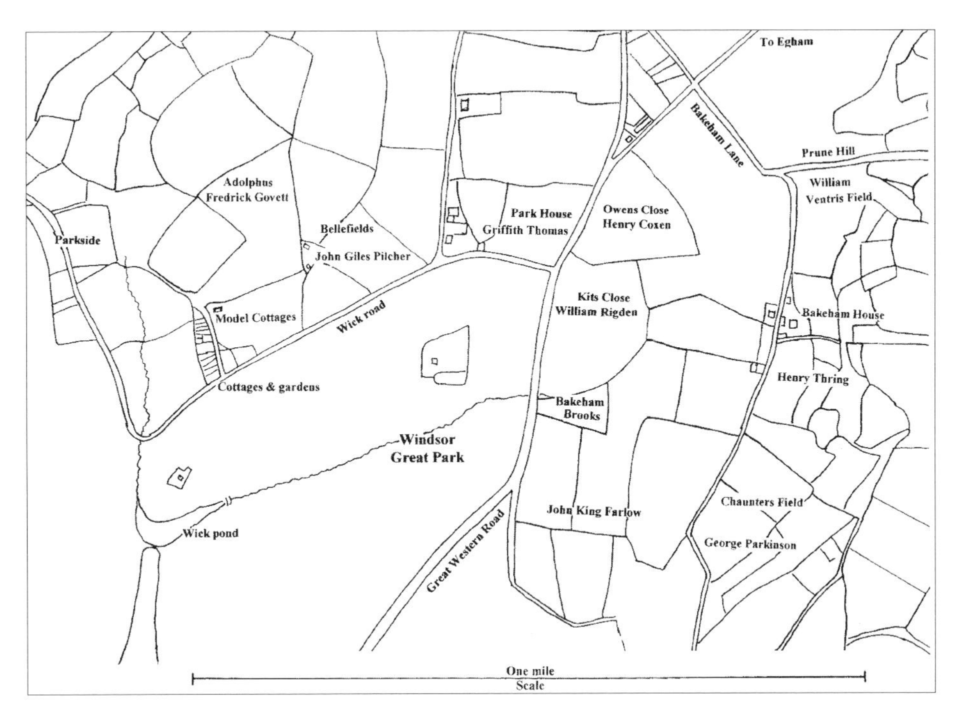

85 *Diagram showing the Bakeham House and Park House Estates, based on The Plan of the Parish of Egham, 1841.*

Like most of the other gentlemen house-builders, his first move was to install his gardener on the site to improve the land. In this case he thought so highly of Henry Kentfield, his gardener at Rusham, that he transferred him to Bakeham to supervise the transformation of the fields into gardens and plantations. By 1876 Farlow's mansion was complete and he with his wife and family moved in. They called the house Woodlee.[95] Its most distinguishing feature was the 'Light Room' on the third floor, used as a workroom; above it was an observatory tower, providing a panoramic view of the surrounding countryside.[96]

John King Farlow was a property developer, buying and selling land and building houses in London and the South East. He worked with John Notley from Dorset and in true entrepreneurial fashion had married Emily, one of Notley's daughters. His acquisitions at Bakeham did not stop with the building of Woodlee. Soon after the Crown bought Kitts Close and Bakeham Brooks, Farlow took a lease on them also. The Brooks he incorporated into his own estate, creating an attractive fishpond, while on Kitts Close he built another house, Queenswood, this time for renting out. His first tenant was William Giles Rigden, a glove manufacturer.[97]

With an increased number of schools for the labouring poor in the district and the implementation of the Foster Education Act of 1870, young men working in Windsor Great Park under Menzies were better educated than

86 *Wood Lee, London Road, built by John King Farlow, print,* c.*1870.*

their fathers and grandfathers had been. Many were ambitious to better themselves further. As a result Menzies found it difficult to keep able young men when he could only pay them average wages for their skills. Early in 1875 Thomas Palmer, the Head Nurseryman, died. His wages were 18s. a week, with a cottage and garden and deadwood for firing. This was only 2s. more than George Tough had received in 1800. Palmer was responsible for the care of a small nursery near Parkside and all ornamental plantings in the park, especially round the new cottages. He also had charge of the young plantations until they were mature enough to hand over to the woodmen.[98] Menzies recommended 28-year-old Robert Collins, one of the forest labourers, for the post of Head Nurseryman. He had been educated at the Queen's School in the park, had an excellent character and, still of considerable importance even in the late 19th century, he was the son of a respectable labourer with many years of Crown service to his credit.[99]

Unfortunately for the Crown, Collins only served as Head Nurseryman for two years when the Duke of Sutherland offered him a job at double the wages. The Deputy Surveyor could not compete and, nothing daunted, appointed another young man to the post. He was Frederick Sumner, aged 23, the son of a forest worker of long service and good character. Sumner had been educated at Cranbourne Free School and trained at an Ascot nursery. He was given one of the cottages at Parkside in which to make a home for his family and remained as nurseryman for 13 years before he too left to accept a more lucrative offer.[100]

William Menzies devoted his whole working life to the park. He lived at Parkside, Egham Wick, throughout his service and died there in 1878, aged only 50 years, from a work-related fever, first contracted five years before his death. His friends remembered him as a most genial companion, while to his men he was 'a kind and considerate overseer'. He had been a great favourite of the Prince Consort in the latter's lifetime and also of Queen Victoria, who had visited her Deputy Surveyor during his illness.[101] Menzies shared with the prince a determination to solve the problem of contaminated water and to improve sanitation. Less than two months before his death Menzies was investigating the water supply at Fort Belvedere. Robert Turner, the bombardier, had fallen ill and on investigation it was discovered that the water from the flat roof of the fort that his family used was unfit for drinking. Menzies ordered pure water to be brought by cart from Wheeler's Yard and recommended the digging of a well, 150ft deep, for the household's use.[102]

William Menzies was succeeded as Deputy Surveyor in the park by Frederick Simmonds, his brother-in-law. Simmonds had lived with the family in 1861 when he was Menzies' pupil. Later he qualified as an architect and worked as a land agent in Sussex and also for Baron John Henry Schroeder, who had an estate at Bishopsgate. Simmonds took over Parkside on his appointment in 1878 and his nephew, William, the late Deputy Surveyor's son, continued to live there.[103] Following in the footsteps of William Menzies cannot have been easy but Simmonds shared with his predecessor a genuine concern for the men who worked for him. Under his regime the park men enjoyed a day's holiday every year, during which they played cricket and other games and dined together in the evening.[104]

The severe weather of 1864 had not been an isolated occurrence. The harvests in the 1870s had been disastrous and Great Britain was importing more food than was good for its agricultural industry. The winters of 1878-9 and 1880-1 were bitter and those who could not work in such conditions were dependent on charity, the casual labourer suffering most. As usual, however, in these circumstances there was the opportunity for the lower classes to share a free entertainment with their betters.[105] In January 1881 a 'few country people, mechanics and labourers' were once more enjoying the ice at Virginia Water when they were joined by the Prince of Wales, his brother-in-law, Prince Christian, and other house guests from Cumberland Lodge.[106]

In 1866 Princess Helena, Queen Victoria's third daughter, had married Prince Christian of Schleswig-Holstein. A year later Prince Christian was appointed Ranger of Windsor Great Park and the couple made their home first at Frogmore and then at Cumberland Lodge. The prince involved himself in park affairs while the princess devoted herself to philanthropic work in the area. She was especially concerned with improving the care of the sick and with the training of nurses.[107] In 1879 a cottage hospital was built at Englefield Green through the generosity of Benjamin Warwick, a merchant who had moved to the area. The hospital would provide nursing care for the poorer members of the community. Princess Christian became patron of its fundraising committee and a ward was named after her. The princess was, however, no mere royal figurehead. One visit was recorded by the hospital's first matron, Mrs Alice Bolton, a lady of self-confessed 'Socialist tendencies'. Having spoken with the patients and enquired especially of one boy, Princess Christian retired to Alice's sitting room where the two women 'talked away' about their mutual interest in nursing.[108] In the informality of her visits, her enthusiasm for local charities and a manner that put ordinary people at ease, the princess was ahead of her time.

The Prince of Wales often stayed in the vicinity of Windsor Great Park during Ascot Racing Week. Many local children were kept away from school for the period because of the danger from increased traffic on the roads. The boldest among them, however, seized the opportunity to distract and amuse the racegoers by their antics and thereby earn themselves some pennies.[109]

Meanwhile, John King Farlow, the developer, had not been idle. He leased more Crown land along Bakeham Lane and Callow Hill, and built another house, Glenwood, in a field called Chaunters, next to Sir Henry Thring's new dwelling. Here, according to family tradition, the younger Farlow children were housed, together with nannies, governesses and nursery maids, so that Woodlee might remain a peaceful sanctuary for the adults.[110]

The plot south of Glenwood, another part of Chaunters Field plus some neighbouring land, about 23 acres in all, Farlow leased to a dentist, George Parkinson. On this site, once enclosed from the common and used as a sandpit by Thomas Burton, Parkinson built his own mansion, later described as a 'charming bijou residence'. He called the house 'Huntersdale', an adaptation of an old place name.[111]

Farlow had not yet finished his development of the Bakeham lands. To the east of Queenswood and fronting Bakeham Lane he built two more houses to rent out, Ulverscroft and Ashleigh. The former was completed by 1881 when its first tenants, Charles Clement Beardsley, a stockbroker, and his wife, Edith, were in residence. Ashleigh was as yet unnamed and unoccupied; only a carpenter, William Micham, was on the site, living in

87 *Glenwood, Callow Hill, 1980, another Farlow mansion, photograph by Mann & Co.*

rooms above the stables and doubtless putting finishing touches to the construction. Ashleigh, like Glenwood, was sometimes used by the Farlow family and sometimes let out.[112]

Near the Clockcase lay the plot bought by John Secker at the time of enclosure. A gardener had continued to live and work on the site and it remained in the Secker family. It was not until John's grandson, John Herbert Secker, came into possession of the land that there were any building plans. Following his marriage in 1876, John Herbert built a mansion on the site and called it Hangmore, from the old name of the hill on which the Clockcase had been built. In 1880 Secker, who, like most of his family, was a solicitor, tried to increase the size of his estate by offering to buy 13 acres of the Clockcase Plantation, arguing that it would straighten his boundary with the Crown. The old fears that a building on the site might overlook the lake were raised and his request was refused.[113]

Thus, in a space of 14 years, the landscape in the vicinity of Virginia Water and Egham Wick had been changed and again the Crown, as the largest landowner, had been closely involved. By 1881, where once men had sown, hoed and harvested in the Bakeham and Wick fields or gathered wood on the waste, 14 mansions had been built. Their reception rooms were spacious, their kitchen areas complex; there were numerous bedrooms for master and family and attics for maids. Outside were lodges, stables and coach-houses, gardens, plantations, shrubberies and driveways, even in some cases small farms, all requiring staff. The local population, hungry for work as ever, was grateful for the opportunities provided by the new gentry. Many of the servants working in these houses and gardens were descendants of the men who had come into the area and learnt their skills with John Robinson and Nathaniel Kent in Windsor Great Park.

In the 1870s another very rich man had been on the lookout for building land in the area, with a particular eye for bargains near railway lines. He was Thomas Holloway, the manufacturer of pills and ointments, who, having no direct descendants, had determined to use his fortune to benefit a wider public. He eventually acquired the freehold of an estate on Egham Hill, blighted by agricultural depression, and at Virginia Water, farmland blighted by the railway itself. At Virginia Water, only a stone's throw from the station, he built a sanatorium for the treatment of the mentally ill of the middle classes and on Egham Hill a college for the higher education of women.[114]

These were no ordinary buildings but bold statements from an entrepreneurial genius who had achieved wealth by hard work and an instinctive understanding of the gullibility of human nature. The architecture of the sanatorium was based on that of a public building in Belgium, the cloth hall at Ypres, while the college owed its basic structure to the Chateau de Chambord in the Loire Valley.[115] The impact of these great buildings on the once impoverished areas near Windsor Great Park was vast. They

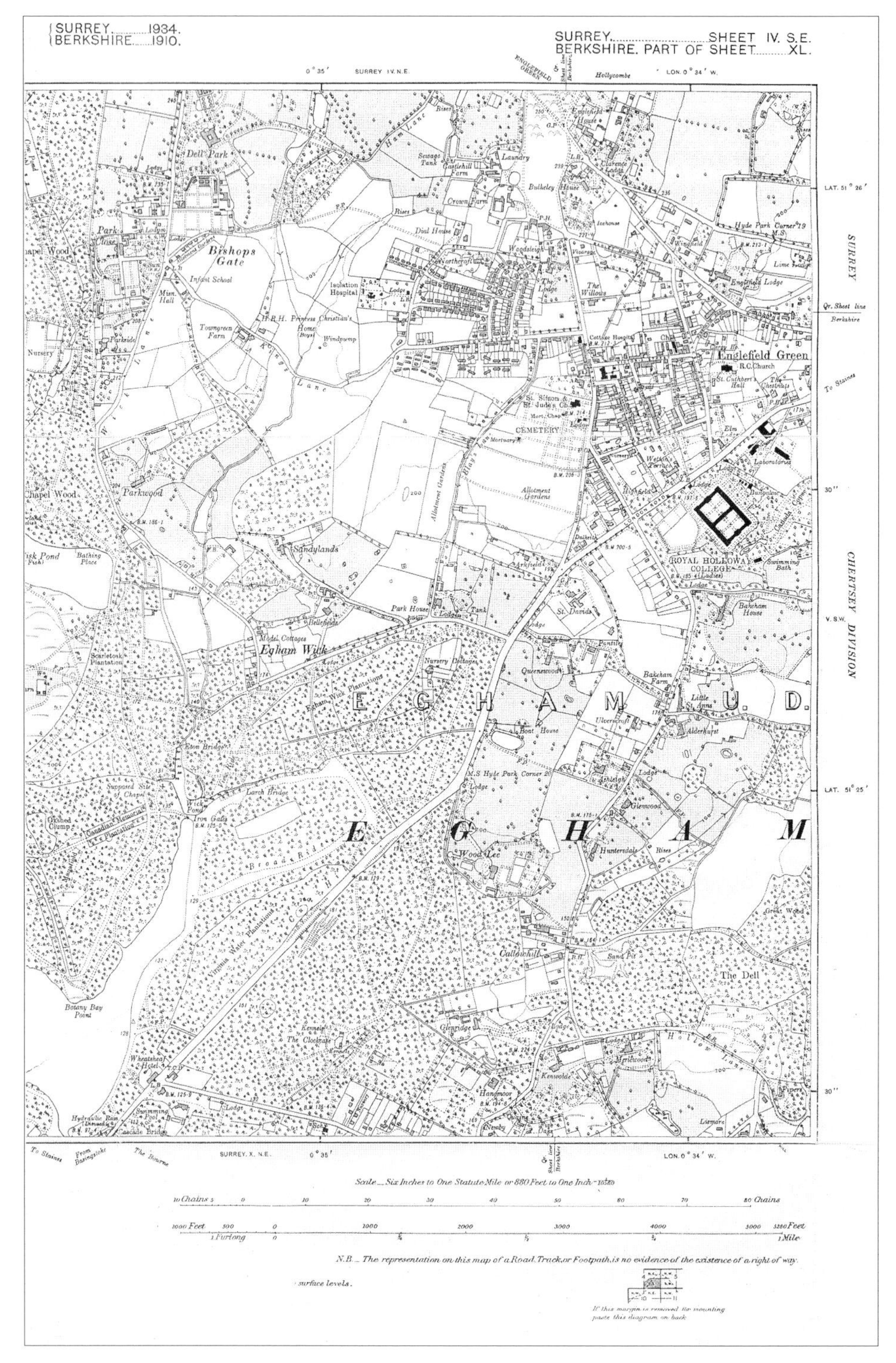

88 *Ordnance Survey map, 1934–8, scale six inches to one mile, showing the Bakeham and Egham Wick mansions.*

provided work for numerous labourers as well as for skilled men; craftsmen were attracted to the district from all over the country and even from the mainland of Europe. The magnificence of the completed buildings and the amount of money involved ensured that their openings were attended by the greatest in the land, the heir to the throne and even the reclusive monarch herself. Holloway Sanatorium was opened in July 1885 by the Prince and Princess of Wales. The children from Christ Church National School were given a holiday in order to line the road and cheer their royal visitors. The following year Queen Victoria herself, encouraged by the country's response to her proclamation as Empress of India and the enthusiasm for her approaching Golden Jubilee, came to Englefield Green to open Thomas Holloway's college for young ladies. By the queen's wish it became known as 'Royal Holloway College'. Once more the children were given a holiday and patriotic banners appeared: 'Egham's Devotion and Loyalty Follow in Your Train' and 'She Has Wrought Her People Lasting Government'.[116] The royal connection did not end there. Prince Christian served on the college's first Board of Governors and Princess Christian visited in 1887 to unveil a statue of her mother in the north quadrangle, afterwards known as Queen's Quad. The sculptor was Count Gleichen, son of Queen Victoria's half-sister.[117]

When, in June 1887, Queen Victoria celebrated 50 years as monarch, there was pride in her achievement. Celebration was in the air. Simmonds' men in the park were given £50 to be shared among them in gratuities.[118] The children of Christ Church, Virginia Water's National School, were given outings and an extra week's holiday that June. The vicar of Virginia Water, the Rev. R.E. Molyneux, inscribed all the pupils' names in books sent over from Windsor. On 15 July some of the older scholars trekked over to Smith's Lawn to see the queen lay the foundation stone of the

89 *An early design for Holloway Sanatorium.*

90 *Royal Holloway College,* c.*1930.*

Women's Jubilee Memorial.[119] The women of Great Britain and the empire had been invited, at the queen's request, to each contribute a small coin in order for a statue of the late Albert, Prince Consort, to be erected. Three years later the statue was complete and once again the children went to Smith's Lawn, this time to witness the unveiling and the military review that followed.[120] So great was the revival of feeling for the queen and empress that a baby girl, born to the Broom family in Virginia Water in the summer of 1887, was baptised Mabel Victoria Jubilee.

Despite the fact that prospects and wages in agriculture were static if not in recession in the 1880s and early '90s, the men working in the park made the best of things, helped each other and found enjoyment where they could.

91 *Unveiling the Prince Consort's statue on Smith's Lawn, 1890, Robert Taylor Pritchett.*

At a time when the government was actively encouraging working men to save, Frederick Simmonds reported to one of his superiors in 1895 on a save-and-enjoy scheme that operated effectively among his men.[121]

Every year since 1884 an excursion by train had been organised with about three hundred park workers taking part. The men each paid 2s. a week into a fund, some of them adding an extra 1s. for their wives to be included. This sum was augmented by a subscription raised by Prince Christian and other gentlemen living in the park. In July 1895 the chosen destination was Portsmouth and, as usual, Bartlett, the foreman in the park, made all the arrangements. A special train was chartered from the London & South Western Railway Company, at a cost of 4s. for each passenger; in addition each man was handed 6s. 6d. spending money for the day. The train left Windsor at 6 a.m. and called at Egham, Virginia Water, Ascot, Bagshot and Camberley to pick up passengers. It left Portsmouth at 8 p.m. for the return journey. For Simmonds himself, as well as his men, the outing was always an enjoyable experience.[122]

The train had done much to improve the quality of life of the working classes. By the end of the century other organisations were regularly chartering trains to take their members on excursions, usually to the seaside. The children of Virginia Water were often absent from school on the day when the Band of Hope Union, a Temperance society, took their members to Bournemouth for the day.[123]

In an age of greater mobility the *Wheatsheaf* inn also prospered. Charles Ratcliffe from Derbyshire became its licensee in 1870 and managed the business until the end of the century.[124] He did much to improve its status and turned many of Henry Jennings's dreams into reality. In 1890 extensive alterations were made to the building, the date of the work being inscribed on the front façade. In a Petty Sessions Licensing list of 1892 the inn was described as catering for the hotel and respectable bar trade with good accommodation and stabling; most important of all for the running of a successful house, the landlord lived in.[125]

92 *Sunningdale station, 1860, photograph by A. Seeley.*

From her home at Cumberland Lodge Princess Christian continued her philanthropic work. In 1896 she started a new enterprise, this time to help disadvantaged boys. She took a lease on a small piece of land adjoining Windsor Great Park near Bishopsgate, where, in a house newly designed by William Menzies, the architect of Englefield Green and son of the former Deputy Surveyor in the park, the princess established a holiday home for disabled boys. These 'poor London waifs who had been injured in accidents or other ways' would profit for a short time from clean country air, good food and an atmosphere more like that of a family home than the institutions they were used to. Away from the corrupting influence of the town they might also learn new skills to improve their employment prospects.[126]

The queen's Diamond Jubilee of 1897 was keenly anticipated. Schoolchildren had lessons on the Union flag and the life of Queen Victoria. On the queen's 78th birthday, the children of St Ann's Heath School, Virginia Water's newly opened Board School, decorated the schoolroom and each child wore red, white and blue flowers. For the jubilee itself the schools were closed for the week and Egham town was illuminated with fairy lamps.[127] As darkness fell 2,000 people gathered at Englefield Green to see a great cone of faggots lit by the magic of science. The ingenious staff and students of the Royal Indian Engineering College on Coopers Hill had combined 'certain chemicals' with a 'cask of petroleum' to create a spectacular blaze.[128]

As Britain moved towards a new century, the Royal Agricultural Society and numerous local agricultural societies encouraged the country to make the best of a depleted agricultural industry. In June 1899 the Royal Counties Agricultural Show was held in the Home Park, near Windsor Castle, with Queen Victoria as nominal president and Prince Christian actively engaged as vice-president. The men who worked in the park, farms and gardens in Windsor Great Park were given a half-day's holiday and free tickets to encourage them to attend.[129] Despite the growth in manufacturing in other parts of the country, most men in Virginia Water and Egham Wick still depended on tilling the soil for their livelihood.

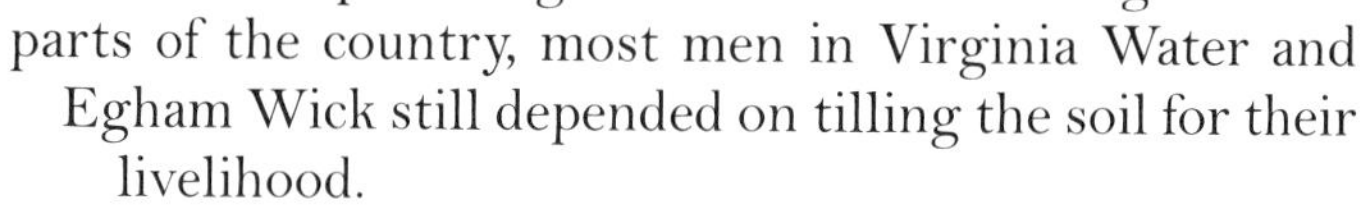

93 *Plan for a Boys' Home at Englefield Green, elevation to road, 1896.*

Chapter Six

Patriotism, War and a People's Pleasure Park: 1901-2006

Queen Victoria died at Osborne House on the Isle of Wight in January 1901. At Virginia Water's Board School at St Ann's Heath, flags flew at half-mast and the queen's photograph was draped in black.[1] Victoria's people mourned a lost era but the patriotic pride in country and empire generated in the last quarter of her reign remained.

A year later thoughts turned to ways of celebrating the coronation of Edward VII and Queen Alexandra—the first such ceremony for more than 60 years. 'Old hands' among the park workers told Frederick Simmonds, the Deputy Surveyor, that when Queen Victoria was crowned all the men received 5s. and two bottles of port each. This recollection was taken with a large pinch of salt by the king's advisors, who proposed giving the men two days' holiday with pay, the old tradition being, in their opinion, 'thoroughly bad'. In the end, however, popular preference prevailed and each man received a gratuity of 5s. with 2s. apiece for their wives.[2]

Unfortunately Coronation Day had to be delayed until August because of the king's illness, but the occasion was celebrated in Egham in July. The town was decorated with greenery, crowns, flags, banners, trophies and heraldic devices. The old folk were treated to a substantial meal and the schoolchildren to mineral water and pies, chocolate and a presentation mug. A procession, accompanied by marching bands and decorated bicycles, wound its way to Englefield Green where sports and tea were provided. In the evening there were fireworks and a bonfire.[3] Frederick Simmonds, with the approval of his superiors, provided faggots free to the Coronation Festivities Committee, as he had for the jubilee celebrations. Simmonds' men and their families, some 400 to 500 in all, gathered at George III's statue in Windsor Great Park, where they illuminated the royal initials with hurricane lamps and lit a great bonfire. A few days later the men went on their annual excursion, again visiting Portsmouth, this time to see the British fleet assembled for the Royal Naval Review.[4]

The pomp and jollification did nothing to bring agriculture out of the doldrums. At the Egham Royal Agricultural Show in 1902 only 12 ploughing teams took part, compared with more than 20 in the 1870s. By 1902 there was more emphasis on horticultural exhibits, with cottagers and others who worked their own gardens encouraged to enter fruit and vegetables. There was also an increase in honorary exhibits with the owners of the large houses entering fruit, flowers and exotic plants grown by their gardeners in hothouses.[5]

Land values had fallen and farmers were urged to diversify. In 1906, at a dinner to celebrate the 50th ploughing match, it was noted that those present were mainly from the trades and professions: the number of farmers present could be counted on the fingers of one hand.[6] In 1908 severe weather once more made work even more scarce. A bread relief fund was started in Egham and a soup kitchen set up in the parish room, where a pint of soup could be bought for a halfpenny.[7]

At Virginia Water the royal brig, the *King Edward VII*, the last non-motorised boat to sail on the lake,[8] was ice-bound and a centre of attraction for skaters and spectators. King Edward himself hosted shooting parties in Windsor Great Park, often entertaining the crowned heads of Europe, to many of whom he was related. The parties were often based at the 'Swiss Cottage', formerly the fishing temple on the north bank of the lake, still inaccessible to the public.

The enthusiasm for all things imperial and the intense patriotism encouraged by Queen Victoria's successful jubilees and by the final triumph over the Boers in South Africa continued into Edward's reign. Nationalism was not unique to Great Britain, but was dangerously widespread throughout Europe. In Virginia Water's schools the boys drilled in military fashion, supervised by ex-army drill instructors. In an attempt to keep the glory days of Victoria's reign alive, Reginald, the 12th Earl of Meath, suggested that the late queen's birthday, 24 May, should be set aside each year for the celebration of the British Empire. The idea caught on and in 1905 St Ann's Heath Board School celebrated Empire Day for the first time. A tradition was established that lasted for more than three decades; school children throughout the land learned about the Empire; saluted the Union Flag, sang patriotic songs and sometimes acted out elaborate tableaux. Even more memorable was the half-day's holiday that followed.[9]

When Edward VII died in May 1910, as a mark of respect, Empire Day passed quietly. The following year the occasion was combined with celebrations for the coronation of George V and Queen Mary.[10] In a few short years many of the boys who had drilled so enthusiastically in the school playgrounds would be fighting for their country in foreign fields.

Great Britain declared war on 4 August 1914 when Germany invaded Belgium. Within days a recruitment meeting was held at the Englefield

94 *Children pausing from skating on Virginia Water near King Edward's Brig, 1907, photograph by William End.*

Green Rifle Club and 12 men, ready to serve king and country, signed up. By the autumn Belgium refugees were seeking asylum in the Egham district and the town was full of soldiers. By the beginning of November, 800 local men, fired with patriotic fervour, were under arms: 10 men had enlisted from one estate alone, Parkwood in Egham Wick. At the Sunday School prize-giving at Christ Church, Virginia Water, in December 1914 there was 'an inspiring military element' and the children spontaneously broke into 'It's a Long Way to Tipperary'. At the Christmas entertainment at St Ann's Heath School not only were khaki uniforms well represented but also families from 'gallant little Belgium'.[11]

Windsor Great Park became a training ground for soldiers. Early in 1915 men of the 2/5th East Surrey Regiment conducted manoeuvres and dug and manned trenches 'near Virginia Water'. On 8 April they were inspected by George V, His Majesty riding out on his charger while Queen Mary, Princess Mary and the two youngest princes rode in a carriage. A march past of 25,000 men took an hour to complete.[12]

The local newspaper noted with approval the young men who volunteered and, as the war intensified, listed the heroes who had given their lives. One who received a particularly detailed obituary was Charles Benn, an all-round sportsman who excelled at rowing, punting, swimming, shooting and gymnastics, killed in action in September 1917. He had been born at the Clockcase, the youngest son of Charles Benn, an under-gamekeeper in the park. Young men from the big houses, Lieutenant Cecil Davis of Hangmore and Herbert Hughes of Glenridge, fell, as well as ploughmen, gardeners and clerks.[13]

95 *Soldiers of the 2/5th East Surrey Regiment trenching near Virginia Water, 1915.*

More centres were needed in which to treat the wounded and, according to the local paper, a score of 'curious huts' were set up on Crown land off Bond Street in Englefield Green to accommodate 200 convalescent men.[14] It was established as a Red Cross Hospital, with Red Cross volunteers working under the supervision of trained nurses. The hospital was well supported by the local community and by Princess Christian, the local princess, who often visited the hospital, persuading George V and Queen Mary to accompany her in 1916.[15] Young women, such as Emily Maud Pocock from Egham Hill, were as eager as their brothers to serve their country and eagerly joined the volunteers at Englefield Green.

96 *Nurses and convalescent soldiers outside one of the huts at the Red Cross Hospital, Englefield Green,* c.*1917—Emily Maud Pocock is seated in the middle row, looking directly at the camera.*

During wartime the Crown, like all other landowners, was expected to turn as much land as possible over to agricultural use. The Egham Agricultural Committee had to find an extra 500 acres to put under cultivation and proposed that the Crown should play its part by letting out the Southcrofts Allotment land at Englefield Green. In the committee's opinion there were acres of Crown land lying idle: the Crown should set an example and encourage working men to grow food on it.[16]

As more and more men were called up for war service, agriculture faced a new crisis: more land needed to be cultivated yet there were fewer men to do the work. Each week the Egham War Tribunal met to hear evidence from farmers and small businessmen pleading for key workers not to be called up. It was not until June 1917 that full-time agricultural workers were finally exempt from military service. Small businesses continued to be under threat if the proprietor was called up.[17]

The pressure on older men still at work and those exempt from war service was considerable. In Windsor Great Park, Arthur Forrest, the Deputy Surveyor, had more land to cultivate than previously as well as routine work to maintain. At the same time many of his young men had been called up and others were thinking of transferring to munitions work where they could earn between 25 and 50 per cent more than park rates.[18]

The Foreman of the Park, George Payne, worked especially hard during 1916-17, giving up his Saturday afternoons and clocking up 700 extra hours. For this he earned £140 per annum that, with extras and a cost of living bonus, amounted to a total of £153. Forrest championed his right to be paid overtime for the extra hours and for his basic salary to be raised to at least £160 or preferably £200, as the purchasing power of money had significantly declined during the war.[19] The agricultural wage, never generous, was proving inadequate to cope with the dramatic rise in the cost of living. A pound was worth only three-quarters of its pre-war value and Forrest was particularly concerned for those of his men on the minimum adult male rate of £1 a week. The national press reported that men working in the London parks were in receipt of an extra 5s. a week war bonus to compensate for this and Forrest, never backward in advocating the cause of his men, claimed parity for his staff.[20]

Most of the under-gamekeepers, woodcutters, carters and permanent labourers earned between 20s. and 30s. a week, depending on age and experience. They were eventually granted the same war bonus as the men in the London parks. Those men earning more than £2 a week received 4s. a week extra as war bonus. The casual men on an hourly rate of between 6d. and 9d. an hour, some of whom had worked in Windsor Great Park for a number of years, were excluded. Instead they received an increase of 1d. an hour, this being regarded as comparable with agricultural wages in the district.[21] This differential treatment was not conducive to good labour relations and the hourly labourers felt let down. They petitioned their superiors and even their local Member of Parliament, Donald McMaster, who lived at Merlewood in Virginia Water. Finally in July 1917 a question was asked in the House of Commons, designed to highlight the anomaly of the long-serving casual labourer. It elicited the desired response: 'A person who has been working for five or six years cannot be considered a casual labourer.'[22]

The war also brought financial hardship to many innkeepers. Restrictive licensing laws designed to stop war workers getting drunk caused a drop in trade. The licensees of the *Wheatsheaf Hotel*, Robert Upcraft and his daughter Lucy, were granted a reduction in rent by the Crown every year throughout the war when their house had to close each afternoon and shut its doors by 9 p.m. each evening.[23]

For some young men the war brought new opportunities and excitements, such as learning to drive motor vehicles. The combination of powerful machines, inadequate roads and inexperienced drivers, however, could be lethal. Many of the road accidents in and around Egham during the First World War involved military vehicles or personnel. An even more exciting machine, the aeroplane, was also observed over Egham, the Royal Flying Corps having a base at Ascot. In the autumn of 1917 a plane frightened onlookers as it suddenly descended over the town, only just missing the telegraph wires. A few months later another pilot was not so lucky: his plane hit a tree at Englefield Green and crashed. To the astonishment of witnesses the pilot wriggled out of the cockpit almost unscathed.[24]

Some things never changed in the relationship between the neighbourhood and Windsor Great Park, war or no war. At a Chertsey Rural Council meeting in September 1917 councillors blamed the recent flooding in Thorpe on mismanagement of the sluices at Virginia Water. The methods

97 Wheatsheaf Hotel, c.*1910*.

used to prevent the lake overflowing were, in their opinion, 'prehistoric, archaic and out of date'. Replying with some indignation, Arthur Forrest reminded the council of the exceptional rainfall that year and of the fact that Thorpe had flooded since prehistoric times. Surveyors on both sides would investigate further.[25]

Apart from perpetual anxiety for the safety of their loved ones overseas, the most obvious outward sign to the people of Virginia Water that the country was engaged in a world war was the presence of Canadian soldiers in Windsor Great Park. In February 1916 the British government appealed to Canada to assist the mother country in the production of timber for the war effort. Skilled labour was urgently required to make trench props, boards and sleepers for export to France. A contingent of Canadian lumbermen was immediately recruited. There was no time for military training: they were 'first and foremost woodsmen'.[26]

There was no shortage of timber in England and the royal forests were a prime source. The Deputy Surveyor of Windsor Great Park, Arthur Forrest, suggested the Clockcase and Belvedere woods as possible sites. The Crown, though anxious to contribute to the war effort, was concerned at the widespread loss of trees. At the suggestion of George V all broad-leaved trees near the road were to be conserved. It was hoped that self-sown Scots pine would naturally replenish what was taken.[27] By 13 May 1916, 150 men from the 224th Canadian Forestry Battalion were encamped at the Clockcase felling spruce, fir, pine and larch and constructing a sawmill from the timber.[28]

The local newspaper was quick to report the arrival of the Canadians and the building of the camp, particularly noting the up-to-date sanitary

98 *Tree cutting in Windsor Forest, 1917.*

arrangements and the provision of hot shower baths. Local people were clearly intrigued by their new neighbours, who had among their number men of African and Native American descent. A member of Egham's Exemption Tribunal assumed that the Canadians were likely to live off the land: on being told that rabbits had to be kept off neighbouring farms, he replied, somewhat facetiously, 'You have some young fellows up there who will have anything living.' That they were free spirits was confirmed by one of their number when he was fined for having no lights on his bicycle: 'They did what they liked in Canada and would do so here.' Within a few weeks of their arrival, however, the Canadians had proved their worth to the local populace by helping to put out an undergrowth fire at Shrubs Hill. The damage would have been much greater without their timely assistance.[29] As well as felling and working timber the lumbermen aimed to be self-sufficient. They farmed 55 acres of neighbouring land, ran their own piggery and produced enough grain and vegetables to supply other Canadian messes.[30]

With the Clockcase an industrial site from the middle of 1916, trackways had to be strengthened so that motor lorries could take the prepared timber from the sawmill to the main road and thence to the railway station.[31] One of the motor transport vehicles belonging to the forestry battalion was involved in an accident in Stroude only a few weeks after the men's arrival. In trying to avoid a tradesman's horses and cart the driver ran the lorry into soft ground. Horsepower failed to haul it out and the driver had to wait for another army vehicle to extricate it.[32]

The camp at the Clockcase was extensive. As well as sleeping accommodation there was a recreation hut, kitchen, bathhouse, hospital, canteens and storerooms, stabling for 50 horses and garaging for motor vehicles.[33] A temporary rail track had to be laid to carry timber from the Belvedere woods. It would be drawn by horses or a light engine and would cross the Great Western Road near the *Wheatsheaf*. The Office of Woods & Forests had no objection to the track running through the archway near the ruins and along the shore of the lake so long as the sites were restored after use.[34]

At the beginning of 1917 more Canadians were drafted into the park: the Central Depot for the Canadian Forestry Battalion was established on Smith's Lawn, to the north of the lake, near Obelisk pond,[35] in another large, well-appointed camp, complete with sawmill. The men worked on a variety of timber, creating prefabricated hut sections to be dispatched to camps all over the country. They were able to send out 72 huts a month.[36]

There was urgent need for more plantations to be made available and Frostfarm Plantation at Shrubs Hill was approved for the felling of conifers but not hardwood.[37] Work continued at the Clockcase and the Belvedere woods until by May 1917 the areas were almost cleared. The Clockcase, described as resembling the case of a grandfather's clock, was visible from the road for the first time in 100 years.[38]

The Canadian soldiers must have felt at home during their first winter in Virginia Water. The temperature in January 1917 was 16 degrees below zero, 6ins of snow fell (the heaviest fall for 36 years) and the ice on the lake was excellent. The children played a dangerous game of 'dare', cutting a slide from the ruins across the royal lake almost to the fishing temple. There was always a gap near the temple where they were told the ice was cut out and put in the icehouse in the grounds. The children had to take a flying leap at the end of their slide and land on the veranda of the fishing temple—forbidden territory to them![39]

The Canadians were very popular with the children of Virginia Water. When the youngsters were sent wooding to the Belvedere or Clockcase woods the soldiers helped them fill their baskets, prams or little trucks. One seven-year-old girl who lived at Blacknest loved to hear the shout of 'Timber!' as a tree fell and to watch the huge trunks being loaded onto the railway. On one occasion a soldier asked her if she could sew, as his socks needed mending. She said her mum and gran would do them for him and thus a 'great friendship built up'.[40]

No one minded scraps of wood being taken from the timber sites—poor people had always done so—but when valuable timber, in wartime the property of HM Secretary of State for War, was removed in sackloads, it was a criminal matter. In February 1917 an Egham labourer and a 15-year-old boy were brought before W.G. Pilcher, the Egham magistrate, for such an offence. The case against the man was dropped, as he was about to join the Royal Flying Corps; the boy was fined 9s., being spared a whipping as he had a good character.[41]

As is inevitable when a large group of men is isolated in a strange environment, there was some misbehaviour among the Canadians and even a few criminal prosecutions against them. Boredom leading to drunkenness was a major problem. A defendant in an assault case early in 1917 claimed that no reliance could be placed on evidence given by men stationed at Virginia

99 *YMCA Hut, Canadian Forestry Camp, Egham,* c.*1917.*

Water 'because they were all drunk most of the time after Christmas'. One Canadian soldier was merely locked up for the night when found drunk in Chertsey and released the next day. Another, whose drunkenness led him to strike out at the policemen trying to arrest him, found himself serving three months' hard labour. The Adjutant of the 224th Canadian Forestry Battalion agreed that the man needed to be made an example of. There were also a few cases of assaults on women, for which sentences of between two and six months' imprisonment with hard labour were handed down. One attack occurring at the lake resulted in a detachment of military foot police being billeted at Virginia Water.[42]

There is one recorded incident suggesting an element of racial tension in the Canadian Forestry Battalion. In the early summer of 1918 a 'coloured' man, Pte. John Munroe, seeing a black comrade struck by a white Canadian soldier, went to his aid and hit the apparent aggressor, knocking him to the ground and causing a fatal blow to the back of his head. The incident took place outside the *Castle* beerhouse on Egham Hill in the presence of local women and may have had as much to do with drink and bravado as race. It was fortunately a rare episode and the offenders were a small minority of the hundreds of soldiers working at the Clockcase and Belvedere woods between 1916 and 1918.[43]

By the time the Canadian Forestry Battalion had been in the district for a year they were well established as members of the community. Church halls were opened for them as recreation centres and they often attended church in Egham and Virginia Water, usually accompanied by a band. Occasionally they went to morning service at Chertsey Parish Church as, for example, when the United States of America entered the war on the side of the Allies in 1917. The band of the Canadian Corps played outside the church to the delight of passers-by. By the autumn of 1917 the Canadians had formed an orchestra, a string band and a concert party, which were much in demand at fundraising events.[44] Several Canadian soldiers married local girls, some returning with their brides to their homeland, while others remained in this country. There were certainly other less regular relationships: one local girl who had a son by a married Canadian soldier received financial support from the Canadian government to help her raise the child when the father returned home at the end of the war.[45] Many of the Canadian soldiers who fell victim to accident or illness while serving in Windsor Great Park were buried in Englefield Green cemetery.[46] The Canadian Plantation near Smith's Lawn in the park is their memorial.

The winter of 1917-18 was worse than the previous year, with rain and floods adding to the lumbermen's difficulties. With the areas near the sawmill cleared, the men were working between five and seven miles from base. The Church Army ran a dry canteen for them and Princess Alice, Countess of Athlone and granddaughter of Queen Victoria, arranged concerts and entertainments. King George and Queen Mary visited. The men of the Canadian Forestry Battalion at Virginia Water had reason to be proud of their achievement for, by the end of the war and despite some criticism of the wasteful nature of the Canadian operation, Virginia Water had produced more cubic feet of timber than any other camp.[47]

The success of the enterprise was due in part to co-operation between Arthur Forrest, Deputy Surveyor of Windsor Great Park, and the officers of the Canadian Battalions. In recognition of his work during the war and especially in the formation of the camps and in supervising the felling of trees, Arthur Forrest was made a Member of the Victorian Order and eventually received his own war bonus.[48]

As the war approached its final year, councillors and clerics turned their thoughts to the post-war period. It was agreed that a fund would be raised to provide a suitable memorial for the fallen. There was also general concern for the future of the survivors that life should be better for them on their return. In the opinion of many, an improvement in housing conditions for working men was a priority. It was reported that poor tenants in Virginia Water and Englefield Green had had to move to make way for the employees of large establishments and weekenders. The council was urged to use its powers, acquire land and build 'homes fit for heroes'.[49]

The First World War ended on 11 November 1918 and thanksgiving services were held at parish churches. The last months of the war had been marked by an influenza epidemic that closed schools and killed thousands. Official celebrations would take place in 1919 and events were held to raise money for memorials to the fallen. In August in Virginia Water, a parade of serving and demobilised soldiers, Boy Scouts and the Egham Brass Band heralded an afternoon of sports with dancing in the evening. By October the community had raised enough money to unveil its war memorial at Christ Church. It commemorates the names of 41 servicemen from Virginia Water who made the ultimate sacrifice.[50]

The servicemen returning from the First World War did not find a much better world awaiting them. The wages of agricultural and horticultural labourers remained low and, despite numerous housing acts designed to help the working class, most house-building in the 1920s and '30s had the owner-occupier in mind.

There was little new housing for park workers at this time. Arthur Forrest retired in 1920 and only then did Parkside at Egham Wick cease to be the official residence of the Deputy Surveyor. When Forrest was appointed in 1909 the house was already described as so old it was not worth further expenditure. Its situation on the south-eastern side of the park was also inconvenient at a time when most work activity was centred on Prince Consort Workshops, two miles distant. Nevertheless, Forrest resided at Parkside for the whole of his term of office, the Treasury being unconvinced that the provision of a new, more centrally located house was a priority.[51] After his retirement a decision was made to lease Parkside out, and throughout the 1920s its occupiers were the Hon. Thomas and Lady Cecily Vesey.[52]

In the 1930s in Windsor Great Park there was a growing interest in horticulture. It started with the granting of residences within the park to the two senior royal princes. In 1929 Edward, Prince of Wales, moved into Fort Belvedere and, as well as redesigning the interior, took a close interest in improving the gardens. Two years later his brother and sister-in-law, the Duke and Duchess of York, made Royal Lodge their Windsor residence and became equally enthusiastic about transforming the garden.[53] In that same year Eric Savill, himself a veteran of the First World War,[54] was appointed Deputy Surveyor in Windsor Great Park and, with the encouragement of the royal family, planned to create a garden in the south of the park for the first time. He selected a site near the old plant nursery at Parkside, formerly the home of the Deputy Surveyor. At first sight there was nothing but a tangle of undergrowth, hiding a stream that flows into Obelisk Pond, but it had the clear potential to become a woodland garden. There was plenty of work to be done—clearing, fencing, digging and planting and this continued throughout the 1930s.[55]

There were other changes in the park, reflecting the mood of the times. The Prince of Wales drove speedboats on the lake, to the consternation of those responsible for safety and the maintenance of the banks. The large boats were removed, the fishing temple demolished and an airstrip built on Smith's Lawn. At Fort Belvedere a tennis court was constructed as well as a swimming pool. This latter innovation caused some consternation among the girls of St David's School on the London Road opposite Windsor Great Park. They were on their regular walk round the lake one day in the 1930s when their noses were assailed by 'horrid smells'. They were astonished to see bare beaches on the edges of the lake and freshwater mussels marooned on them. Pipes were being laid from the lake to feed the pool at the fort.[56] Despite such incidents Virginia Water continued to be a popular venue for excursions.

100 *HRH The Prince of Wales and HRH The Duke of York with two gardeners, cutting back laurel in the gardens of Fort Belvedere, 1930s.*

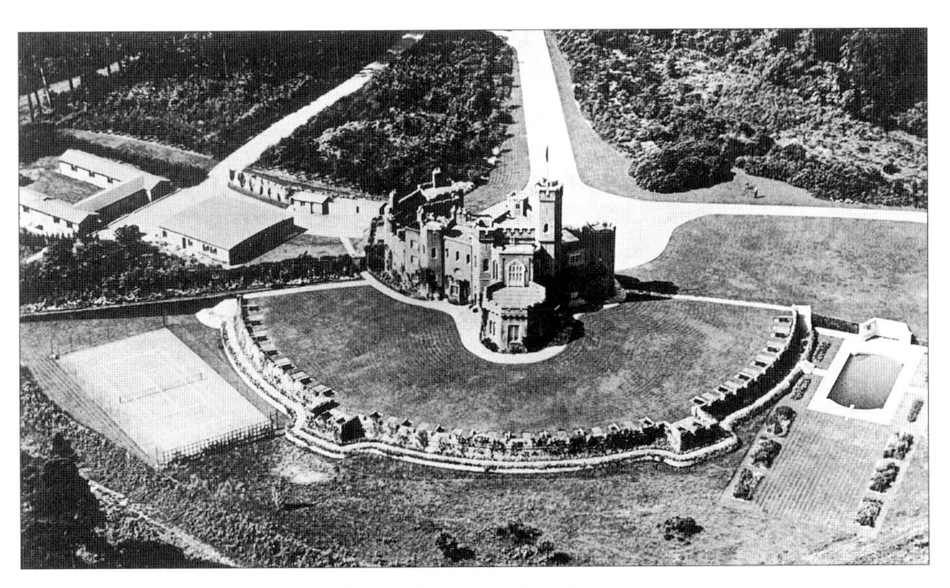

101 *Fort Belvedere and gardens,* c.*1940*

The Silver Jubilee of George V and Queen Mary was celebrated in May 1935 with the issue of a medal to long-serving members of the Windsor Park staff. Eric Savill was delighted that 16 of his own men were honoured and doubted if there was an estate in the country with so good a record for long service.[57] In Virginia Water on 6 May the *Rose & Olive Branch* beerhouse on Callow Hill hung out bunting and flags in celebration. Higher up the hill and higher up the social scale, the *Glenridge Hotel*, once the home of the Pocock family, advertised attractions for Virginia Water's new middle class. The hotel planned to hold a Jubilee tennis tournament followed by a dinner and dance.[58]

George V died less than a year after the celebrations and his eldest son was proclaimed Edward VIII in January 1936. With the new king determined to marry Wallis Simpson, a twice-divorced American woman,

102 *Day-trippers enjoying Virginia Water.*

however, a constitutional crisis erupted. The opinion of government, Church, Commonwealth and many ordinary people that such a marriage was unsuitable, prevailed. Edward made his abdication broadcast from Fort Belvedere on 11 December and left for France. The responsibilities of monarchy fell to his brother, George V's second son, formerly the Duke of York. As George VI he was crowned king with his consort, Queen Elizabeth, on 12 May 1937. The Southern Railway ran special trains to London on the day, beginning as early as two in the morning so that as many people as possible could line the processional route and share in the celebrations.[59]

Royal Holloway College should have celebrated its Golden Jubilee in 1936 but the national crisis delayed the event. Instead, Queen Mary visited the college in October 1937, accompanied by her sister-in-law, Princess Alice of Athlone, the newly appointed chairman of the college governors, to plant an oak tree in commemoration.[60]

In Virginia Water the building development that had begun slowly in the 1920s received a new impetus in the 1930s. So many new private houses were erected that Egham's Rates' Clerk must have been hard pushed to keep up with all the new assessments there and elsewhere. In 1936 more cottages for Crown employees were built at Egham Wick, Virginia Water and Cumberland Gate. Virginia Water got its very first council houses, built between the hamlets of Trumps Green and Knowle Hill. The first occupants moved in just as the Second World War was about to begin.[61]

Preparations for war, as far as the general population was concerned, had begun in 1937, with lectures on air raid precautions and first aid being organised in school halls. These continued into 1938, when anti-gas instruction was added to the syllabus. In the summer of 1939 schoolchildren practised how quickly they could evacuate their building and regularly checked their gasmasks. On 1 September the government arranged for children in potentially dangerous areas to be evacuated to places of safety and Egham, Virginia Water and cottages in the park took in evacuees initially from London.[62] The Second World War began two days later.

The War Office was actively looking for large properties in rural areas for military use. Fort Belvedere, unused since Edward VIII's departure, was considered too small. Instead, the fort became the headquarters of the Local Defence Volunteers, later known as the Home Guard. On the London Road the War Office requisitioned the mansion, Woodlee, the land of which adjoined the Clockcase, and established a mechanisation unit there. There was adequate space and plenty of tree cover to enable the testing, storing and servicing of armoured vehicles to take place unseen. By the end of 1943 this was discontinued and the estate transferred to the Ministry of Labour & National Service. Woodlee became 'a residence and hutted hostel' for the rehabilitation of wounded servicemen. Queenswood, the neighbouring estate to Woodlee on the London Road, became the main mess for soldiers working in the Egham Wick area.[63] At Egham Wick two mansions in Wick

Road, Sandylands and Bellefields, were also requisitioned, the latter being used as a headquarters for the Royal Corps of Signals after having short-wave masts erected there.[64]

Ashleigh, on Bakeham Lane, one of the Farlow mansions, was empty at the outbreak of war and immediately requisitioned by the local council. As 'a safe area', taking in evacuees not only from London but also from the south coast, Egham needed to use all available accommodation.[65]

In the park Virginia Water was drained to confuse enemy navigators but the streams still flowed in their habitual beds, leaving a ghostly image of the lake. Engineers were able to check the penstock thoroughly for structural damage and rectify the decay of a century and a half.[66] In time a new beauty was created in the bed of the lake as rushes flowered in profusion and tree saplings took root in the damp soil.[67]

In August 1940 the war began in earnest for the civilian population. German bombers began their systematic bombing of the capital and other important strategic targets. The Battle of Britain was being fought in the skies over south-east England. Leslie Vaughan worked as draughtsman and later as Head Clerk in the Crown Estate Office in the park and also served as a Local Defence Volunteer. During the war, while living at the Clockcase with his family, he recorded the raids and other events in his diary. Bombs fell in and all around the park, on Wentworth, Sunningdale, Shrubs Hill, Egham and Thorpe. Mostly they fell in open country and left a crater or at worst a fire but there were inevitably some casualties.[68]

At lunchtime on 4 September, no air-raid warning having sounded, the children of St Ann's Heath School were enjoying a break in the playground. Suddenly they saw German bombers diving towards the south-east. Explosions were heard and the teachers hurried the children inside.[69] They had witnessed the start of the attack on Vickers Aviation Ltd's aircraft

103 *Inspecting a bomb crater somewhere in the Egham Urban District.*

factory at Weybridge, where 83 workers were killed and many more seriously injured.[70] The raid was calamitous and, as a result, a policy of establishing smaller, more inconspicuous units was devised and a Vickers factory was set up in the obscurity of Egham Wick.

So routine did the raids become that a night without a warning was noteworthy: Leslie Vaughan reported on 26 September the first undisturbed night for many weeks. It was a false dawn. The end of September and the beginning of October were especially bad. A German Messerschmitt 109 fighter plane was brought down near Queen Anne's Gate, numerous high explosive and incendiary bombs fell on the park and the Belvedere woods were set alight. Christchurch School suffered broken windows and had to close the following day. In April 1941 a German bomber crashed in the park, killing two of its crew and injuring two others.[71]

A wartime use was finally found for Fort Belvedere when, at the beginning of 1941, the Commissioners for Crown Lands evacuated their London office and established themselves at Shrubs Hill. It was felt that no camouflage was required there, except to hide the cars: the enemy might become suspicious of what the fort was being used for if it suddenly 'disappeared'.[72] There was more activity at the Clockcase with soldiers digging in Rhododendron Ride to make a hard surface for tanks. As at Woodlee, the canopy of trees provided a natural cover for the parking of military vehicles.[73]

The nation was urged to dig for victory and in 1941 George VI ordered that Norfolk Farm in Windsor Great Park should be recreated, it having been allowed to return to parkland 70 years previously. The deer were culled and the remainder moved to a confined area, driven by 800 soldiers in a scene reminiscent of that described by Thomas Love Peacock in 1817. In all, 2,000 acres of parkland were put under cultivation.[74]

In the autumn of 1941 the local Home Guard detachment moved its headquarters from Fort Belvedere to the Vickers factory at Egham Wick. The factory canteen soon became a centre for recreational activities for park and factory workers alike, in October 1942 providing a harvest supper for 260 people.[75]

The park, as in the First World War, played host to a variety of military personnel. The airstrip at Smith's Lawn, made for the use of Edward VIII, was enlarged to accommodate 25 men and 14 Dakotas of the American Air Force. Later the RAF set up a training camp there.[76]

In July and August 1943 Virginia Water, from Blacknest to Wick Bridge, became a prohibited area. A temporary camp was set up so that the army could carry out secret training activities on the bed of the lake. Repair work that was underway at the penstock had to be suspended until military operations were complete. Little more than a year later, amphibious tanks underwent trials at the lake and after some days of rehearsal gave a demonstration of their effectiveness. It was, however, forbidden for the vehicles to go over the reconstructed penstock.[77]

Early in 1944 there was renewed aerial activity over south-east England. At the end of February bombs fell at Egham Wick and Tite Hill. A house on Wentworth was hit and its occupants killed. Windows were broken as far away as the Clockcase. In June rumour was rife as the civilian population was subject to a new and frighteningly unpredictable threat: flying bombs, V1s, popularly known as 'doodlebugs', Nazi Germany's revenge weapon for the successful Allied landings in Normandy the previous week. Part of the *Bells of Ouseley* inn at Old Windsor was destroyed, killing two people; another doodlebug fell in the Clockcase woods near the A30, badly damaging Woodlee Lodge. An even more deadly weapon, the V2—a jet-propelled missile—was launched on south-east England in September. One landed near the Obelisk in the park. The civilian population could not relax until Allied forces finally captured all the launch sites in northern Europe. Only then could the Home Guard stand down.[78]

Victory in Europe was in sight and in the summer of 1945 informal street parties were held throughout the district. The cessation of hostilities was finally celebrated when the war against Japan was concluded later in the year. A church parade was held at Christ Church in November with the salute being taken by returned prisoners of war. In the afternoon a concert was given at the Woodlee Rehabilitation Centre with the theme of 'Thanksgiving for Peace', ending with a tribute to the United Nations.[79]

Most of the Vickers factory sheds at Egham Wick were speedily demolished in the summer of 1945. The canteen building, however, was carefully dismantled and rebuilt in the village in the park to become a recreational centre for the community under a new name—York Hall.[80]

104 *Some members of the Virginia Water Home Guard outside the* Rose & Olive Branch, *Callow Hill, c.1940.*

The mansions requisitioned by the War Office were returned to their former occupiers, sometimes a little worse for wear. The Ministry of Labour, however, retained Woodlee and it was officially opened in December 1946 by the Foreign Secretary, Ernest Bevin, as a rehabilitation centre. Bevin had planned the project as wartime Minister of Labour and expressed the government's determination to look after those who had sustained a disability as a result of their war service rather than leave the task to charitable organisations, as had been the situation after the First World War.[81] The centre was the first of its kind in the country and provided accommodation for disabled servicemen and civilians 'in the difficult and often disheartening period between convalescence and new employment'. During their one to three months' stay the men toned up physically, brushed up their basic education and received vocational training. They were given free board and lodging and an allowance of 30s. a week for a married man and 20s. for a single man.[82] Once a fortnight girls from Egham went up to Woodlee on the Aldershot bus to attend a dance at the centre.[83] The post-war task of rebuilding wounded men's careers and rebuilding an exhausted country had begun.

There was considerable interest in the post-war future of the lake and local people wanted to have their say. It was known that George VI's main interest in the park was in its potential for recreation and horticulture rather than in hunting and shooting. Local newspapers considered that swimming for the general public should be allowed when the lake was refilled and suggested that the king favoured the idea.[84] In addition, with the royal boats removed from the lake in the 1930s, there was an opportunity, it was argued, for everyone to enjoy pleasure boating. Tom Taylor & Sons, boat-builders of Staines, asked if they could rent the boating and fishing rights. The depth of the lake—27ft in places—and the profusion of waterweed, however, make Virginia Water too dangerous a place for watersports. Moreover, the thicket of sapling trees that had grown up in the empty bed of the lake provided an additional hazard. There was no alternative but for Sir Eric Savill to recommend that all such applications be refused.[85]

Returning the lake to its former glory brought its own problems. The state of the waterfalls continued to cause concern: as the lake slowly refilled, weaknesses were revealed and torrents of water occasionally burst through. The engineers and contractors were handicapped by the fact that no plans or records of the original construction could be found. While work was underway, no water was allowed over the cascade for fear of flooding Thorpe and Chertsey. Cavities in the banks of the lake, caused by being dried out for so long, also had to be repaired.[86] It was not until 1948 that the local paper could report that the lake was filling up again.

With park employees returning from war service, work could resume at the woodland garden at Egham Wick. Extensive propagating houses and a new plant nursery of several acres would help realise the next phase of the horticultural expansion of Windsor Great Park, the creation of the Valley

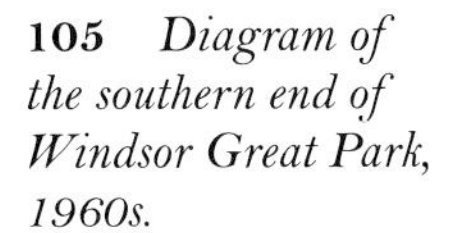

105 *Diagram of the southern end of Windsor Great Park, 1960s.*

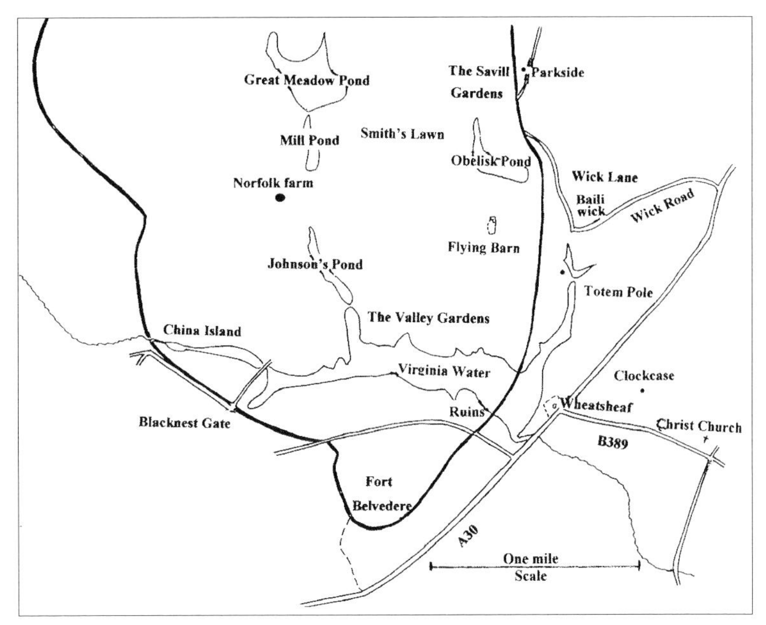

Gardens, which would be freely open to the public. The most ambitious redesigning and planting scheme since John Robinson had redeveloped the Wick branch of the lake for George III was about to take place on the north bank of the lake. As in the 18th century, tons of earth had to be moved to provide new valleys and sweeping slopes. Sir Eric Savill's men had the advantage of earth-moving machinery but much of the basic work was very similar to that of the 18th century. Scrub trees and bracken had to be removed, paths laid and forest trees retained to provide vistas and shade. Once more many trees and shrubs were planted and the Valley Gardens began to take shape.[87] Pride of place was given to shrubs that would thrive in the natural acidic soil of the area: rhododendrons and magnolias in the main arena, while the steep Punch Bowl was to become a spectacular amphitheatre for azaleas.[88] Like his predecessors in office, Sir Eric was assiduous in maintaining the status and standard of living of his employees. He emphasised particularly the exceptional skills required by his foreman in Windsor Great Park, Thomas Hope Findlay, in carrying out the grand new horticultural design.[89]

It was an exciting, though exhausting, time for the men. They worked from 7.30 a.m. to 5 p.m. and till noon on Saturdays, with a break at 10 a.m. and half an hour for lunch. Their wages were around £4 10s. a week with extra for tea, sugar and cheese and there was also a cycle allowance. The basic workforce was a team of six men: Bill Hunt, Jack Bowden, Bill Barrie, Ted Hancock, Arthur Wakely and George Dibley. In the 1950s 2,000 rhododendron plants were removed from Tower Court at Ascot to the north bank of the lake. George Dibley described the hard work involved in digging out and transporting mature plants, often with a root ball of 6ft across, and the subsequent replanting at Virginia Water.[90]

106 *Valley Gardens under construction: the team lowering a plant into its new home, 1950s, photograph by R.W. End.*

To provide colour and interest throughout the year, other trees and shrubs were planted—an intermingling of winter flowering shrubs and of camellias, hydrangeas and Japanese maples. Like John Robinson, Sir Eric cultivated the natural look: there were to be no straight lines or regimental planting.[91] New features were added to the garden at Egham Wick. In 1951 a wall was built on its northern boundary from bricks collected from bombsites in London. This would provide support and shelter for climbing plants. In the same year George VI decreed that in future the garden should be known as the Savill Garden in honour of its creator, Sir Eric. In 1952 the Crown Estate Commissioners decided to charge 1s. for admission to the garden.[92]

In 1958 the southern end of the park received its most exotic adornment. A 100ft totem pole, cut from a single tree, was given to Queen Elizabeth II to mark the centenary of British Colombia. The totem pole is carved in the authentic style of the tribes and clans inhabiting the northern part of Vancouver Island. It was erected at the eastern end of the lake by the 22nd Field Engineer Regiment. In order to accommodate the totem pole before it was set up in the park, a very large lay-by had to be constructed on the old Great Western Road, the present A30.[93]

Despite the post-war building boom, the village of Virginia Water retained much of its rural character. Buildings were never allowed to dominate the landscape: all the new properties had moderate to large gardens; forest trees were retained wherever possible along the main roads and even in some gardens, while new roads were planted with flowering trees and shrubs. Flowing through the district from the lake, the River Bourne provides a natural oasis where no building can take place.

Knowle Grove, once Crown forest, had been sold in 1919 and its valuable deposits of sand extracted. When the mineral reserves were exhausted,

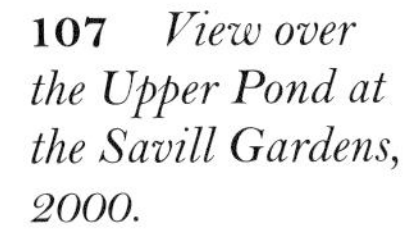

107 *View over the Upper Pond at the Savill Gardens, 2000.*

permission was given for building development to take place on the land. Scrub woodland, much of it silver birch, was cleared in 1954 to make way for roads and the building of more houses. In Knowle Grove and elsewhere, small havens of land were left to nature or planted with shrubs—in fact everything possible was done to please 'the discerning purchaser'.[94]

The mansions built on Crown land in the 19th century suffered varied fortunes but all the plots eventually passed into freehold ownership. There was some anxiety among Crown leaseholders in the 1950s about the covenants on their properties. These prevented them from carrying on any trade or business on site and also restricted building development. The owners of Park House successfully argued in 1955 that such a covenant was by then out of date.[95] The following year Production Engineering Consulting bought the property and established a training school on the site. In 1987 a purpose-built office block was built.[96] At Egham Wick, Parkside, Sandylands and Bellefields survive as private residences.

Opposite the park on the London Road, by the 20th milestone, Woodlee, John King Farlow's mansion, ceased to be

108 *Totem pole near Wick Ponds, 1966, photograph by Donald Bostock.*

109 *Housing development at Knowle Grove, 1954, photograph by E.W. Rawnsley.*

a rehabilitation centre in 1992. It was sold by the Employment Services in 1994 and became an American Community School. The neighbouring house, Queenswood, never recovered from its military occupation in the Second World War. As its Crown lease came to an end in the late 1960s, it fell into dereliction and was demolished.[97] St David's School for Girls, once Coxen's mansion, Bendemere, closed in the 1960s. The building was later so damaged by fire that it too was pulled down. In 1997 its site, being close to the urban area of Englefield Green, was released for building development. Sixty-one luxurious houses and apartments, protected by electronic gates, have since been constructed on the 11-acre estate.[98] Along Bakeham Lane, Bakeham House, built in the Victorian era, as well as the old farmhouse, renamed Little St Anne's, remain in private hands. Glenwood, another mansion built by John King Farlow, was converted into eight apartments in the early 1960s and the owners acquired the site's freehold.[99] A smaller mansion, Ashleigh, continued to be used for housing the homeless after the war. Like its neighbour, Ulverscroft, it has been reconstructed in the building extravaganza of the early 21st century. Two of the Bakeham Lane mansions received a new lease of life in the 1960s when they were acquired by nearby Royal Holloway College, then in the process of expansion. Alderhurst housed the Zoology Department until 1991 when the site was sold to the International Mycological Institute. Huntersdale, with 21 acres of adjacent woodland, became an ideal centre for the Botany Department and later for the Institute for Environmental Studies.[100]

Princess Alice, Countess of Athlone, resumed her close working relationship with Royal Holloway College after the war, becoming Chairman of the College Council, a task she carried out with energy and charm. Another royal connection was made in 1955 when Queen Elizabeth, The Queen Mother, succeeded the Earl of Athlone as Chancellor of London University and in that capacity often visited her local college.[101] In 1986, when the college celebrated the centenary of its foundation, it was fitting that the reigning monarch joined staff and students to celebrate the occasion. Her Majesty joked with students that 100 years ago, in a time of very different architectural taste, her great-great-grandmother, Queen Victoria, had found the college chapel 'gaudy'. The energy and vision of Royal Holloway's founder, however, were still in evidence in the extraordinary changes that had taken place on the campus in the 1970s and '80s.[102]

The Queen Mother had a special relationship with the area south and east of Windsor Great Park as she often stayed at Royal Lodge, only a short drive from Bishopsgate. This residence, once a favourite home of George IV, had been granted to her and her husband in the 1930s and had been a welcome refuge for them from wartime duty in London. When she was at Royal Lodge the Queen Mother often made informal visits to the Egham area and, as Princess Christian had once done, endeared herself to her neighbours by her interest in and support for small community-based charities. In December 1980, for example, the Queen Mother inaugurated the newly refurbished Egham Museum and then moved on to the Egham Hospital, formerly the Cottage Hospital, at Englefield Green to open a lift, funded by the 'Friends' of the hospital. Her visit closely mirrored one made by Princess Christian to the same hospital at the beginning of the 20th century.[103] A few years later the Queen Mother explained her interest in the vicinage: 'As a neighbour and living as I do so close to the village of Englefield Green, it gives me great pleasure to come here today.' The occasion was the opening of Queen Elizabeth House, The Queen Mother's Care Home, the successor to the Cottage Hospital.[104]

The Crown, once the chief landowner in Egham parish, no longer retains that position of influence, holding in the early 21st century only some open fields, laid to grass, between Bakeham Lane and London Road.[105] The two pieces of common land that William, Duke of Cumberland, took into the park in 1750, however, are still Crown property, but the buildings built as

110 *Wentworth Gate, London Road, c.2000, photograph by Hamptons International.*

vantage points on the elevated sites, Fort Belvedere and the Clockcase, are leased as private residences. The two houses adjoining the Clockcase have suffered differing fates. Hangmore still survives, having been divided into two residences in 1955. Glenridge became a country house hotel in the 1920s but by the 1970s was in a ruinous state and demolished. An attractive residential retirement complex was built on the site.[106]

At the same time as the Crown's ownership of land in Egham was on the decrease, more and more of the landscape around Virginia Water was opened to the public. What was once jealously guarded as a royal pleasure ground by the loyal servants of George IV is now enjoyed by walkers, cyclists, runners, dog-owners, birdwatchers, fishermen and families. The day-trippers that Henry Jennings, the licensee of the *Wheatsheaf* in the 1850s, hoped to attract now come in their millions.

As a tourist amenity and accountable to the Treasury, however, the area at the southern end of Windsor Great Park needs to attract even more visitors. In 2005, therefore, a marketing company representing the Crown Estate announced ambitious new plans for redevelopment at the Savill Garden at Egham Wick. A new visitors' centre, including restaurant and shop with exhibition and conference facilities, was planned. Its architecture would be revolutionary, 'a futuristic gateway to the Royal Landscape' in the words of the company. The most recent technology would be used to construct an undulating roof, incorporating four layers of interlocking English oak.[107] Nothing so striking had been built at the southern end of the park since the reign of George IV.

When it became clear, however, that further plans for the area included a children's playground, a Land Rover train to transport visitors, the fencing in of the Valley Gardens and a charge for admission, there was an immediate reaction from regular visitors, walkers and nature enthusiasts. Fear was expressed that the royal landscape was being turned into a theme park and an action group was set up to fight the proposals.[108] The most controversial aspect of the plan was the enclosure of the Valley Gardens, Sir Eric Savill's 'flowering forest'[109] of rhododendrons and azaleas on the northern bank of the lake, since its inception freely accessible to the public. It was recalled that it had been originally laid out as an open garden, where visitors could discover new vistas at every turn.[110] The Crown Estate justified the building of the fence on the grounds that it would prevent erosion and damage from an increasing population of deer and rabbits. This argument was refuted by academics who pointed out that the vast majority of plants in the Valley Gardens were unpalatable to deer and rabbits and had been selected for that very reason.[111] There were also concerns, more reluctantly expressed, that the gardens, containing as they did plant collections of national importance, were threatened by 'unmanaged' public access.[112] Strong feelings were expressed in the local papers and the activists themselves were accused of regarding Windsor Great Park as their own back garden rather than the queen's.[113]

Within a few weeks, however, the movement to keep the Valley Gardens accessible had caught the popular imagination and gained the backing of the local press, councillors, Members of Parliament and thousands of ordinary people. The campaigners gathered in Windsor Great Park, not as their ancestors had done in 1679 to harass keepers or kill deer, but to discuss the new plans with visitors and collect signatures for their petition that the Valley Gardens should remain open to all.[114]

By the end of April 2006, with the petition containing nearly 20,000 signatures, the Crown Estate agreed to defer the plans for the Valley Gardens for a few years. 'Public pressure', according to one newspaper, had prevailed. A spokesman conceded that, 'When people make their views known so strongly we should think again.'[115] Ordinary people had welcomed the opportunity in the 19th century to walk along the banks of Virginia Water and over the years to enjoy even more royal acres. The park that had once been the preserve of kings, where deer were paramount and the general public excluded, had become a people's pleasure ground. The people had established their right to be heard in matters concerning the park and, over the years, their own traditions on where they might roam.

Windsor Great Park no longer threatens to encroach on its neighbours; the time is long gone when it was the largest and most influential employer in the district. Its presence today is wholly beneficent, a valuable asset to any community. As Virginia Water becomes even more urbanised in the 21st century, with high-density building, smaller gardens and security fences replacing hedges, and with the village threatened with gravel-raising and a waste incinerator on its perimeters, the vast acres of Windsor Great Park are an increasingly welcome retreat, a tranquil landscape where over the years nature has been enhanced by the skill of the gardener.

111 *Virginia Water, winter 2007, photograph by Alan Bostock.*

Appendix I

Known owners and tenants of Wick manor

1545 John Worsopp
1564 Edward Worsopp and Edmund Hogame, merchants
William Russell, Keeper in the Great Park at Windsor—Value: £60
1617 Edward Anthony
Francis Anthony of London, Doctor of Physic
1619 Rented to George Mortimer, gentleman
1621 Onslow Winch and Richard Taylor of Lincoln's Inn—Value: £255 and London house
1624 John Fabian of Thorpe, gentleman—Value: £400
1638 Thomas Bennett of Great Fosters, Egham, gentleman (Part of manor)
1654 Richard Legh, of Enveild, Staffs., gentleman, John Phillips of New Inn and John Lyddialt of Woolaston, Staffs.—Value: £800
1655 George Billingshurst
1681 John Pratt of London, skinner and Peter Smith, of London, merchant
Thomas Detton of Chertsey, gentleman—Value: £500
1750 James Richards
Elizabeth Richards
1768 William Robert Jones of Egham, Clerk in Holy Orders and Elizabeth Richards Jones
1786 John Pitt for His Majesty King George III

(Compiled from PRO LR 2/190; SHC 2642 and EMT DOC 2256)

Known owners and occupiers of other properties at Wick

One tenement with barn, orchard, garden and three acres, near Wick farmhouse
1598 John Gallis of Darthford
William Gallis of Egham
1635 John Elliott of Clewath, husbandman
John Bramley of Egham, husbandman—Value: £53 15s.
Jeremy May (occupier)
1708 Marmaduke Bramley, son of Thomas Bramley
William Ventum of Egham, corn chandler—Value: £30 (part of property)
John Tindsley and Thomas Slann (occupiers)
1714 Andrew Mackason of Egham, butcher—Value: 29 14s.

One tenement with barns, orchard, garden and three plots of pasture (3.5 acres)
1685 John Fabian, the younger
Richard Frame and --- Wheatley (occupiers)
Ann Fabian
Arnold Miles, of Chertsey, currier
1697 Henry Newbury of Stoke
1728 Andrew Mackason of Egham, butcher

One cottage, barn and one rood of land
n/k Thomas Haywood
Stephen Frimley
1697 John Hanks of Egham, carpenter

One cottage
1695 Henry Field (occupier)
John Field (occupier)

(Compiled from PRO CRES 38/1932 and 1929; SHC 2355/1/5/19/23 and 51, 1201/13, 2642/14/14 and 548/2/42 A-C)

Appendix II

The Sanders, alias Goodwin, family and the land at Harpesford

In June 1666 William Slanne surrendered to the manor of Broomhall a close of land containing one acre 'more or less' called Harpers Ford at Park Corner, Egham. John Sanders, alias Goodwin, was admitted in his place. Members of the Sanders/Goodwin family had acquired other lands in Egham in 1556 when John Hypysley made over 37 acres to them and William Reynolles.

The family flourished in Egham in the late 16th and early 17th century, a Robert Goodwyne being listed in a muster roll in 1569 as 'a bill man of ye best sort'. Two members of the family appear in the Lay Subsidy Assessment of 1593, a tax to replenish the exchequer after the expenses of fighting the Armada. Thomas Sanders paid 21s. 4d. on goods worth £8, while Robert paid 10s. 4d. on goods worth £4.

The Sanders/Goodwin family seems to have lived in Egham Hythe; their daughters married well and they were substantial craftsmen—basket-makers, bargemen, watermen and carpenters. They were closely connected with other branches of the family in Staines.

The lessees of Harpesford 1666-1783

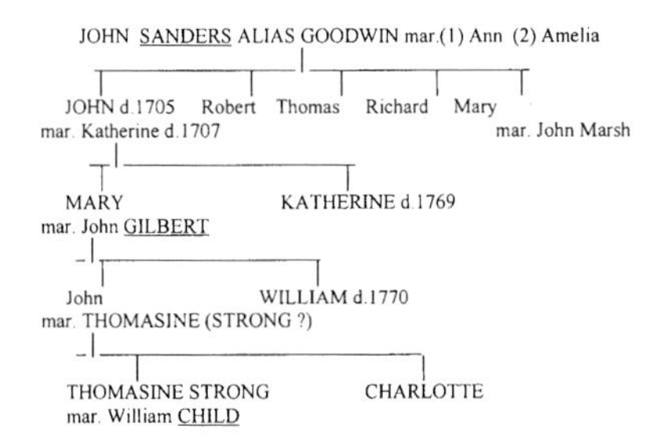

The John Sanders admitted to the Virginia Water lands had moved to London and was a coach-maker. The first John appeared again at the Manor Court of Broomhall in 1669 to include his four sons in the admission, in 1673 to include his wife, Ann, and to let it be known that they had 'lately erected' a house on the one acre at Harpesford. In 1678 he was readmitted with his second wife, Amelia.

The second John had no sons and, apart from bequests to his daughters, Mary and Katherine, and his brothers, Thomas and Richard, left the remainder of his estate to his wife, Katherine, on his death in 1705. She in turn bequeathed everything to their daughters, who were admitted to the Harpesford land in 1707. Mary married John Gilbert, by whom she had two sons, John and William. When Mary died intestate, Katherine became the sole legatee.

By her will, proved in 1769, she left Harpesford in trust for any children of her nephew, William Gilbert, and for Thomasine Gilbert, daughter of her deceased nephew, John Gilbert. William Gilbert died unmarried the following year, leaving his share to his brother's widow.

By 1775 the sole heiresses were Katherine's great nieces, Thomasine Strong Gilbert, married to William Child, coach-harness maker of St Giles, London, and Thomasine's younger sister, Charlotte. The latter was aged only 14 and William Child was her guardian. On her surrender of the Broomhall land at a special Court Baron in 1785 Thomasine was interviewed apart from her husband and was presumably able to testify her direct descent from John and Katherine Sanders.

(Compiled from: PRO CRES 38/1932 and LR 3.65/9; St John's College Cambridge, Mr Doyley's Book; SHC 86/10/35, SRO Vol. XIX No. 903; Turner pp.100 and 103 and Egham Parish Registers)

APPENDIX III

The fields of Wick Farm 1782

Lands ofthe Manor or Reputed Manor ofEgham Wick:

Arable Fields:

Nine-Acre Close
Eight-Acre Close
Walnut Tree Six Acres
Ten-Acre Close
Six-Acre Close
Hyde One Close
Colts Hill Close
Arable Fields
Cottage Field Close

Colts Hill Meadow Close
Rushy Brook—Two Closes
Black Brook Close
Wick Heath Coppice
Long Slip Close — Containing Together 86 acres

A Messuage with the Barns, Stables and other Outhouses, Yards, Gardens and Orchards belonging, called Egham Wick Manor House.

And all those several Closes, Inclosures and Parcels of Land belonging thereto: Viz:-

	A. R. P.
Home Meadow Close and House Meadow Close	01-1-29
Grubbs Grove and Oatfield Close (arable)	02-2-22
And a Piece Adjoining	02-0-06
Hithes and Middle Running—Two Closes (arable)	
And the Runnings—Two Closes together	10-2-18
Rickyard Close (arable)	00-2-16
Bramblebys—Two Closes (meadow)	03-0-34
Part of Warren Hill Field Close	01-1-33
Part of Shoulder of Mutton	00-3-32
Field Close	2 [*sic*]
Containing Together:	23-1-04
(Correction in red) Should be:	22-2-32
Great Hides	07-3-23
Little Hides	06-0-31

(Lately Part of Wick Farm, given to John Ashby in exchange)

(Based on PRO CRES 35/146)

Appendix IV

ARTIFICERS AND LABOURERS WORKING IN WINDSOR GREAT PARK, MARCH 1791

Surname	Christian name	Age	Family	Residence	Occupation	Service
Aldridge	Robert	21	single	At the Lodge	Mixed work	-
Bail	Thomas	-	-	Near the Lodge	Servant to Mr Sandby	-
Bateman	John	38	wife only	Sunning Hill	Mixed work	5yr
Beauchamp	Richard	30	wife & 1 child	Sunning Hill	Mixed work	21yr
Bignall	Thomas	-	-	Bishops Gate	Brick maker	-
Blay	Richard	21	wife & 1 child	Egham Wick	Carrier	1yr
Booth	William	54	wife & 2 children	Beachnest(sic)	Mixed work	-
Bradley	Thomas	43	wife & 5 children	At the Spittle	Haymaker & Foreman	22yr
Brown	Thomas	26	wife & 2 children	Sunning Hill	Mixed work	1yr
Burcher	George	33	single	Bishops Gate	Joiner	20yr
Burcher	John	71	-	Bishops Gate	Master carpenter	35yr
Burrett	Benjamin	20	single	Englefield Green	Mixed work	7yr
Burrett	Thomas	25	wife & 2 children	Englefield Green	Mixed work	10yr
Cam	Thomas	48	wife & 2 children	Chaw Lane Gate	Sawyer	22yr
Chase	Daniel	47	wife & 8 children	Egham Wick	In the rides	13yr
Chase	George	12	boy	Egham Wick	Weeder	3yr
Coster	William	-	-	At the Lodge	Stable keeper	-
Dewes	Robert	62	wife & ? children	Sunning Hill	Superannuated has 5sh. a week-	
Dewley	Richard	50	wife & 3 children	Clewer	Mixed work	30yr
Dormer	John	40	wife only	Winkfield	Mixed work	6yr
Eades	John	28	wife & 3 children	Egham Wick	Mixed work	3yr
Finch	James	53	wife & 1 child	Egham Wick	Labourer	29yr
Finch	Mary	50	married woman	Egham Wick	Weeder	21yr
Fisher	John	37	wife & 4 children	Egham Hill	Mixed work	4yr
Floyd	Richard	50	single	At the Lodge	Carter	8yr
Frost	[Joseph]	-	single	At the Lodge	Farmer	-
Godfrey	Jeremiah	23	wife & 2 children	Englefield Green	Mower	-
Godfrey	John	30	wife & 3 children	Winkfield	Mixed work	4yr
Goodchild	William	25	single	Sunning Hill	In the rides	4yr
Gray	Thomas	22	single	Englefield Green	Mixed work	1yr
Griffith	Thomas	52	wife & 2 children	Near Sand Pit Gate	Mixed work	-
Harris	Thomas	60	wife & 3 children	Sunning Hill	Mixed work	34yr
Herbert	James	28	wife & 1 child	Windsor	Hay binder	14yr
Hicks	John	35	single	Cragg's Hole	Mixed work	-
Hodges	William	50	wife & 1 child	Bishop's Gate	Tree nailer	-
Humphreys	John	27	wife & 1 child	Englefield Green	Labourer	1yr
Humphreys	Thomas	-	-	In the Forest	Mole catcher	-
Jackman	James	18	single	At the Lodge	Mixed work	-
Jackson	Elizabeth	50	widow & 4 children	Near the Garden	Weeder	6yr
Johnson	John	43	wife & 5 children	Brook's Corner	Shepherd	3yr
King	John	46	wife & 6 children remaining of 17	Egham Wick	Labourer	18yr
King	William	28	single	Egham Wick	Labourer	16yr
Lenham	William	50	-	Near Barretts Lodge	Boatman	-
Long	John	37	no wife but 3 children	At the Lodge	Carter	24yr
Mayham	William	26	single	In the Garden	Foreman	4yr
Morris	William	22	wife & 1 child	Englefield Green	Mixed work	-
Payne	Thomas	40	wife & 3 children	Egham Wick	Mixed work	16yr
Pike	John	30	single	Egham Wick	Labourer	2yr
Priestwood	Paul	38	single	At the Lodge	Mixed work	-
Ride	Samuel	52	single	Egham Wick	Labourer	3yr
Roper	John	30	single	At the Lodge	Mixed work	-
Saw	Thomas	50	wife & 5 children	Cragg's Hole	Chaff-cutter	20yr
Sayers	John	42	wife & 3 children	Winkfield	Mixed work	4yr
Slade	Jonathan	20	single	In the Garden	In melon ground	-
Smith	John	21	wife only	Bishop Gate	Mixed work	3yr
Smith	Samuel	40	single	Winkfield	Mixed work	17yr
Smith	William	28	single	Winkfield	Mixed work	15yr
Spring	Michael	23	single	In the Garden	Fruit carrier	3yr
Spring	Peter	22	single	Bishop's Gate	In hot house	1yr
Starling	William	37	wife & 2 children	In the Garden	Gardener	-
Stevens	Daniel	40	wife & 6 children	Near Sand Pit Gate	Carter	13yr
Stroud	William	30	wife & 1 child	Near Sand Pit Gate	Butcher	2yr
Sutton	William	21	single	Bishop's Gate	Labourer	1yr
Taylor	Richard	22	single	Near the Garden	Labourer	1yr
Taylor	Thomas	60	wife & 2 children	Sunning Hill	Mixed work	42yr
Taylor	Thomas	50	wife only	Sunning Hill	Sawyer	11yr
Tellis	Thomas	43	wife & 6 children	Egham	Mixed work	19yr
Terry	John	27	wife only	Egham Hill	Mixed work	5yr
Thackery	William	60	wife & 1 child	Brocks Corner	Labourer	6yr
Tilts	William	38	wife only	Sunning Hill	Ox carter	4yr
Tindall	John	47	wife & 6 children	Englefield Green	Labourer	13yr
Tindall	Robert	17	single	Egham Wick	Carter	3yr
Tirrett	John	33	wife & 2 children	Winkfield	Carpenter	8yr
Walker	John	41	wife & 3 children	Englefield Green	Wheelwright	21yr
Watts	Richard	35	widower & 1 child	At the Lodge	Mixed work	22yr
Wood	Jonathan	21	single	Near the Garden	In melon ground	-

From vol. 1 of Nathaniel Kent's *Journal of Progressive Improvements in Windsor Great park 1791*, in the Royal Library, Windsor Castle. By gracious permission of Her Majesty The Queen

APPENDIX V

The parish boundaries of Christ Church, Virginia Water

> From the obelisk in the Great Park to the point of the triangle on the North side of the Great Western Road which is opposite to Bakeham Lane; from thence crossing the Great Western Road to the cluster of cottages called Pruen [Prune] Hill; from thence running parallel with a Bye road through Rusham to Stroude until it reaches the farm occupied by Mr Deane [Whitehall Farm], from thence it takes nearly a straight line to the junction of the road from Trumps Mill with that from Thorpe; thence taking the same line as the boundary of the [Egham] parish to the bend towards the North beyond lower Portnall Farm [Warren Farm]; from whence it passes to the twenty-second mile stone on the Great Western Road and taking a circuit so as to exclude the Belvidere [Fort Belvedere] reaches the point where the [Egham] Parish Boundary crosses the Virginia Water in the Park.

(From the first Baptismal Register of Christ Church, Virginia Water, 4 March 1839)

APPENDIX VI

Selection of maps consulted (in chronological order)

Survey of the Honour of Windsor, John Norden (1607) (Reproduced in *The History of Windsor Great Park & Windsor Forest* (1864), William Menzies)
Review of the Great Park called Windsor Great Park (1662) (RL RCIN 711290
The Road from London to the Land's End, John Ogilby (1671-5)
Plan of Windsor Forest, Charles Bridgeman (PRO MR1/279) (1720)
Plan of the Great Park, John Vardy (PRO MR1/280) (1750)
Surveys of Surrey & Berkshire, John Rocque (1752)
A New & Accurate Description of all the Direct & Principal Crossroads in Great Britain, Daniel Paterson (1771)
Plan showing land taken into Windsor Great Park (PRO MPEI/1493) (*c.*1780)
Plan of Virginia Water, Bassett (PRO MR1/698) (1788)
Plan of Windsor Forest, William Faden (PRO MR1/687) (1788-91)
Plan of the Old Road from the Western Turnpike Road to Priests Hill, Windsor (SHC QS 2/6 1790 p.27/2) (1789)
Plan of the Parish of Egham, William Crosley (SAOCS & EMT M656 copy) (1790)
Part of Virginia Water with adjacent portions of Windsor Great Park (PRO MPE1/565) (1798)
Plan of the Manor of Egham, Abraham & William Driver (SAOCS & EMT M669 copy) (1802-5)
Inclosure Map of the Parish of Egham (EMT M73) (1817)
Plan of the Parish of Egham, William Sherborn (EMT M42 copy) (1841)
Plan of the Parish of Egham, May & Collins (PRO MR1/679 & EMT M49 copy) (1856)
Ordnance Survey Maps (1868-present)

Endnotes

Abbreviations used:

CPR	Calendar Patent Rolls
Eg&StN	*Egham & Staines News*
EMT	Egham Museum Trust
LMA	London Metropolitan Archives
PRO	Public Record Office (The National Archives)
SAOCS	The Sidney Oliver Charitable Settlement
SHC	Surrey History Centre
SRS	*Surrey Record Society*
SyAS	Surrey Archaeological Society
SyAC:	Surrey Archaeological Collections
VCH	*The Victoria History of the County of Surrey*
W&EE	*Windsor & Eton Express*

Chapter One: From Forest and Waste to Hamlets and a Turnpike Road: 12th to mid-18th centuries

1. 'St Ann's Heath School [excavations]', *Connection, the Parish Magazine of Christ Church, Virginia Water* (hereafter *Connection*), May 2007, p.9.
2. Hunt, Roger, *Hidden Depths: An Archaeological Exploration of Surrey's Past* (2002), p.53.
3. Welsh, Thomas C., 'The Devil's Highway', *Surrey Archaeological Society Bulletins* (January 1982), pp.2-3, (June/July 1982), p.3.
4. Gover, J.E.B., Mawer, A. and Stenton, F.M., *The Place Names of Surrey* (1934), pp.119, 121 and 124.
5. *VCH*, vol. 3 (1911), p.404 and SHC 86/10/12.
6. Barnes, Patricia (ed.), 'The Chertsey Abbey Cartularies (concluded)', *SRS*, vol. 12, vol. 2, part 2 (1963) 1305, vii.
7. Blair, John, *Early Medieval Surrey* (1991), p.87.
8. Guiseppi, Montague S., Hudson, the Rev. William and Jenkinson, Hilary (eds.), 'The Chertsey Abbey Cartularies (continued)', *SRS*, vol. 12, vol. 2, part 1 (1958) 721 and 738.
9. Blair, pp.40-2.
10. Meeking, C.A.F. and Crook, David, 'The 1235 Surrey Eyre', *SRS*, vol. 31 (1979) (hereafter SRS, vol. 31) vol. 1, pp.222 and 235.
11. Turner, Frederic, *Egham, Surrey: A History of the Parish under Church and Crown* (1926), p.20.
12. Manning, the Rev. Owen and Bray, William, *The History and Antiquities of the County of Surrey (1804-14)*, vol. 1, p.v.
13. Magna Carta caps. 48 and 53.
14. Malden, H.E., *A History of Surrey* (1900), p.121 and Manning, the Rev. Owen and Bray, William, *The History and Antiquities of the County of Surrey (1804-14)*, vol. 1, pp.vi and vii.
15. Roberts, Jane, *Royal Landscape: the Gardens and Parks of Windsor Great Park* (1997), pp.9 and 249.
16. CPR (PRO) I Edward III, 26 December 1327.
17. *VCH Berkshire* (1907), vol. 2, p.80 and SRS, vol. 12, vol. 2, part 2, p.xlv.
18. Hughes, G.M., *The History of Windsor Forest, Sunningdale and the Great Park* (1890), p.345.
19. Turner, pp.56-7 and 59.
20. SRS, vol. 12, vol. 2, part 2, 1281 and 1282.
21. SRS, vol. 12, vol. 2, part 1, p.liv, CPR Elizabeth, 1569-72 and SHC 2642/14/45.
22. SRS, vol. 31, vol. 2, 431.
23. SRS, vol. 12, vol. 2, part 2, 1271.
24. SRS, vol.12, vol. 2, parts 1 and 2, 168 and 1425. Southbrooks sometimes appears as 'Sowsbrooks' on later plans.
25. CPR 3 Edward III.
26. Turner, p.53.
27. SRS, vol. 12, vol. 2, part 2, 1279.
28. *Ibid.* and 1305, iv.
29. SRS, vol. 12, vol. 2, part 1, 719.
30. Turner, p.226.
31. *Ibid.*, p.59.
32. SHC 2642/14/27.
33. PRO CRES 38/1932 and see Appendix I.
34. CPR Elizabeth, 14 March 1571-2.
35. SHC 86/10/12 and 16 and see Davis, R.G., 'A History of Portnall and Trotsworth' (University of London, Thesis in Local History, 1974).
36. Turner, pp.146-8.
37. *Ibid.*, p.147.
38. Turner, p.127.
39. EMT DOC 1396. The original document is Finch Hatton ms. 2256 in the Northampton Record Office
40. SHC 2642/14/16, 19 and 31.
41. Turner, p.165.
42. *Ibid.*, p.151 and Manning, the Rev. Owen and Bray, William, *The History and Antiquities of the County of Surrey (1804-14)*, vol. 1, p.xiii.
43. Turner, pp.151-2. William Purse was buried on 17 February 1656, being described as 'a very old Thefe'.
44. *Ibid.*, p.152.
45. Calendar of State Papers Domestic, Charles 1639-40, p.16.
46. Turner, pp.153-4.
47. *Ibid.*
48. PRO SP 28/178 and see Davis, Ron and Dorothy, 'The Civil War and its Aftermath: Egham and Thorpe, 1642-75', *Surrey History*, vol. 6, no. 5 (2003).
49. SHC 2642/14/31.
50. PRO SP 28/178, 194 and 334.
51. SHC 2642/14/20, 30 and 39.
52. PRO PROB/11/38 f.71 and SHC 1201/13.
53. Royal Library, 2075.
54. *Ibid.*

55. Laslett, Peter, *The World We Have Lost* (1971), pp.63 and 193.
56. Manning and Bray, vol. 3, p.lxxx-lxxxiii.
57. Turner, p.155.
58. PRO PC 2.68, pp.127 and 138-9.
59. *Ibid.*
60. SHC 2642/14/7 and 39. Dean was one of the alternative names given to Egham Common.
61. PRO PROB/11/38 f.71 and SHC 1201/13 and 548/2/42 A-C.
62. EMT DOC 4276, transcript of Henry Strode's diary. The original is in the Verney Family Archives, Claydon House Trust, 11/68.
63. SHC 2355/51/19/1/5 and 23.
64. PRO CRES 38/1929.
65. SHC 2642/14/14 and 25.
66. SAOCS and EMT Key to the Survey of the Parish of Egham (1790) and Pitt's Estate Act 1782.
67. Thompson, E.P., *Whigs and Hunters: The Origin of the Black Act* (1990), pp.30 and 62-3.
68. Hudson, Helen, *Cumberland Lodge* (1989), p.29.
69. Thompson, pp.65 and 98.
70. Roberts (1997), p.361.
71. PRO T 1/244.
72. *Ibid.* and Thompson, p.73 and note 4.
73. Thompson, p.75.
74. Thompson, pp.234-5.
75. Defoe, Daniel, *A Tour through the Whole Island of Great Britain* (reprint 1989), p.99.
76. Thompson, p.220.
77. SHC 548/2/42 A-C and PRO CRES 38/1930.
78. Manning and Bray, vol. 3, Appendix, p.l.
79. 1 George II cap.6.
80. *Ibid.*
81. LMA Acc. 809 Tp BED/1, May and June 1728.
82. *Ibid.*, 19 June and 5 August 1728.
83. *Ibid.*, May-August 1728.
84. PRO CRES 38/1930.
85. PRO MR 1/280, John Vardy's Plan of the Great Park (1750) and John Rocque's Surveys of Surrey & Berkshire (*c.*1752).
86. PRO CRES 38/1928.
87. PRO MPE 1/1403 and 565.

Chapter Two: The First Lake at Virginia Water and Life on the Great Western Road: 1746-76

1. Roberts, Jane, *Royal Landscape: the Gardens and Parks of Windsor Great Park* (1997), pp.9 and 409.
2. *Ibid.*, pp.375-6.
3. PRO MR 1/280.
4. PRO LR 3/67 and 69 and see SAOCS & EMT Key to the Survey of the Parish of Egham (1790).
5. South, Raymond, *Royal Lake: The Story of Virginia Water* (1983), pp.28-9.
6. Roberts, Jane, *Views of Windsor: Watercolours by Thomas and Paul Sandby* (1995), pp.17-18 and 20.
7. Roberts (1997), p.287.
8. Turner, Frederic, *Egham, Surrey: A History of the Parish under Church and Crown* (1926), p.215.
9. Rawlins, F.T., *Notes on Virginia Water* (1867), p.9 and South, pp.25-6.
10. Ward, W.R. (ed.), 'Parson and Parish in the 18th Century: Replies to Bishops' Visitations', *Surrey Record Society*, vol. 34, p.25 (hereafter SRS, vol. 34).
11. Hudson, Helen, *Cumberland Lodge* (1989), p.77.
12. Roberts (1997), p.43.
13. *Ibid.*, p.462.
14. *Ibid.*, p.462.
15. *Ibid.*, pp.393-4 and notes 20 and 21.
16. Manning, the Rev. Owen and Bray, William, *The History and Antiquities of the County of Surrey (1804-14)*, vol. 3, p.252.
17. *The Gentleman's Magazine*, December 1765.
18. Roberts (1997), pp.424-6.
19. LMA Acc. 809 Tp BED/1, July 1753 - March 1754.
20. Turner, pp.212-3.
21. Roberts (1997), p.449.
22. *Ibid.*, pp.487-8.
23. *Ibid.*, pp.397 and 487.
24. SAOCS & EMT Key and Survey of the Parish of Egham (1790).
25. LMA Acc. 809 Tp BED/4, 7 May 1763.
26. Worsley, Giles, 'Stiff but not Dull', *Country Life*, 25 July 1991. The author is grateful to Jane Roberts for this reference.
27. LMA Acc. 809 Tp BED/4, 20 May and 21 June 1763 and 16 January 1748.
28. *Ibid.*, 12 July 1763 and 9 July 1765.
29. South, p.26.
30. LMA Acc. 809 Tp BED/4, 11 April and 29 August 1764.
31. *Burke's Peerage* (1934).
32. Whitworth, Rex, *William Augustus, Duke of Cumberland: A Life* (1992), pp.205-23.
33. Turner, p.199.
34. Roberts (1997), pp.36-7 and note 44.
35. LMA Acc. 809 Tp BED/4, 11 October and 1 November 1763.
36. *Ibid.*, February 1764 to July 1766.
37. Roberts (1997), p.53.
38. LMA Acc. 809 Tp BED/4, June 1764 to July 1768.
39. PRO LR 3/67 1767.
40. SHC 2642/14/25.
41. SRS, vol. 34, p.107 and see Hill, Christopher, *The Century of Revolution: 1603-1713* (1972), pp.84-5.
42. Maryfield, Pamela, *Henry Strode's Charity* (1994), pp.27-38.
43. Memorial in Egham Parish Church; Manning, the Rev. Owen and Bray, William, *The History and Antiquities of the County of Surrey (1804-14)*, vol. 3, p.262.
44. Turner, pp.180-1.
45. PRO CRES 2/46, 4 March and 27 May 1768.
46. Delany, Mary, *The Autobiography and Correspondence of Mary Granville, Mrs Delany*, 2nd series (1862), vol. 1, p.159, 6 September 1768.
47. PRO CRES 2/57, 20 August 1807.
48. LMA Acc. 809 Tp BED/4, 24 October 1768 and 21 February 1769.
49. PRO CRES 38/1955.
50. Egham Parish Registers and Silverthorne, Elizabeth (ed.), 'The Deposition Book of Richard Wyatt, 1767-76', *SRS*, vol. 30 (1978), p.vii.
51. SRS, vol. 30, 218.
52. *Ibid.*, pp.xiii and 269.
53. *Ibid.*, p.269.
54. *Ibid.*, p.276.
55. *Ibid.*, p.270.
56. Aubrey, John, *The Natural History and Antiquities of the County of Surrey* (reprinted 1973), vol. 3, p.167.
57. Hughes, G.M., *The History of Windsor Forest, Sunningdale and the Great Park* (1890), pp.21-2.
58. SRS, vol. 30, pp.236 and 237.
59. *Ibid.*, p.235.
60. *Ibid.*, p.281.
61. *Ibid.*
62. *Ibid.*, pp.277, 278 and 281.
63. *Ibid.*, p.282.
64. Turner, p.222.
65. LMA Acc. 809 Tp BED/1, May-December 1752; January and July 1753.
66. SRS, vol. 30, p.xiii.
67. *Ibid.*, pp.146 and 147.
68. *Ibid.*, p.206.
69. *Ibid.*, pp.209-211.

Chapter Three: The Cost of Restoring 'an Ancient Piece of Water': 1778-1803

1. 22 George III cap. 9 (Pitt Estate Act 1782).
2. PRO CRES 38/1974.
3. PRO CRES 38/1932 and 38/1974. See also St John's College, Cambridge Archives.
4. PRO CRES 38/1932.
5. SHC 86/10/35.
6. PRO CRES 35/146 and SHC 86/18/43.
7. PRO CRES 38/1930.
8. SRS vol. 30, pp.vii-viii.
9. Turner, Frederic, *Egham, Surrey: A History of the Parish under Church and Crown* (1926), p.232.
10. Smith, J.T., *The Book for a Rainy Day*, 2nd edn. (1845), p.102.
11. PRO CRES 35/146.
12. *Ibid.*
13. PRO T 25/1, p.218.
14. PRO CRES 2/1204 and see Egham Parish Registers.
15. PRO CRES 2/60A, 20 March 1791.
16. PRO CRES 38/1928 and T 25/1, p.218.
17. PRO CRES 38/1928 and see Egham Parish Registers.
18. PRO CRES 35/146.
19. Roberts, Jane, *Royal Landscape: The Gardens and Parks of Windsor* (1997), pp.462-3.
20. Rawlins, F.T., *Notes on Virginia Water* (1867), p.10.
21. PRO T 25/1, pp.217 and 372-3 and see Roberts (1997), pp.470-5.
22. From Salmagundi's *A Miscellaneous Combination of Original Poetry* (1791). The author is indebted to Jane Roberts for this reference.
23. PRO CRES 2/57, 21 March 1792.
24. PRO CRES 2/57, 20 August 1807.
25. PRO T 25/1, pp.372-3 and 390.
26. Menzies, William, *The History of Windsor Great Park and Windsor Forest* (1864), p.27.
27. Smith, p.102.
28. Roberts (1997), p.400.
29. SAOCS & EMT Key and Survey of the Parish of Egham (1790).
30. PRO CRES 2/57, 7 October and 9 May 1788.
31. *Ibid.*, 19 and 20 May and 4 September 1788.
32. PRO CRES 2/58, 15 January and August 1789; 2/60A, 12 June 1789.
33. PRO CRES 2/58, November and December 1789 and see *Dictionary of National Biography.*
34. PRO CRES 2/57, 4 February 1789 and 19 August 1788.
35. *Ibid.*, 1 December 1788.
36. *Ibid.*, 11 March 1789.
37. *Ibid.*, 13 March 1789.
38. PRO CRES 2/54, pp.44, 46 and 54-6; 2/57, 29 November 1788.
39. PRO CRES 2/57, 4 and 25 February and 11 August 1789; 2/60A, 1 June 1789; 2/58, 19-20 August 1789 and 2/54.
40. PRO CRES 2/57, 9 September 1788 to 13 January 1789; 2/58, 17-24 October 1789.
41. PRO CRES 2/57, 1 and 15 December 1788 and 13 January 1789.
42. *Ibid.*, 25 December 1788.
43. *Ibid.*, 18 April 1788.
44. *Ibid.*, 10 October 1790.
45. *Ibid.*, 4 September 1788 and 6 and 11 March 1789.
46. PRO CRES 2/1207, 16 May 1789.
47. PRO CRES 2/60A, 1 and 14 June and 4 July 1789; 2/58, 16 July 1789 and 2/57, 8 August 1789.
48. PRO CRES 2/57, 20 September 1789.
49. PRO CRES 2/58, 17-24 October 1789.
50. SHC QS 2/6/1790, p.27/1.
51. PRO CRES 2/57, 30 August 1788.
52. SHC QS 2/6/1790, pp.27/1 and 27/2. See also QS 5/8/4 Easter 1790.
53. PRO CRES 2/54, p.30.
54. SHC QS 2/6/1790, pp.26/1 and 26/2.
55. PRO CRES 2/57, 30 August 1788.
56. *Ibid.* and 22 June 1792. See also SAOCS and EMT Key to the Survey of the Parish of Egham (1790).
57. PRO CRES 2/57, 22 June 1792 and 2/1207, 28 December 1799. In fact, the Nunn family had served the Crown since the reign of Charles II.
58. PRO CRES 2/57, 30 August 1788 and 22 June 1792 and 2/1234.
59. PRO CRES 2/57, 22 June 1792.
60. *Ibid.* and 30 August 1788 and PRO CRES 2/1206 11 December 1798.
61. PRO CRES 2/57, 22 June 1792 and 2/1207, 27 April and 23 May 1793.
62. SAOCS & EMT Key to the Survey of the Parish of Egham and EMT DOC 2753.
63. SHC 2642/14/22.
64. PRO T 25/1, p.372; CRES 2/57, 9 September 1788 and 25 February 1789 and PRO MR 1/687.
65. PRO CRES 2/57, 22 June 1792; 35/146.
66. Turner, p.263.
67. Roberts (1997), pp.73-4 and see *Dictionary of National Biography.*
68. Menzies, p.29 and Kent, Nathaniel, *Journal of the progressive improvements in Windsor Great Park* (1791-7), vol. 1, pp.18, 28-9, 39 and 96.
69. *Kent Journal*, vol. 1, pp.5 and 10.
70. *Ibid.*, pp.6-9 and Egham Parish Registers.
71. *Kent Journal*, pp.13-14, 19-21, 38 and 129-31.
72. Kent, Nathaniel, *An Account of all the money received and paid by Messrs Kent, Claridge & Pearce on His Majesty's account relative to Windsor Great Park and Farms* (1790-1801), October 1791 and *Kent Journal*, vol. 1, p.43. See also Roberts, pp.74-5.
73. Menzies, p.30.
74. *Kent Accounts*, November 1790, June 1791, June and July 1792.
75. Eedle, Marie, *A History of Bagshot and Windlesham* (1977), p.58.
76. *Kent Journal*, vol. 1, pp.91-2 and 128-34.
77. *Ibid.*, pp.13, 18, 26, 29 and 34-6.
78. Roberts, p.305.
79. *Kent Journal*, vol. 1, pp.37-8 and 170 and vol. 2, pp.98-100 and see Roberts (1997), pp.280 and 381.
80. *Kent Journal*, vol. 2, pp.26-7 and 29-34; vol. 3, p.9; vol. 1, pp.58-60 and Kent Accounts, February, March, May, June and September 1792.
81. *Kent Journal*, vol. 1, pp.46, 54 and 137 & *Kent Accounts*, May 1792.
82. *Kent Journal*, vol. 1, pp.20, 73 and 80; *Kent Accounts*, July, September and December 1791, February and March 1792.
83. *Kent Accounts*, June and September 1792 and *Cheesman Genealogical Notes*, quoting *Kent Accounts*, October 1798.
84. *Kent Accounts*, January, June and August 1792; *Kent Journal*, vol. 1, p.69 and vol. 2, pp.56, 73, 145 and 133.
85. *Kent Accounts*, December 1791 and January, February, July and September 1792.
86. *Kent Journal*, vol. 1, pp.142-6 and vol. 2, p.22.
87. *Kent Journal*, vol. 1, p.69 and vol. 2, pp.23-5 and 36 and March 1794.
88. *Kent Journal*, vol. 2, pp.59-61 and vol. 1, pp.143-5.
89. *Kent Journal*, vol. 3, pp.122 and 125-6.
90. *Cheesman Genealogical Notes*, quoting *Kent Journal*, vol. 3 (1796).

91. *Kent Journal*, vol. 1, pp.58, 84-7 and vol. 3, p.195. See SAOCS & EMT Plan of the Manor of Egham (1802-5) and Egham Parish Registers.
92. *Kent Journal*, vol. 3, pp.8-13.
93. *Ibid.*, pp.47 and 50-52.
94. *Kent Journal*, vol. 2, pp.131 and 161.
95. *Kent Journal*, vol. 3, pp.55 and 64-6.
96. *Ibid.*, pp. 266-7.
97. PRO CRES 2/60A, 20 March 1791, LR 4/19/1204 and Egham Baptismal Registers.
98. PRO CRES 2/60A, 16 March and 2 and 20 April 1791.
99. *Ibid.*, 12, 19 and 26 December 1791 and 2/60B, 9 March 1793.
100. PRO CRES 2/60B, 4 March 1794.
101. PRO CRES 2/60B, 4 and 10 March 1794.
102. PRO CRES 2/58, 16 February and 12 December 1796.
103. PRO CRES 35/339, 5 April and 4 July 1796, 4/104, 9 April and 5 July 1796, 2/58, 10 June 1792 and 2/57, 20 October 1790.
104. PRO CRES 35/339, 5 April 1799.
105. PRO CRES 2/57, 5 April 1797.
106. Roberts (1997), p.500; PRO CRES 2/58, 1 February 1796 and 2/57, 29 June 1801.
107. PRO CRES 2/60A, 16 and 28 March 1791 and 2/60B, 19 June 1795.
108. PRO CRES 2/1206, 2/57, 4 February 1789 and SAOCS & EMT Plan of the Manor of Egham (1802-5).
109. LMA Acc. 809 Tp BED/4, 13 and 16 July 1789.
110. PRO CRES 35/146, 16 July 1789, 38/1955 and 2/57, 22 June 1792.
111. PRO CRES 35/146, 2/57, 22 June 1792 and 38/1955.
112. PRO CRES 35/146 and 38/1955.
113. PRO CRES 2/60C, 2 November 1798.
114. Roberts (1997), p.313.
115. SAOCS & EMT Key & Survey of the Parish of Egham 1790 and see Manning, Rev. Owen and Bray, William, *The History and Antiquities of the County of Surrey (1804-14)*, vol. 3, p.251.
116. PRO CRES 2/1206.
117. *Ibid.*
118. *Ibid.*, and PRO CRES 2/57, 7 October and 20 December 1805.
119. PRO CRES 2/1206.
120. PRO CRES 4/15.
121. *Ibid.*, 20 April 1805.
122. *Ibid.*, 10 May 1805.
123. PRO LR 4/18/176.
124. PRO CRES 2/1204.
125. PRO LR 4/19/188 and CRES 2/58.
126. PRO CRES 35/339, 4 July 1803, 21 July 1806 and 2/57, September 1804.
127. PRO CRES 2/1208 1789; Manning, Rev. Owen and Bray, William, *The History and Antiquities of the County of Surrey (1804-14)*, vol. 3, p.106 and PRO CRES 2/60B, 4 March 1794.
128. PRO CRES 4/15 and 39/30.

Chapter Four: Enclosure, Unrest and More Activity at the Lake: 1802-32

1. PRO CRES 4/15; 2/57, August-September 1804 and 35/339, 21 July 1806.
2. PRO CRES 4/94, 23 and 30 October and 1 November 1809.
3. Poster advertising the Celebration, October 1809, John End Collection.
4. '100 Years Ago', *Egham & Staines News*, 15 October 1909 and see Lord, Maurice, *Egham Races 1734-1884* (1988), pp.18 and 28.
5. SHC 2088/1, 22 and 23 March and 19 June 1810.
6. SAOCS & EMT Map of the Manor of Egham (1805) and PRO CRES 2/1212.
7. *Ibid.*
8. PRO CRES 2/1214.
9. PRO CRES 2/57, 20 December 1805.
10. PRO CRES 2/1214.
11. Roberts, Jane, *Royal Landscape: the Gardens and Parks of Windsor Great Park* (1997), pp.75 and 313.
12. PRO CRES 2/1234.
13. *W& EEx*, 11 September 1812. The newspaper was founded in August 1812 by the Charles Knights, father and son, of Windsor.
14. PRO CRES 35/339, 14 November and 22 December 1812.
15. PRO CRES 35/342, 4 February 1813.
16. Turner, *Frederic, Egham: Surrey, A History of the Parish under Church and Crown* (1926), p.215 and see *Dictionary of National Biography.*
17. Manning, the Rev. Owen and Bray, William, *The History and Antiquities of the County of Surrey (1802-14)*, vol. 3, pp.cii and 198 and vol. 1, p.483.
18. *W&EEx*, 26 November 1815, 8 February 1818 and 8 September 1816, 16 January 1815 and 29 September 1816.
19. SHC 86/1/10/42 and see Davis, Ron and Dorothy, *The Virginia Water Picture Book* (1989), p.24.
20. See Aspinall, A. (ed.), *The Letters of Princess Charlotte* (1949), Janaway, John, *The Surrey Bedside Book* (2002), p.81 and Holme, Thea, *Prinny's Daughter* (1976).
21. SHC 2088/2.
22. *W&EEx*, April 1814 and 54 George III cap.153.
23. *W&EEx*, 17 July, 14 and 28 August 1814 and January 1815.
24. 54 George III cap. 153 and *W&EEx*, 16 April 1815.
25. 54 George III cap. 153 and Lord, p.27.
26. SHC PSH/EG 7/1, 14 and 17 April 1814.
27. PRO CRES 2/1210, 31 March 1815 and 12 September 1816.
28. PRO CRES 2/1210 Printed Subscription List and 19 April 1816 and SHC 2088/2 (Edgell Wyatt Edgell Diaries).
29. SHC PSH/EG 7/1, 6 January 1817 and PRO CRES 2/1210, 28 December 1816.
30. *W&EEx*, 23 July 1815, 18 February and 1 September 1816, 19 January 1817 and EMT Egham Enclosure Award.
31. *W&EEx*, March 1817 and EMT Egham Enclosure Award.
32. *W&EEx*, 13 April 1817.
33. SHC PSH/EG/6/1, 1, 8 and 10 November 1820 and 29 January 1818.
34. *Ibid.*, 1816-17.
35. PRO CRES 35/339, 20 April 1816 and 35/345, 26 May 1816 and 6 April 1819.
36. PRO CRES 35/339, 27 June and 28 August 1817.
37. PRO CRES 35/342, 21 October and 15 December 1817.
38. PRO CRES 35/345, 6 February, 6 April and July 1819.
39. *W&EEx*, 27 September 1818.
40. *Ibid.*, 1 November 1818.
41. PRO CRES 39/31.
42. EMT Egham Inclosure Award 1817.
43. *W&EEx*, March 1816.
44. EMT DOC 2753.
45. *W&EEx*, 30 May 1819 and see EMT Plan of the Parish of Egham 1841.
46. *Cheesman Genealogical Notes.*
47. PRO CRES 2/1206, 11 December 1798.
48. Roberts (1997), p.76.
49. Fedden, Robin, 'The Passing of Windsor Forest', *Country Life Annual* (1962).
50. Cobbett, William, *Rural Rides* (reprinted 1957), vol. 1, p.124.

51. Pardoe, B.F.J., 'Glenridge, Virginia Water and the Pococks', *Egham-by-Runnymede Historical Society*, Carta 8 (February 1975) and EMT Plan of the Parish of Egham 1841.
52. Huish, Robert, *Memoirs of George IV* (1831), vol. 2, pp.295-7 and see Frazer, Flora, *The Unruly Queen* (1996), p.347.
53. Roberts (1997), p.81.
54. *W&EEx*, October 1820.
55. Huish, vol. 2, p.303.
56. Roberts (1997), p.219.
57. *W&EEx*, November 1820.
58. *Ibid.*, 10 December 1820.
59. *Ibid.*, 10 March and 27 May 1821.
60. Huish, vol. 2, p.359.
61. *W&EEx*, 3 December 1815 and 30 May 1819.
62. PRO CRES 2/57, 30 August 1824.
63. *W&EEx*, 18 and 25 September 1824.
64. Huish, vol. 2, p.362.
65. LMA Acc 809 Tp BED/4, 21 November 1782.
66. LMA Acc.809, Tp BED/92, 93, 94, 96, 99 and see Rowse, A.L., *Windsor Castle in the History of the Nation* (reprinted 1974), pp.179-80.
67. Rawlins, F.T., *Notes on Virginia Water* (1867), p.31.
68. For detailed descriptions of all these features see Roberts (1997), pp.79, 413-21, 438-9, 449-53 and 457-60.
69. LMA Acc.809 Tp BED/113, 121, 127 and 130.
70. *W&EEx*, 12 August 1826.
71. SHC QS 5/10/2 1805-14 and 1814-24.
72. PRO CRES 38/1955. The Deed of Sale was dated November 1824 but not recorded until February 1826.
73. PRO CRES 35/1415.
74. *Ibid.*
75. Royal Archives GEO/34627, 31 May 1826. The author is grateful to Jane Roberts for this reference.
76. PRO CRES 35/345 and 352.
77. PRO CRES 35/352.
78. Pardoe, 1975.
79. PRO CRES 35/354.
80. Aspinall A. (ed.), *The Letters of King George IV* (1938), 2 May 1828.
81. PRO CRES 2/57, 7 June 1828.
82. Huish, vol. 2, p.361.
83. *W&EEx*, 9 June 1827 and 5 April 1828.
84. Fear, Diana, *Ploughing Matches and Mangel Wurzels* (1991), p.1.
85. SAOCS & EMT Survey of the Parish of Egham, 1790 and PRO CRES 2/1208.
86. *W&EEx*, 4 January 1823. For more details about the Knowle Hill families see Davis, Ron and Dorothy, 'The Saga of Charles Hackett of Knowle Hill', *Connection* (November 2001).
87. EMT Transcripts of Egham Vestry Papers (hereafter EMT Transcripts), monthly vestry meetings, January-October 1825. Original documents SHC 2615.
88. EMT Transcripts, monthly vestry meetings, March 1825, August 1827 and January 1828.
89. PRO CRES 2/1214.
90. EMT Transcripts, monthly meetings, October and December 1825.
91. *Ibid.*, December 1825, September 1826, June, August and September 1827.
92. Cobbett, vol. 2, pp.1-2.
93. PRO CRES 4/15.
94. *Ibid.*
95. PRO CRES 2/50 and EMT Plan of the Parish of Egham 1841.
96. PRO CRES 2/1233 and 30/30.
97. EMT Transcripts, monthly vestry meetings, 2 December 1826, January 1827, March 1829 and December 1830.
98. *W&EEx*, 14 May 1825.
99. Corpus Christi College, Oxford, Muniments of the Manor of Milton Ga/16/7. The undated document is written in a copperplate hand as if by a clerk but it has notes at the foot in Edgell Wyatt's Edgell's handwriting.
100. *W&EEx*, 8 October 1825.
101. *Ibid.*, 29 March 1828 and see Hammond, J.L. and B., *The Village Labourer 1760-1832* (1987), pp.186-202.
102. Corpus Christi College, Oxford, Muniments of the Manor of Milton Ga/16/7.
103. Falkner, Richard, *Church and School at Englefield Green* (1973), p.2 and see SAOCS and EMT Map of the Manor of Egham (1802-5).
104. PRO CRES 2/1233.
105. EMT Transcripts, vestry room meeting, May 1829.
106. *Ibid.*, December 1826. Rusham End, together with its chapel, was pulled down in the late 19th century by order of Baron de Worms, the successor to the Edgell family at Milton Place.
107. *Ibid.*, and January 1827.
108. *DNB.*
109. EMT Transcripts, vestry room meetings, December 1826 and January 1827.
110. PRO WORK 4/29, pp. 415-6 and 1/17, pp.478-81.
111. PRO CRES 2/57, 4 March 1830.
112. Cobbett, vol. 2, p.1.
113. Huish, vol. 2, p.360-note.
114. Roberts (1997), pp.84-5 and see PRO CRES 4/89.
115. *W&EEx*, 6 November 1830. See also Hobsbawm, E.J. and Rude, G., *Captain Swing* (1970).
116. *W&EEx*, 13 November 1830 and EMT Transcripts, vestry room meetings, August-September 1827.
117. EMT Transcripts, General Meeting of the Inhabitants of Egham, 16 November 1830 and see Hobsbawm and Rude.
118. *W&EEx*, 27 November 1830.
119. *Ibid.*, 25 December 1830.
120. *Ibid.*, 1 January 1831.
121. See Hobsbawm and Rude.
122. Pardoe, 1975.
123. EMT Transcripts, Parish Officers' Meeting, 13 November 1832.
124. *The Penny Magazine*, 9 February 1833, pp.52-3. The author is grateful to Mavis Collier for this reference. Charles Knight, the younger, one of the founders of the *Windsor & Eton Express*, was actively involved in this publication.

Chapter Five: From Spade Husbandry to the Gentrification of Virginia Water: 1831-1901

1. EMT Transcripts of Egham Vestry Papers (hereafter EMT Transcripts), Officers' Meetings, March, November and December 1831: original documents SHC 2516.
2. *Ibid.*, Answers to Poor Law Commissioners' Questions, October 1834; Parish Officers' Committee, February, March, November and December 1832 and Parish Officers' Meeting, September 1832.
3. *Ibid.*, Parish Officers' Committee, March 1832.
4. *Ibid.*, Parish Officers' Meeting, November 1832 and Parish Officers' Committee, June and December 1833.
5. PRO CRES 2/50.
6. PRO CRES 2/1204.
7. PRO CRES 4/15.
8. EMT Transcripts, Answers to Poor Law Commissioners' Questions, October 1834.
9. *The Penny Magazine*, October 1841. The author is grateful to Diana and Ivan Fear for this reference.
10. SHC PSH/V/WAT 11/1-9,

25 May 1837.
11. *Ibid.*, 29 April and 22 March 1837.
12. *Ibid.*, 7 and 14 October 1837.
13. *Ibid.*, 2 December 1837; 8 and 15 January and 10 September 1838.
14. *Ibid.*, 10 September and 8 and 20 October 1838.
15. *Ibid.*, 30 November 1838.
16. PRO CRES 4/94, 6 February 1840.
17. SHC PX/56/73. The author is grateful to Jill Hyams for this reference.
18. *Ibid.*
19. EMT Egham Census Returns 1841, 51 and 61.
20. PRO CRES 4/15.
21. Turner, Frederic, *Egham, Surrey: A History of the Parish under Church and Crown* (1926), p.216.
22. Roberts, Jane, *Royal Landscape: The Gardens and Parks of Windsor Great Park* (1997), pp.302-3.
23. SHC 2225/11/68 and Turner, p.263.
24. EMT Plan of the Parish of Egham & Egham Census Returns 1841.
25. *Ibid.*
26. *Ibid.*
27. The National Society for Promoting the Education of the Poor in the Principals of the Established Church: Christ Church, Virginia Water file: Application Form.
28. *Ibid.*, 20 October 1843 and 5 January 1844 and Presentation of Accounts 1844. See Davis, Dorothy, *Country School, 1843-1900* (1982).
29. PRO CRES 35/362, 22 February, 24 June and 22 July 1854.
30. PRO CRES 4/5, 6 June 1847.
31. PRO CRES 2/1204.
32. PRO CRES 4/82 and 4/21.
33. PRO CRES 2/50, 4/21 and 4/82.
34. PRO CRES 2/50.
35. PRO CRES 4/21 and 2/50.
36. PRO CRES 4/21 and EMT Egham Census Return 1851.
37. Davis, Ron, *Railways from Staines to Sunningdale, 1856-1996* (1996), pp.6-7.
38. PRO CRES 2/1207.
39. PRO CRES 4/5, 4 March1852.
40. *Ibid.*, January 1854-7.
41. PRO CRES 35/362, 2 June 1854.
42. PRO CRES 2/1208.
43. Letter from Crown Estate Commissioners, 2 July 1979.
44. PRO CRES 35/1415 and EMT Egham Census Return 1851.
45. PRO CRES 35/1415.
46. *Ibid.*
47. PRO CRES 35/1419.
48. Pardoe, B.F.J., 'Glenridge, Virginia Water and the Pococks', *Egham-by-Runnymede Historical Society Newsletter*, Carta 8 (February 1975).
49. PRO CRES 35/362.
50. *W&EEx*, 2 July 1853.
51. *W&EEx*, 9 July 1853.
52. *Ibid.*, and see MacFarlane, Charles, *The Camp of 1853* (1853).
53. *W&EEx*, 9 July 1853.
54. *Ibid.*, 2 and 9 July 1853.
55. Roberts (1997), pp.99-100.
56. Pearce, B.L., *Old Ascot—the Diaries of George and G.L. Longhurst 1831-81* (privately printed 1964), 4 September 1858 and 24 August 1865.
57. Rawlins, F.T., *Notes on Virginia Water* (1867).
58. McDougall, P.L., 'The Roman Road between Silchester and Staines', pp.61-5 and Lance, E.J., 'Remarks on the Roman Road from Silchester (Vindonum) in Hampshire to Egham (Pontes) in Surrey', pp.66-8, *Surrey Archaeological Collections*, vol. 1, 1858.
59. Roberts (1997), p.96 and Menzies, William, *The History of Windsor Great Park and Windsor Forest* (1864), p.41.
60. EMT Egham Rate Books and Census Return 1861.
61. Fear, Diana, *Ploughing Matches and Mangel Wurzels* (1991), pp.1 and 3.
62. Davis, R. (1996), p.14.
63. PRO CRES 35/1415.
64. EMT Egham Rate Books and Egham Census Returns 1851 and 1861.
65. EMT Egham Burial Registers and Egham Rate Books.
66. SAOCS and EMT Survey of the Parish of Egham (1790), Egham Inclosure Award (1817), Plan of the Parish of Egham (1841).
67. Virginia Water Memorial Inscriptions.
68. PRO CRES 2/1225 and 35/1197, Sale Particulars.
69. Roberts (1997), pp.463-5 and see *DNB.*
70. Walford, Edmund, *The County Families of the United Kingdom* (1868), p.99.
71. Memorial in Christ Church, Virginia Water and EMT Egham Census Returns 1881 and 1891.
72. Pearce, 15 December and 4-20 January 1861.
73. *W&EEx*, 2 May 1862 (piece dated 8 March 1862).
74. SHC PSH/V.WAT 16/3 School Acc. Book 1857-69.
75. PRO CRES 4/94, 2 March 1863.
76. *W&EEx*, 9 Jan 1864.
77. Roberts (1997), pp.421-2.
78. Menzies, pp.5-6, 25-6 *et passim.*
79. *Ibid.*, pp.27 and 32-5.
80. Pearce, 28 November and 3 December 1866.
81. Obituary of Robert Turner, June 1910.
82. Letter from A.M. Fox, June 1933 in the John End Collection.
83. Best, Geoffrey, *Mid-Victorian Britain 1851-75* (1971), pp.99, 115-6 and 137-8.
84. PRO CRES 35/1197.
85. EMT Egham Rate Books; Egham Census Return, 1871 and May and Collins Map of the Parish of Egham (1856).
86. PRO CRES 35/1197, Sale Particulars.
87. *W&EEx*,, 23 March 1867.
88. PRO CRES 35/1197.
89. *Ibid.*
90. EMT Egham Rate Books.
91. PRO CRES 35/1200.
92. Dennis, Graham, *Englefield Green in Pictures* (1993), p.61.
93. LMA Acc.809 Tp BED/284/12.
94. EMT Egham Rate Books and Census Returns.
95. EMT Egham Rate Books; Egham Census Return 1871.
96. Sale Catalogue 1927.
97. Farlow Family Tree, conversations with Mary Chaplin and Daphne Bousfield, EMT Egham Rate Books and Egham Census Return 1881.
98. PRO CRES 4/15, 30 January 1875.
99. *Ibid.*
100. *Ibid.*, 8 February 1877 and 25 March 1890 and see EMT Egham Census Return 1881.
101. PRO CRES 4/21 and see *W&EEx*, 11 May 1878.
102. PRO CRES 35/375.
103. PRO CRES 4/119 and see EMT Egham Census Returns 1861, '71 and '81.
104. PRO CRES 4/94, 28 July 1895.
105. Gregg, Pauline, *A Social and Economic History of Britain 1760-1970* (6th ed. 1971), pp.377-8.
106. *Surrey Advertiser*, 29 January 1881.
107. Hudson, Helen, *Cumberland Lodge* (1989), Chap. 9.
108. Davis, Dorothy, 'The Cottage Hospital at Englefield Green' and 'Princess Christian Visits', *Connection*, June and July 2005.
109. Christ Church School Logbooks, June 1881-2, 1886-8.
110. Conversation, Daphne Bousfield.

111. EMT Egham Rate Books; Map of the Manor of Egham (1802-5) and SAOCS 125 Sale Catalogue 1901.
112. EMT Egham Rate Books and Egham Census Return, 1881. See Davis, Dorothy, 'Woodlee, Queenswood, Ulverscroft and Ashleigh', *Connection*, July-November 1991.
113. PRO CRES 35/352.
114. Davis, Ron, 'Thomas Holloway—Entrepreneur and Philanthropist', *Surrey History*, vol.3, no. 2 (1986), pp.67-75.
115. Davis (1986) and Williams, Richard, *Royal Holloway College: A Pictorial History* (1993), pp.7-8.
116. Davis (1986) and Christ Church School Logbooks, 19 June 1885 and 2 July 1886.
117. Williams (1993), pp.10-11 and 16 and Bingham, Caroline, *The History of Royal Holloway College 1886-1986* (1997), pp.60-6.
118. PRO CRES 4/94 23 July 1895.
119. Christchurch School Logbooks, 17 June, 1 and 8 July 1887 and 12 May 1890.
120. Programme of the Unveiling Ceremony 1890, John End Collection.
121. PRO CRES 4/94 23 July 1895.
122. *Ibid.*
123. Christchurch School Logbooks, 15 July 1897, 4 July 1898 and 3 July 1899. See also St Ann's Heath Board School Logbooks 1898 and 1899.
124. EMT Egham Rate Books and Census Returns 1861-91.
125. EMT DOC 379.
126. PRO CRES 35/2824 and see Davis, Dorothy, 'Princess Christian and the Boys' Home at Englefield Green', *Connection*, May 2005.
127. Christchurch School Logbooks, 12 January, 18 June and 8 July 1897: St Ann's Heath School Logbooks, 11 January, 4 and 27 May, 18 June and 8 July 1897.
128. *Eg&StN*, 19 June 1897. See Davis, Ron and Dorothy, 'Victorian Celebrations—Diamond Jubilee 1897', *Connection*, May 1998.
129. PRO CRES 4/94, 3 June 1899.

Chapter Six: Patriotism, War and a People's Pleasure Park: 1901-2006

1. St Ann's Heath School Logbooks, 25 January and 4 February 1901.
2. PRO CRES 4/94, 12 and 18 March, 26 April and 6 and 8 May 1902.
3. *Eg&StN*, 12 July 1902.
4. PRO CRES 4/94, 11 August 1902.
5. Fear, Diana, *Ploughing Matches and Mangel Wurzels* (1991), p.4.
6. *Ibid.*, p.8.
7. *Eg&StN*, 18 January 1908.
8. Roberts, Jane, *Royal Landscape: The Gardens and Parks of Windsor Great Park* (1997), p.428-9.
9. Davis, Dorothy, *St Ann's Heath School through the Century* (1996), pp.19-20 and St Ann's Heath School Logbooks, 15 July 1901 and 24 May 1905 *et passim.*
10. St Ann's Heath School Log Books, 24 May 1910 and 24 May 1911.
11. EMT Newspaper Cuttings Files—First World War, compiled by Diana Fear and the late John Hardaker (hereafter NCF WW1), 14 August and16 October 1914; 5 and 19 March and 16 and 30 April 1915; 6 November, 9 October and 25 December 1914.
12. SHC 7502/ES/17A, April and May 1915.
13. EMT NCF WWI, 14 January 1916, 27 August 1915, 14 and 21 September 1917 *et passim.*
14. *Ibid.*, 22 September 1916 and 22 June 1917.
15. Dennis, Graham and Williams, Richard, *The Englefield Green Picture Book* (1992), p.59, Dennis, Graham, *Englefield Green in Pictures* (1993), p.57.
16. EMT NCF WWI, 22 June and 24 August 1916.
17. *Ibid.*, 12 May and 23 and 30 June 1916; 8 and 22 June and 6 July 1917 and 4 January 1918.
18. PRO CRES 4/141, 21 August 1917.
19. PRO CRES 4/150.
20. PRO CRES 4/141.
21. *Ibid.*
22. *Ibid.*
23. PRO CRES 35/1422.
24. EMT NCFWWI, 21 July 1916; 12 January, 11 May, 1, 11 and 15 June, 7 September, 5 and 26 October 1917; 15 February, 1 March 1918, 12 October 1917 and 22 March 1918.
25. *Ibid.*, 28 Sept. 1917.
26. Bird, C.W. and Davies, J.B., *The Canadian Forestry Corps: Its Inception Development and Achievement* (1919), pp.5 and 18. The author is indebted to Rick Parker for this reference.
27. PRO CRES 35/399, April and July 1916.
28. Bird, C.W. and Davies, J.B., *The Canadian Forestry Corps: Its Inception Development and Achievement* (1919), p.18.
29. EMT NCFWW1, 5, 12 and 26 May and 22 September 1916 and conversation with Eamonn Priestley.
30. Bird, C.W. and Davies, J.B., *The Canadian Forestry Corps: Its Inception Development and Achievement* (1919), p.20.
31. PRO CRES 35/399.
32. EMT NCF WWI, 23 June 1916.
33. Bird, C.W. and Davies, J.B., *The Canadian Forestry Corps: Its Inception Development and Achievement* (1919), p.19.
34. PRO CRES 35/399, May and July 1916.
35. PRO CRES 35/400, December 1916.
36. Bird, C.W. and Davies, J.B., *The Canadian Forestry Corps: Its Inception Development and Achievement* (1919), pp.21-2.
37. PRO CRES 35/400, May 1917.
38. Bird, C.W. and Davies, J.B., *The Canadian Forestry Corps: Its Inception Development and Achievement* (1919), p.18.
39. Thake, Margaret, 'Memories of Virginia Water', *Egham-by-Runnymede Historical Society Newsletter*, February 1990.
40. *Ibid.*
41. EMT NCFWWI, 23 February 1917.
42. *Ibid.*, 23 June and 18 and 25 August 1916, 2 February and 2 March 1917.
43. EMT *Surrey Herald*, 7 June 1918 (hereafter *SH*).
44. EMT NCF WWI, 10 August, June, 4 May and 5 and 26 October 1917.
45. Conversations with Kathleen Lewis and Susan Midson and letter from John Luckhurst, May 2006.
46. EMT NCFWWI, 21 July 1916, 11 May 1917 and Bird, C.W. and Davies, J.B., *The Canadian Forestry Corps: Its Inception Development and Achievement* (1919), p.33.
47. Bird, C.W. and Davies, J.B., *The Canadian Forestry Corps: Its Inception Development and Achievement* (1919), p.20.
48. PRO CRES 4/152, 29 May and 4 June 1917 and 27 September 1918.
49. EMT NCFWW1, 22 June and 7 and 14 September 1917.
50. *SH*, 15 November 1918 and *SH*, 8 August and 24 October 1919.
51. PRO CRES 4/152, 17 February 1909.

52. EMT Egham Rate Books and Register of Electors.
53. Roberts (1997), p.102-3.
54. Press Release from Dartmouth Town Council, 2002.
55. Roper, Lanning, *The Gardens in the Royal Park at Windsor* (1959), pp.28 and 30-3.
56. St David's Chronicle 5. The author is grateful to Miss E. MacFarlane for this reference. The school was previously known as Northlands, and was originally the mansion called Bendemere. See Davis, Dorothy, 'St David's School for Girls', *Connection*, June 1991.
57. PRO CRES 4/94.
58. Davis, Ron and Dorothy, *The Virginia Water Picture Book* (1989), p.39 and *SH*, 3 May 1935.
59. *SH*, 30 April 1947.
60. Bingham, Caroline, *The History of Royal Holloway College 1886-1986* (1997), pp.123 and 164, and Williams, Richard, *Royal Holloway College: A Pictorial History* (1993), p.44.
61. EMT Egham Rate Books 1936 and 1938-9, including Additional Assessments. Most of the development in Virginia Water took place on Wentworth and Trotsworth land, not on land previously owned by the Crown.
62. SHC C/EM/67/5 and St Ann's Heath School Logbooks, January and September 1938, 24 and 27 July and 1 August 1939. See Glicksman, Ruth, 'Evacuation of School Children from London, 1 September 1939', *Connection*, September 1992.
63. PRO CRES 35/417 and 3/35; EMT Egham Rate Books. The War Office also requisitioned mansions on the Wentworth Estate.
64. Dennis, p.60.
65. EMT Egham Rate Books.
66. PRO CRES 35/1428.
67. Conversation with Madge Tayler and Parker, Eric, *Surrey* (1947), pp.7-8.
68. Vaughan,Leslie,Diaries:1939-45 (unpublished), August-September 1940. The author is grateful to Mrs Anne Long, Leslie Vaughan's daughter, for allowing her access to a transcript of the wartime diaries.
69. St Ann's Heath School Logbooks, September 1940, and see Leaney, Victor, 'Wartime at St Ann's Heath School', *Connection*, September 1996.
70. Gale, Vic, 'The Air Raid at Brooklands in September 1940', *Addlestone History Society Newsletter*, October 1993.
71. Vaughan, September-October 1940 and January-April 1941.
72. PRO CRES 3/35.
73. Vaughan, November 1941.
74. Roper, pp.35-6 and Elliott, R.J., *The Story of Windsor Great Park* (undated), p.45.
75. Vaughan, October 1941 and October 1942.
76. Roberts (1997), pp.105 and 379-81.
77. PRO CRES 35/1428 and letters to local residents in the Graham Dennis Collection.
78. Vaughan, February, June, July and October 1944. See Ogley, Bob, *Surrey at War 1939-45* (1995), pp.176-7 and 183.
79. *SH*, 16 November 1945.
80. Elliott, p.46.
81. *Surrey Herald & News*, 10 December 1996, 'Fifty Years Ago'.
82. 'Egham Centre', Ministry of Labour Pamphlet, May 1946.
83. Conversation with Bruce Greatheart
84. *SH*, 31 August 1945.
85. PRO CRES 35/1428, 31 August 1945.
86. PRO CRES 35/1428, 1946-8 and *W&EEx*, 16 April 1948.
87. Roper, pp. 40-1, 45-6 and 57-8.
88. *Ibid.*, p.57.
89. PRO CRES 4/170, 12 May 1947.
90. Dibley, George, *Estate Times*, June 2001. The author is indebted to Mark Flanagan for this reference.
91. Roper, pp.48-50.
92. *Ibid.*, pp.38-9.
93. Information on site and conversation with Madge Tayler.
94. Tarrant Builders Ltd Brochures (though Tarrant built mainly on Trotsworth and Wentworth land).
95. PRO CRES 35/1200.
96. Dennis, p.61.
97. Davis, Dorothy, 'Woodlee' and 'Queenswood', *Connection*, August and October 1991.
98. Knight Frank, Sales Catalogue, 1997.
99. EMT Egham Rate Books.
100. Williams (1993), p.50.
101. Bingham, pp.192-3, 219, 238 and 266 and see Williams (1993), p.49.
102. *Surrey Herald and News*, 22 May 1986.
103. *Eg&StN*,12 December 1980.
104. *Eg&StN*, 13 April 1989.
105. Letter from the Crown Estate Office, 12 November 2003.
106. EMT Egham Rate Books.
107. 'A New Year at the Savill Gardens', *Royal Landscape Pamplet*, February 2007.
108. *Eg&StN*, 1 March 2006 and *The Leader*, 20 April 2006.
109. Flanagan, Mark, *Valley Gardens, Windsor Great Park* (2002), back cover and p.4.
110. *Eg&StN*, 3 May 2006.
111. *Ibid.*, 1 March 2006.
112. *Guardian*, 17 April 2006.
113. *Eg&StN*, 17 May 2006.
114. *The Villager*, 31 May 2006.
115. *Eg&StN*, 26 April 2006.

INDEX

(a page number in bold denotes an illustration)